English Poetry, 1900-1950

AMERICAN LITERATURE, ENGLISH LITERATURE, AND WORLD LITERATURES IN ENGLISH: AN INFORMATION GUIDE SERIES

Series Editor: Theodore Grieder, Curator, Division of Special Collections, Fales Library, New York University

Associate Editor: Duane DeVries, Associate Professor, Polytechnic Institute of New York, Brooklyn

Other books on English literature in this series:

ENGLISH DRAMA TO 1660 (EXCLUDING SHAKESPEARE)—*Edited by Frieda Elaine Penninger*

ENGLISH DRAMA, 1660-1800—*Edited by Frederick M. Link*

ENGLISH DRAMA AND THEATRE, 1800-1900—*Edited by L.W. Conolly and J.P. Wearing*

ENGLISH DRAMA, 1900-1950—*Edited by E.H. Mikhail*

MODERN DRAMA IN AMERICA AND ENGLAND, 1950-1970—*Edited by Richard H. Harris*

ENGLISH FICTION, 1660-1800—*Edited by Jerry C. Beasley*

ENGLISH FICTION, 1900-1950 (volume 1)—*Edited by Thomas Jackson Rice*

ENGLISH FICTION, 1900-1950 (volume 2)—*Edited by Thomas Jackson Rice**

CONTEMPORARY FICTION IN AMERICA AND ENGLAND, 1950-1970—*Edited by Alfred F. Rosa and Paul A. Echholz*

OLD AND MIDDLE ENGLISH POETRY TO 1500—*Edited by Walter H. Beale*

ENGLISH POETRY, 1660-1800—*Edited by Donald C. Mell**

ENGLISH ROMANTIC POETRY, 1800-1835—*Edited by Donald H. Reiman*

CONTEMPORARY POETRY IN AMERICA AND ENGLAND, 1950-1970—*Edited by Martin E. Gingerich**

ENGLISH PROSE, PROSE FICTION, AND CRITICISM TO 1660—*Edited by S.K. Heninger, Jr.*

ENGLISH PROSE AND CRITICISM IN THE NINETEENTH CENTURY—*Edited by Harris W. Wilson and Diane Long Hoeveler*

THE ENGLISH LITERARY JOURNAL TO 1900—*Edited by Robert B. White, Jr.*

ENGLISH LITERARY JOURNALS, 1900-1950—*Edited by Michael N. Stanton*

*in preparation

The above series is part of the
GALE INFORMATION GUIDE LIBRARY

The Library consists of a number of separate series of guides covering major areas in the social sciences, humanities, and current affairs.

General Editor: Paul Wasserman, Professor and former Dean, School of Library and Information Services, University of Maryland

Managing Editor: Denise Allard Adzigian, Gale Research Company

English Poetry, 1900-1950

A GUIDE TO INFORMATION SOURCES

*Volume 33 in the American Literature, English
Literature, and World Literatures in English
Information Guide Series*

Emily Ann Anderson

*Special Education Department
Northwest High School
Shawnee, Kansas*

Emily Ann Anderson Allen
September 23, 1993

Gale Research Company
Book Tower, Detroit, Michigan 48226

Library of Congress Cataloging in Publication Data

Anderson, Emily Ann.
   English poetry, 1900-1950.

   (American literature, English literature, and
world literatures in English information guide
series ; v. 33) (Gale information guide library)
   Includes indexes.
     1. English poetry—20th century—Bibliography.
I. Title. II. Series.
Z2014.P7A54 [PR610]   016.821'52   74-32505
ISBN 0-8103-1360-X   AACR2

I dedicate this book, with deepest love and gratitude, to my mother Emily M. Anderson, to my sisters Mary Jo Cashner and Ellen Volk, and to the memories of my father Joseph, my brothers Michael and Stephen, and my grandmother, Agnes M. Martin.

VITA

Emily Ann Anderson is currently head of the special education department at Shawnee Mission Northwest High School in Kansas City. She received her B.A. degree in philosophy from Fontbonne College in St. Louis, an M.A. in theology from Marquette University in Milwaukee, an M.A. and Ph.D. in English literature from the University of Wisconsin-Milwaukee, and certification in special education from Stritch College in Milwaukee.

Academic honors include a Knapp Dissertation Fellowship awarded in 1975 and a Knapp Travel Fellowship awarded in 1977 by the University of Wisconsin-Milwaukee.

CONTENTS

Contents

ACKNOWLEDGMENTS

I want to thank Theodore Grieder and Duane DeVries for their advice during the preparation of this book. Professor Grieder's patience and good humor during my long-distance conferences with him were comforting, encouraging, and, at times, even amusing. I gratefully acknowledge the enormous amount of financial support given me by my sister Ellen and her husband, George E. Volk, M.D., during the final stages of editing, and also the clerical aid from my mother, Emily M. Anderson and my sister and brother-in-law Mary Jo and Cecil Cashner. To Justin M. Replogle, my teacher and dear friend, who, along with another steady and loyal friend, Pru Byers, is always able to tell a poem from a pig, I owe a special debt of thanks, because it is he who arranged this project for me. To Dean William F. Halloran, whose support never flagged, I also say thanks. I am grateful for the unhesitating cooperation of the interlibrary loan librarians of the University of Wisconsin-Milwaukee and University of Missouri-Kansas City Libraries and for the generosity of the Knapp Fellowship Committee for awarding me a grant for study at the British Museum in 1977.

INTRODUCTION

This guide, designed as a resource tool for students of twentieth-century British poetry, is divided into three parts. Part 1, "General Aids," includes selective listings of autobiographies and diaries, bibliographies, bibliographies of bibliographies, and various other kinds of reference resources useful to the student of modern poetry. The entries in part 1 are annotated and listed alphabetically.

Part 2, "Background Readings," lists selected studies directed toward the literary criticism history of twentieth-century British poetry. The entries in part 2 are alphabetical and annotated. The annotations frequently contain quotations from the entry cited.

Part 3, the longest section of this guide, is concerned with "Individual Authors." Included here are twenty-one modern British poets representative of various literary movements and schools of poetry that have flourished from the turn of the century to 1950. The kinds of information given for each individual author are enumerated below (information in numbers 1-8 is listed chronologically; information in number 9 is listed alphabetically by author of the critical resource cited or the critical title itself if there is no author):

1. Principal works. This section is subdivided into two parts: under "Poetry," there is a checklist of first editions of major works of poetry; under "Other Works," there is a selective listing of various kinds of other literary titles, which are identified as prose, criticism, translation, and so forth. The purpose of this section is to give the reader an overview of the nature of an author's literary contributions. Imprints (place, publisher, date) are cited for titles listed under "Poetry." If English and American publication occurred the same year, the English edition is cited. This is the case for imprints throughout the book. Date of publication only is cited for titles listed under "Other Works."

2. Bibliography.

3. Checklists of criticism. As differentiated from bibliography, which is concerned with works by a given author, these checklists are, when available, concerned with citing critical and biographical titles about a given author.

4. Autobiography.

5. Biography. Where there are many, the most important are cited; where there are no biographies, the reader is referred to works that are partially biographi-

cal. Biographies containing a great deal of literary criticism are listed again under "Criticism," number 9, below.

6. Letters. Important collections are cited. Where such collections have not appeared, the reader is referred to letters appearing in such other publications as articles, biographies, critical studies, and so forth.

7. Dictionary, companion, yearbook, notebooks and papers, concordance. These are listed where available.

8. Periodicals. Author newsletters and journals devoted to a particular author are cited where available.

9. Criticism. Because of the wealth of critical resources available, selection here has necessarily been severe. In general, works providing insight into the critical reputations of particular authors, those surveying the state of scholarship on a particular author, and those that give a broad or overall approach to particular authors, were included.

Critical entries are annotated throughout. The annotations frequently contain quotations from the entry cited.

Part 1

GENERAL AIDS

AUTOBIOGRAPHIES AND DIARIES

Matthews, William. BRITISH AUTOBIOGRAPHIES: AN ANNOTATED BIBLIOG-
RAPHY OF BRITISH AUTO-BIOGRAPHIES PUBLISHED OR WRITTEN BEFORE 1951.
Berkeley: University of California Press, 1955.

Alphabetically arranged by author with an index indicating profes-
sions and occupations, places and regions, reminiscences, wars,
and general topics. The full name of each author, abbreviated
title and date of publication are presented with an annotation.

_____. BRITISH DIARIES. AN ANNOTATED BIBLIOGRAPHY OF BRITISH
DIARIES PUBLISHED BETWEEN 1442 AND 1942. Berkeley: University of California Press, 1950.

Published diaries, diaries in manuscript form, and diaries published
in periodicals are listed in chronological order for each author.
Each listing is annotated. There is an author index and library
or owner locations for unpublished items.

BIBLIOGRAPHIES

See also "Autobiographies and Diaries," page 3, "Biographies" and "Serial Biographies," pages 13, 17.

Altick, Richard D., and Andrew Wright, eds. SELECTIVE BIBLIOGRAPHY FOR THE STUDY OF ENGLISH AND AMERICAN LITERATURE. 4th ed. New York: Macmillan, 1971.

> Altick and Wright present a highly selective, reasonably authorita-
> tive guide to research materials for the study of English and Ameri-
> can literature. They list the books that are indispensable to re-
> searchers--the best histories of literature, the best social and in-
> tellectual histories, the best aids to historical and biographical
> research. They also suggest works that are useful for incidental
> reference and include sections called "Some Books Every Student
> of Literature Should Read" and "A Glossary of Useful Terms."
> The order of entries is determined within each section by its in-
> ternal logic.

Dyson, A.E., ed. ENGLISH POETRY: SELECT BIBLIOGRAPHICAL GUIDES. London: Oxford University Press, 1971.

> The essays in this guide call attention to the best critics, editions,
> biographies, background readings, and special studies on twentieth-
> century authors.

Kennedy, Arthur G., and Donald B. Sands, eds. A CONCISE BIBLIOGRAPHY FOR STUDENTS OF ENGLISH. 5th ed. Stanford, Calif.: Stanford University Press, 1974.

> Intended as a guide for advanced undergraduate and graduate stu-
> dents in English, the book "offers a list of older works of demon-
> strated usefulness to the student and new works that show great
> promise." Material in languages other than English are few, as
> are materials in ancillary fields and works of narrow specialization.
> Works on drama and theatre are treated together, and national dis-
> tinctions are drawn only when necessary. No reference is made
> to literary works by single authors; periodical essays are not includ-

ed, but reprinted collections of specialized articles have been listed. In the areas of linguistics and folklore, only basic works are included.

In part 1 the arrangement moves from general bibliographies to specific bibliographies and guides, to general surveys, and finally to general studies in a specific literary period. Part 2 considers the preservation and transmission of literature, examining the early forms and production, distribution, and preservation of books. Following this is consideration of specialized forms, such as the periodical. Part 3 concerns itself with the theory and practice of research and scholarly writing, and with the tools of the trade.

Pownall, David E., ed. ARTICLES ON TWENTIETH CENTURY LITERATURE: AN ANNOTATED BIBLIOGRAPHY, 1954 TO 1970. 7 vols. Millwood, N.Y.: Kraus-Thomson: 1973-- .

Subtitled "An Expanded Cumulation of Current Bibliography" in the journal TWENTIETH CENTURY LITERATURE, volumes 1 to 16, 1955-70. This work offers an enormous number of annotated entries on articles concerned with the major international authors of the twentieth century.

Preminger, Alex, ed. ENGLISH LITERATURE: A BIBLIOGRAPHICAL SURVEY. Carbondale: Illinois University Press, 1967.

This is a critical account of the publications that regularly produce bibliographies of English literature as annual volumes or as bibliographical numbers of journals. It also takes account of the standard larger works such as the CAMBRIDGE BIBLIOGRAPHY OF ENGLISH LITERATURE.

Watson, George, ed. CONCISE CAMBRIDGE BIBLIOGRAPHY OF ENGLISH LITERATURE, 600-1950. 2nd ed. Cambridge, Engl.: Cambridge University Press, 1965.

This work "provides a concise statement of the bibliography of all periods of English literature from Caedmon to Dylan Thomas." It is, apart from the final section which covers 1900-1950, a compression of the CAMBRIDGE BIBLIOGRAPHY OF ENGLISH LITERATURE (Cambridge, Engl.: Cambridge University Press, 1940), the only comprehensive work in this field. It treats six periods: Old English (600-1100); Middle English (1100-1500); Renaissance to Restoration (1500-1660); Restoration to Romantic Age (1660-1800); Nineteenth Century (1800-1900); and Early Twentieth Century (1900-1950). It includes only articles written by authors native to or mainly resident in the British Isles. Excluded, then, are Anglo-Indian, English-Canadian, English-South African, Australian and New Zealand literature, and American literature. No national limits were exercised, however, in the choice of bibliographies or critical material pertinent to the British or Irish writers included in the book.

The book begins with lists of general bibliographies, literary histories and criticism, collections and anthologies, prosody studies,
studies on book production and distribution, grammars, dictionaries
of histories of the language. This initial section is followed by
the six periods, each of which begins with general works concerned with that period. These general works are followed by
treatment of the period's authors, arranged in alphabetical order.
Four hundred writers are considered, including almost all of the
literary writers ranking as major in CBEL. The canon of each
author's work is represented only in selection; and when a list of
biographical and critical works is added, only standard biographies
and major and general critical works are entered. There are more
books listed than articles; some critical essays of importance are
mentioned but specialist articles are never included. The canon
is preceded by standard bibliographies, concordances, and other
reference books concerned with individual authors. See also NEW
CAMBRIDGE BIBLIOGRAPHY OF ENGLISH LITERATURE, below.

Willison, Ian, ed. THE NEW CAMBRIDGE BIBLIOGRAPHY OF ENGLISH LITER-
ATURE. Vol. 4: 1900-1950. New York: Cambridge University Press, 1973.

The poetry section of this volume is divided into two parts, "General Works" and "Individual Poets." Under "General Works" are
listed the bibliographies, histories and studies, and anthologies
most important to the study of modern British poetry. Under "Individual Poets" are detailed, extensive reference listings for the
work of T.S. Eliot, Robert Graves, W.H. Auden, and Dylan Thomas. These comprehensive guides are followed by shorter reference
guides to the work of over 120 modern British poets, alphabetically
arranged. They include the canon of the poet's work, collections
and selections by the poet, contributions to books, translations,
and a list of secondary materials, both in books and periodicals,
arranged chronologically. Secondary materials are not annotated.

BIBLIOGRAPHIES OF BIBLIOGRAPHIES

Besterman, Theodore, ed. A WORLD BIBLIOGRAPHY OF BIBLIOGRAPHIES AND OF BIBLIOGRAPHICAL CATALOGUES, CALENDARS, ABSTRACTS, DIGESTS, INDEXES AND THE LIKE. 5 vols. 4th ed. Lausanne: Societas Bibliographics, 1965-66.

> The most comprehensive recent index to bibliographies, Besterman's study is international in scope and restricted to some 117,000 bibliographies in forty-nine languages that appeared as separately published monographs. It records bibliographies published through 1963, with some later additions. Entries are arranged by sixteen thousand subjects in alphabetical order, and there is a comprehensive index of authors and subjects in volume 4.

Collison, Robert, ed. BIBLIOGRAPHIES: SUBJECT AND NATIONAL. A GUIDE TO THEIR CONTENTS, ARRANGEMENT AND USE. 3rd ed. New York: Hafner, 1968.

> Chapter 9 in part 1 of Collison's work lists the major bibliographies pertinent to the study of language and literature. Under the subheading "Literature in the English Language" Collison includes the literatures of the Commonwealth and the United States. Most of the entries are annotated.

Howard-Hill, Trevor H., ed. BIBLIOGRAPHY OF ENGLISH LITERARY BIBLIOGRAPHIES. Oxford: Clarendon Press, 1969.

> The first volume of the INDEX TO BRITISH LITERARY BIBLIOGRAPHY, this work aims to cover books, substantial parts of books, and periodical articles written in English and published after 1890 in English-speaking countries, the Commonwealth, and the United States, whose concern is the bibliographica and textual examination of English manuscripts, books, printing and publishing. The work also includes any other literary bibliographies published in Great Britain or by British authors abroad from the establishment of printing in England, with the exception of material on post-1890 printing and publishing not primarily of bibliographical or literary interest.

A second volume will list the bibliographies of the works of Shakespeare and present bibliographical and textual discussions of them. The third and final volume, BIBLIOGRAPHY OF BRITISH BIBLIOGRAPHICAL AND TEXTUAL CRITICISM, will list material not included in the first two volumes. Each volume will be separately indexed and may be employed separately.

Mellown, Elgin W., ed. DESCRIPTIVE CATALOGUE OF THE BIBLIOGRAPHIES OF 20TH CENTURY BRITISH WRITERS. Troy, N.Y.: Whitston, 1972.

Mellown lists bibliographies of works by and about twentieth-century British authors. He includes the most famous writers in the social sciences and the more imaginative writers in the humanities. He lists bibliographies that appear as parts of books, in periodicals, and as separate publications; he also cites bibliographical information published in biographical dictionaries and standard reference sources. Many entries are annotated.

Sheehy, Eugene P., ed. GUIDE TO REFERENCE BOOKS. 9th ed. Chicago: American Library Association, 1976.

Includes a literature section under the headings bibliography, dictionaries, handbooks, atlases, history, biography, drama, parodies, and individual authors. The work is mainly helpful to advanced literature students. However, its importance as a recent and comprehensive guide to national bibliographies and research resources in the humanities cannot be overestimated. This is a basic tool, all too often unknown to serious students of English literature.

Temple, Ruth Z., and Martin Tucker, eds. MODERN BRITISH LITERATURE: A LIBRARY OF LITERARY CRITICISM. 3 vols. New York: Ungar, 1966.

Temple and Tucker present excerpts from critical writings on about four hundred authors. The author entries are arranged alphabetically and the excerpts are in chronological order to indicate the rise or decline of the literary reputation. For each author chosen, this guide discusses: "his qualities, definition of his status, indication, if he is well known, of something of his life and personality, and specification, if he is notable otherwise than as an author, his other pursuits." Bibliographies of each author's separately published works are at the end of each volume. There is a cross reference index and an index of critics in the third volume.

Walford, Albert J., ed. A GUIDE TO REFERENCE MATERIAL. 2 vols. 3rd ed. New York: Bowker, 1973-77.

The aim of this guide is "to provide a guide to reference books and bibliographies, with emphasis on current material and on material published in Britain."

BIBLIOGRAPHIC MANUALS

Sanders, Chauncey. AN INTRODUCTION TO RESEARCH IN ENGLISH LITER-
ARY HISTORY. New York: Macmillan, 1952.

> Sander's volume is a textbook for courses in bibliography and me-
> thod. He discusses tools, materials, and methods of research and
> covers problems related to editing, biography, authenticity and at-
> tribution, source study, chronology, success and influence, inter-
> pretation and technique, and the history of ideas and folklore. In
> the last chapter he forwards suggestions on the writing of theses.

Spargo, John W., ed. A BIBLIOGRAPHICAL MANUAL FOR STUDENTS OF
THE LANGUAGE AND LITERATURE OF ENGLAND AND THE UNITED STATES.
New York: Hendricks House, 1956.

> An informal short-title checklist of references for students beginning
> advanced studies. The book is aimed at helping the student during
> the initial stages of investigation. Every section or sub-section is
> a cross-reference to every other. The book is divided into three
> major sections. The first discusses works of general reference, the
> second scholarly journals, and the third books and articles of spe-
> cial interest.

SERIAL BIBLIOGRAPHIES

ABSTRACTS OF ENGLISH STUDIES: AN OFFICIAL PUBLICATION OF THE
NATIONAL COUNCIL OF TEACHERS OF ENGLISH. Boulder, Colo.: National Council of Teachers of English, 1958-- . Monthly, except July and August.

This journal presents abstracts of articles that have appeared in
American and foreign periodicals and are concerned with English,
Commonwealth, and American literature and with English philology.
Each issue has a subject index and arrangement is by periodical.

BIBLIOGRAPHIC INDEX: A CUMULATIVE BIBLIOGRAPHY OF BIBLIOGRAPHIES.
New York: H.W. Wilson, 1938-- . Quarterly.

This is a subject index only. It includes bibliographies published
separately as pamphlets and those that have appeared as parts of
books, pamphlets and periodical articles. It includes references
to new editions and supplements and presents information on new
bibliographic materials.

CURRENT BIBLIOGRAPHY OF TWENTIETH CENTURY LITERATURE: A SCHOL-
ARLY AND CRITICAL JOURNAL. Hempstead, N.Y.: Hofstra University, 1955-
56-- . Quarterly.

This provides a list of periodical articles on twentieth-century literature in English and some foreign languages. The entries are annotated. The cumulation is David E. Pownall's ARTICLES ON
20TH CENTURY LITERATURE: AN ANNOTATED BIBLIOGRAPHY,
1954 TO 1970. Vols. 1-3. New York: Kraus-Thomson, 1973-- .
(In progress). See Pownall under "Bibliographies," above.

MLA INTERNATIONAL BIBLIOGRAPHY OF BOOKS AND ARTICLES ON THE
MODERN LANGUAGES AND LITERATURES. New York: MLA, 1921-- . Annual.

From 1921 to 1955 this bibliography was entitled AMERICAN BIB-
LIOGRAPHY, and was limited to writings by Americans on literatures of various countries. The coverage varied throughout the
years. In 1956-62 its title was the ANNUAL BIBLIOGRAPHY and

the coverage extended to include writings in other languages. From 1963, the title has been as cited above. This comprehensive annual bibliography of literary and linguistic scholarship is divided into four volumes. Volume 1 covers the following areas: general, English, American, medieval and Neo-Latin, and Celtic literatures. Volume 2 covers Portuguese and Brazilian, Rumanian, general Germanic, German, Netherlandic, Scandinavian, modern Greek, Oriental, African, and East European literatures. Volume 3 covers linguistics. Volume 4 constitutes the ANNUAL BIBLIOGRAPHY of the American Council on Teaching Foreign Languages. The arrangement is by national literature, the sections of which are subdivided into literary periods. The names of authors covered appear in boldface. Some volumes have author indexes. There are no annotations.

Modern Humanities Research Association. ANNUAL BIBLIOGRAPHY OF ENGLISH LANGUAGE AND LITERATURE. Cambridge, Engl.: Cambridge University Press, 1921-- .

This bibliography covers English and American literature from 1920 and includes books, pamphlets, and periodical articles. It lists reviews of the cited works. Subject arrangement is followed in the language section; chronological arrangement in the literature section. There are name indexes.

THE YEAR'S WORK IN ENGLISH STUDIES. London: Murray, published for the English Association, 1921-- . Annual.

This work covers English literature from 1919 that appears in books and articles published in Britain, Europe, and America. The survey is selective and critical and groups its subjects chronologically. Since 1954 it has taken into account material on American literature and on the English language. There are author and subject indexes.

BIOGRAPHIES

AUTHORS' AND WRITERS' WHO'S WHO. London: Burke's Peerage Limited, 1934-- .

These volumes provide biographical and bibliographical material on authors, editors, and journalists who write in English, and includes a listing of pseudonyms. The sixth edition was published in 1971.

Combs, Richard E. AUTHORS: CRITICAL AND BIOGRAPHICAL REFERENCES. Metuchen, N.J.: Scarecrow, 1971.

Combs lists about five hundred books that contain critical and biographical material on some fourteen-hundred authors. The references cited are selected as at least six pages in length and mainly critical in nature. Critical works exclusively on one author are excluded.

Kay, Ernest, ed. INTERNATIONAL WHO'S WHO IN POETRY. 4th ed. Cambridge and London: International Who's Who in Poetry, 1974.

Brief biobibliographical accounts of poets worldwide, writing in all languages. Information includes date of birth, occupation, educational background, titles and dates of published works, prizes won, honors conferred, and address.

Kunitz, Stanley, and Howard Haycraft, eds. TWENTIETH CENTURY AUTHORS. New York: Wilson, 1942.

Kunitz and Haycraft include writers from all over the world. Many of the entries are autobiographical and all of them list the author's principal works, dates of publication, and sources for biographical and critical study. Kunitz and Vineta Colby also published a FIRST SUPPLEMENT in 1955.

Murphy, Rosalie, and James Vinson, eds. CONTEMPORARY POETS OF THE ENGLISH LANGUAGE. New York: St. Martin's Press, 1970.

Murphy and Vinson cover eleven-hundred modern poets, offering short biographies, selected author bibliographies, and some critical material.

Seymour-Smith, Martin. WHO'S WHO IN TWENTIETH CENTURY LITERATURE. London: Weidenfeld and Nicolson, 1976.

> The biographical-critical author entries are arranged in alphabetical order. They provide dates of birth and death, identify the genre or genres the author is noted for, list the major works and publication dates, and discuss critical reputation.

Stephen, Leslie, and Stephen Lee. THE DICTIONARY OF NATIONAL BIOGRAPHY. 63 vols. with seven supplements. London: Oxford University Press, 1917-- .

> This concise and authoritative dictionary contains biographies of English writers from the beginnings of English literary history to 1960. It also presents bibliographies on its subjects. The twentieth-century volume relates information only on deceased persons of historical significance.

_____. THE DICTIONARY OF NATIONAL BIOGRAPHY: THE CONCISE DICTIONARY. Part 1: To 1900. London: Oxford University Press, 1953-61. Part 2: 1901-1950. Oxford: Oxford University Press, 1961.

> This is a concise version of the original with abstracts about one-fourteenth of the length of the original articles and as such is both an index and an independent biographical dictionary. It has corrections and additions and extends coverage to 1950.

_____. CORRECTIONS AND ADDITIONS TO THE DICTIONARY OF NATIONAL BIOGRAPHY. CUMULATED FROM THE BULLETINS OF THE INSTITUTE OF HISTORICAL RESEARCH, UNIVERSITY OF LONDON, COVERING THE YEARS 1923-1961. Boston: G.K. Hall, 1966.

Thorne, J.O. CHAMBERS' BIOGRAPHICAL DICTIONARY. Rev. ed. New York: St. Martin's Press, 1969.

> This dictionary lists, in alphabetical order, sketches of some fifteen thousand men and women from different time periods and countries. The entries on literary figures mention their major works and dates of publication.

200 CONTEMPORARY AUTHORS: BIOBIBLIOGRAPHIES OF SELECTED LEADING WRITERS OF TODAY WITH CRITICAL AND PERSONAL SIDELIGHTS. Ed. Barbara Harte and Carolyn Riley. Detroit: Gale Research Co., 1969.

> Updated and revised sketches of those presented in CONTEMPORARY AUTHORS: A BIO-BIBLIOGRAPHICAL GUIDE TO CURRENT AUTHORS AND THEIR WORKS (Detroit: Gale Research Co., 1962--), see "Serial Biographies," page 17. 200 CONTEMPORARY AUTHORS includes checklists of articles on individual authors, studies by critics, and sources for study.

SERIAL BIOGRAPHIES

See also "Biographies," page 15.

BIOGRAPHY INDEX: A CUMULATIVE INDEX TO BIOGRAPHICAL MATERIAL IN BOOKS AND MAGAZINES. New York: Wilson, 1946-- . Quarterly (November, February, May, August).

> This index to biographical material "includes current books in the English language wherever published, biographical material from the 1500 periodicals now regularly included in the Wilson indexes, plus a selected list of professional journals in the fields of law and medicine; obituaries of national and international interest from the NEW YORK TIMES. All types of biographical material are covered: pure biography, critical material of biographical significance, autobiography, letters, diaries, memoirs, journals, genealogies, fiction, drama, poetry, bibliographies, obituaries, pictorial works and juvenile literature. Works of collective biography are fully analyzed. Incidental biographical material such as prefaces and chapters in otherwise non-biographical books is included. Portraits are indicated when they appear in conjunction with indexed material . . . ."

CONTEMPORARY AUTHORS: A BIO-BIBLIOGRAPHICAL GUIDE TO CURRENT AUTHORS AND THEIR WORKS. Detroit: Gale Research Co., 1962-- . Semi-annual.

> This source presents up-to-date sketches of current authors in various fields. The sketches, which are alphabetically arranged, have three parts: the first part, "Personal," contains date and place of birth, parents, spouse, children, educational background, and present address; the second part, "Career," lists places and nature of various employments and other pertinent information; the third part, "Writings," consists of a bibliography of the publications of each writer. The second volume each year provides an index that directs the reader to all listings in all previous volumes of the series.

CURRENT BIOGRAPHY. New York: Wilson, 1940-- . Monthly.

This serial presents articles on prominent people from all over the world in various fields. Information includes full name and pronunciation, dates of birth and death, occupation, address, and a biographical sketch. Most sketches are accompanied by portraits and references to sources for further biographical information. This publication has a bound annual cumulation called CURRENT BIOGRAPHY YEAR BOOK. Each monthly issue has a cumulative index for the issues of the current year, and each yearbook has a cumulative index to all preceding volumes for ten-year periods.

COMPANIONS

Daiches, David, et al, eds. THE PENGUIN COMPANION TO LITERATURE.
4 vols. London: Allen Lane, 1969-71.

Volume 1 is devoted to writers in the British Isles and to writers
who use the English language in the Commonwealth countries.
French-Canadian writers are included. PENGUIN COMPANION
covers English literary history from Anglo-Saxon times to the present. The work functions to tell the reader what the significance
of a writer is, the kind of interest his work possesses, the major
facts of his career, and where added information on him may be
obtained. The short essays on individual writers are followed by
bibliographies of editions of texts and of translations of texts not
already given in the entry itself, and by selective bibliographies
of critical works concerning the subject of the entry.

Harvey, Sir Paul, ed. OXFORD COMPANION TO ENGLISH LITERATURE.
4th ed. Rev. by Dorothy Eagle. Oxford: Clarendon Press, 1967.

This dictionary presents short articles on authors, literary works,
characters in novels, plays, and so forth, and common literary
allusions. The aim of the latest edition is to bring the twentieth-
century literature entries up to date.

Ward, A.C., and Christopher Gillie, eds. LONGMAN COMPANION TO
TWENTIETH CENTURY LITERATURE. 2nd ed. London: Longman Group Limited,
1975.

This work is designed as a "guide to home reading and for consul-
tation in schools and colleges, public and institutional libraries
and offices, and by journalists and other professional workers."
It is arranged alphabetically and is fully cross-referenced. The
contents are comprised of biographical and bibliographical entries
on many well-known and many lesser-known writers of the twentieth
century, mainly English and Scottish but including also those Commonwealth, African, American, French, German, Spanish and Russian
writers with international reputations whose books have appeared in
English editions. There are articles on literary categories, such

as autobiography, biography, criticism, drama; summaries of outstanding novels, plays, and other literary works; descriptions of
fictional characters; authors' pseudonyms; literary terms, topical
phrases, and references and allusions to persons and institutions;
advice for authors on the preparation and publication of manuscripts; articles on censorship, copyright, literary societies, and
other organizations.

DICTIONARIES

Barnet, Sylvan; Morton Berman; and William Burto, eds. A DICTIONARY OF LITERARY TERMS. Boston: Little, Brown, 1960.

This book provides detailed definitions of major literary forms and ideas and dramatic and cinematic terms.

de Vries, Ad. DICTIONARY OF SYMBOLS AND IMAGERY. Amsterdam and London: North-Holland, 1974.

The author supplies background information on the symbols, allegories, metaphors, signs, types, images of Western civilization. Entries are alphabetically arranged.

Evans, Ivor H., ed. BREWER'S DICTIONARY OF PHRASE AND FABLE. London: Cassell, 1970.

This dictionary discusses colloquial, proverbial and foreign phrases, mythological terms, biographical references, characters of fiction, titles, names of organizations, and so forth.

Fowler, H.W., ed. A DICTIONARY OF MODERN ENGLISH USAGE. 2nd ed. Oxford: Clarendon Press, 1965.

On the proper use of modern English words.

FUNK AND WAGNALLS STANDARD DICTIONARY OF FOLKLORE, MYTHOLOGY, AND LEGEND. New York: Funk and Wagnalls, 1972.

This dictionary discusses and defines customs, beliefs, games, heroes, and tales of cultures all over the world. It includes articles with bibliographies on regions and special subjects.

Myers, Robin, ed. DICTIONARY OF LITERATURE IN THE ENGLISH LANGUAGE FROM CHAUCER TO 1940. 2 vols. Oxford: Pergamon Press, 1970.

This dictionary provides biographical and bibliographical material on about thirty-five hundred authors from all over the world who have used the English language as their medium, from Chaucer to 1940. The material is arranged in chronological order by author. A short biographical sketch is followed by a list of the author's works and dates of publication. Volume 1 has geographical and chronological indexes to authors. Volume 2 has a title-author index.

Scott, Arthur F., ed. CURRENT LITERARY TERMS. London and New York: Macmillan; Toronto: St. Martin's Press, 1965.

Scott presents the etymology and concise definitions of the principal terms used in all kinds of literature. The book is alphabetically arranged and cross-referenced.

Shaw, Harry, ed. DICTIONARY OF LITERARY TERMS. New York: McGraw-Hill, 1972.

Shaw presents brief definitions of hundreds of literary terms.

Shipley, Joseph, ed. DICTIONARY OF WORLD LITERARY TERMS, FORMS, TECHNIQUES, CRITICISM. Rev. and enl. Boston: Writer, 1970.

This work is divided into three major parts. Part 1 provides concise definitions of world literary terms. Part 2 presents critical surveys of the history of American, English, French, German, Greek, Italian, Latin, Medieval, Russian, and Spanish literary criticism. Part 3 presents a selected list of critics and works from countries other than those discussed in part 2.

ENCYCLOPEDIAS

Fleischmann, Wolfgang Bernard, ed. ENCYCLOPEDIA OF WORLD LITERATURE IN THE TWENTIETH CENTURY. 3 vols. Enl. and updated ed. of LEXIKON DER WELTLITERATUR IM 20. JAHRHUNDERT. New York: Frederick Ungar, 1967.

> The aim of this work is to cover "the major aspects of the litera-ture of the twentieth century on a global scale." The survey articles discuss almost all literatures "with claim to a substantial productivity." Also discussed in articles are literary movements of consequence, movements in ideas, literary criticism in its his-torical and functional roles, the major genres of literature, perti-nent connections between literature and the related arts, and les-ser genres with claim to outstanding authors. Separate bio-biblio-graphical articles consider authors alive or living in the twentieth century whose contributions to literature may be considered partic-ularly significant. Entries are alphabetically arranged.

Grigson, Geoffrey, ed. THE CONCISE ENCYCLOPEDIA OF MODERN WORLD LITERATURE. New York: Hawthorn, 1971.

> This encyclopedia has three major sections. The first concerns it-self with articles on Anglo-American, French, German, Greek, Italian, Japanese, Latin American, Russian, and Spanish literature. The second presents articles on the forms of literature: drama, the novel, poetry, and the short story. The third provides biographical-critical sketches of the most important authors of the modern age. There is a list of Nobel Prize winners for literature, 1901-1969, at the end of the work, as well as notes on the contributors, an author index, and a title index.

Preminger, Alex, ed. PRINCETON ENCYCLOPEDIA OF POETRY AND POETICS. Enl. ed. Princeton, N.J.: Princeton University Press, 1974.

> Preminger presents a comprehensive treatment of poetry and poetics. It deals with history, theory, technique, and criticism of poetry from earliest times to the present. It contains about one-thousand individual entries ranging from twenty to more than twenty-thousand

words. The entries are supplemented by bibliographies and general cross-references. There are no articles on individual authors, poems, or allusions, since other reference works provide these. The entries are arranged under the four headings of history of poetry, techniques of poetry, poetics and criticisms, and poetry and its relationship to other fields of interest.

Spender, Stephen, and Donald Hall, eds. THE CONCISE ENCYCLOPEDIA OF ENGLISH AND AMERICAN POETS AND POETRY. New York: Hawthorn, 1963.

Spender and Hall provide sketches of poets and short articles on literary movements, genre, and so on.

Steinberg, S.H., ed. CASSELL'S ENCYCLOPEDIA OF WORLD LITERATURE. Rev. ed. 3 vols. London: Cassell, 1953.

Refers to the literature of all periods and all peoples. Volume 1 contains histories of individual literatures, definitions of literary terms, descriptions of literary genres, accounts of schools and movements, of themes explored by writers and of topics of general interest. The revised edition adds an importance to non-European writing absent in the original. There is more extensive treatment in this edition of the literatures of Africa and Asia. Other new material includes discussions of Petrarchism and Baroque, accounts of shifts of critical interest, and information on subjects developing in the last twenty years. Some articles have undergone complete revision. Separate entries have been made for the Koran and the Talmud. There are ninety new articles.

Volumes 2 and 3 are comprised of bibliographical material. Writers are presented in one continuous alphabetical sequence (A-K and L-Z). Incorporated into these volumes are the articles on individual works of literature that appeared in volume 1 of the first edition. Volumes 2 and 3 take into account recent scholarship and reevaluation of individual author's contribution. Some new writers are included.

GUIDES

"American Literature, English Literature, and World Literatures in English: An Information Guide Series." Series ed.: Theodore Grieder; assoc. ed.: Duane DeVries. Detroit: Gale Research Co., 1974-- . In progress.

> The aim of this multivolumed endeavor is ultimately to provide information guides to most English-language literatures. Many volumes are heavily annotated.

Bateson, F.W., ed. A GUIDE TO ENGLISH LITERATURE. 2nd ed. Garden City, N.Y.: Doubleday, 1968.

> Bateson discusses the principal editions of reference resources and commentaries that a reader should use if he is to investigate any of the major areas of English literature from its beginnings to the present day. The book opens with descriptions of the most important general works on English literature. Four "interchapters" function to assist the reader to a historical point of view toward the principal periods, designated by the author as the Middle English period (1150-1500), the Renaissance period (1500-1650), the Augustan period (1650-1800), and the Romantic period (1800-1960). The discussion of each period is followed by reading lists that cover bibliographies, literary histories, anthologies, special studies, and principal authors. There is a general section on literary criticism that covers the major bibliographies; histories of criticism; anthologies; symposia; critical journals; general critical theories; and critical books on poetry, prose fiction, drama, style and stylistics, and prosody. Professor Harrison T. Meserole of Pennsylvania State University provides a final chapter on literary scholarship.

Beckson, Karl, and Arthur Ganz, eds. A READER'S GUIDE TO LITERARY TERMS: A DICTIONARY. New York: Noonday, 1975.

> This guide presents definitions of important terms and discusses their meanings. Many examples and references to literature are provided.

Bell, Inglis F., and Jennifer Gallup, eds. A REFERENCE GUIDE TO ENGLISH, AMERICAN, CANADIAN LITERATURE. Vancouver: University of Columbia Press, 1971.

>Designed for the specific needs of the undergraduate, the book is divided into two sections, one dealing with general reference books and the other with bibliographies of major authors. Section 1 lists bibliographies, indexes, and surveys and periodicals pertinent to the major periods of English literature and its major genres. It lists book reviews; indexes to collections; universal, British, American, and Canadian biographies; handbooks and dictionaries; literary histories; critical surveys; resources for such auxiliary subjects as language, linguistics, style and rhetoric, myth, folklore, symbolism and social and intellectual history. The arrangement is alphabetical.

>Serial bibliographies and annual surveys are added at the end of each section in a separate alphabetical sequence. Section 2 lists major authors alphabetically and bibliographies of criticism chronologically. The approach is selective, the aim being to list the best available material. Writers are included who have published major works in Britain, the United States, or Canada. All entries are annotated.

Bond, Donald F., ed. A REFERENCE GUIDE TO ENGLISH STUDIES. 2nd ed. Chicago: University of Chicago Press, 1971.

>This guide is designed as an introduction to the methods and materials of graduate study in English. It calls special attention to universal bibliographies, bibliographies of bibliographies, indexes and classified lists of books and articles, and bibliographies of dissertations, so that an investigator will "avoid the necessity of repeating operations already performed by others and spare himself . . . discovering that the matter under discussion has already been adequately treated." The guide is restricted to the indispensable references in each field. American literature is kept separate from other literatures, and a section on language is included.

Dick, Aliki Lafkidou, ed. A STUDENT'S GUIDE TO BRITISH LITERATURE. Littleton, Colo.: Libraries Unlimited, 1971.

>Dick's book provides students with a selective guide to the most important authors and writings from the Anglo-Saxon period to the present. The materials are restricted to those the editor considers indispensable. The first chapter presents basic reference materials pertaining to English literature in general. Chapters 2 through 5 are devoted to specific literary periods: Old English, medieval, Renaissance, Restoration, nineteenth century, and twentieth century. A chronological arrangement is used. The last six chapters list bibliographies and critical works pertaining to a particular period as a whole and then list each genre alphabetically and divide it into two parts: works pertaining to the genre as a whole,

and those pertaining to individual authors or works of unknown authorship. The individual author entries fall into four sections: the author's most important works chronologically arranged with date of writing or publication, bibliographies, texts, and selective criticism. Selection of individual authors has been based on their significance as reflected in standard histories of English literature.

LITERARY RESEARCH GUIDE. Ed. Margaret C. Patterson. Detroit: Gale Research Co., 1976.

This is one of the best, certainly the most recent, of the guides to literary research, with emphasis on American and British literature but dealing as well with comparative, continental, and world literatures. The text is logical and comprehensive, and is particularly sound in its organized listing of resources and its descriptive annotations. For any student of literature--undergraduate, graduate, post-doctoral--it represents a very solid beginning point for the study of the literatures it covers. See also John Press, A MAP OF MODERN ENGLISH VERSE, under "Background Readings," below. These are two basic resources from which to begin investigations into modern English poetry.

Sheehy, Eugene P., ed. GUIDE TO REFERENCE BOOKS. 9th ed. Chicago: American Library Association, 1976.

A standard work, international in coverage, it is arranged according to subject, is annotated, and fully indexed. See also under "Bibliographies of Bibliographies," page 9.

Temple, Ruth Z., and Martin Tucker, eds. 20TH CENTURY BRITISH LITERATURE: A REFERENCE GUIDE AND BIBLIOGRAPHY. New York: Ungar, 1968.

Designed for the student of contemporary British literature, this book is divided into two major parts. Part 1 is a reference guide to British literary books of the twentieth century. It lists general reference books, bibliographies of contemporary English literature, special reference guides, general bibliographies, author bibliographies, annual bibliographies, sources for biography, reference books, journals, histories, general histories of modern literature, special studies of modern literature, autobiographies, diaries, memoirs, reminiscences, collections of essays, encyclopedias, and special studies on criticism, drama, the novel, and poetry.

Part 2 consists of the bibliographies of some four-hundred modern British authors. Each author's bibliography is arranged in chronological order, and the genre of each book cited. A bibliography of each author's work is noted, if one has been published, and one or two critical books about him.

Vitale, Philip H., ed. BASIC TOOLS OF RESEARCH: AN ANNOTATED GUIDE FOR STUDENTS OF ENGLISH. 3rd ed. Rev. and enl. Woodbury, N.Y.: Barron's Educational Series, 1975.

Intended for undergraduate and graduate English majors as a reference work or as a text for bibliographical courses, the work is composed of a relatively short list of some six-hundred items that will meet most if not all of the student's needs. The list includes concordances, author bibliographies, and guides to book selection and book reviews. The principle of arrangement is from general to specific and early to current. All items are annotated on their first listing. Brief excerpts from reviews follow the formal annotation of a given work.

HANDBOOKS

Barnhart, Clarence Z., and William D. Halsey, eds. NEW CENTURY HAND-
BOOK OF ENGLISH LITERATURE. Rev. ed. New York: Appleton-Century-
Crofts, 1967.

This handbook is designed to answer questions about English writers,
works of literature, characters from works of literature, and various
related items which are most likely to be asked by American students of English literature. It includes more than fourteen-thousand
entries arranged in alphabetical order and covers Anglo-American,
Canadian, Australian, Irish, and South African literatures. Pro-
nunciations are given.

Deutsch, Babette, ed. POETRY HANDBOOK: A DICTIONARY OF LITERARY
TERMS. New York: Funk and Wagnalls, 1969.

Deutsch presents concise definitions of literary terms and offers il-
lustrations. Intended for the general reader as well as for students
of poetry.

Holman, Clarence Hugh. A HANDBOOK TO LITERATURE. 3rd ed. New
York: Odyssey, 1972.

Based on the original edition by William Thrall and Addison Hibbard, Holman's resource explains literary terms, genres, classifications, prosodic terms, and important names, places, magazines.

Malof, Joseph. A MANUAL OF ENGLISH METERS. Bloomington: Indiana
University Press, 1970.

A detailed presentation of all that is involved in meter. Prosody
is defined, illustrated, and explained.

Shapiro, Karl, and Robert Baum. A PROSODY HANDBOOK. New York:
Harper, 1965.

On the intricacies of prosody, this study explains what makes up
poetry--syllables, feet, lines, stanzas--and illustrates with examples

from poems. Prosody's ultimate connection to theme, imagery,
and structure is emphasized. The book contains a glossary, select
bibliography, and index to poetic terms.

Thorpe, James. LITERARY SCHOLARSHIP: A HANDBOOK FOR STUDENTS
OF ENGLISH AND AMERICAN LITERATURE. Boston: Houghton Mifflin, 1964.

Thorpe emphasizes a well-organized and methodical approach to
literary research. He illustrates his methodology with examples
from literature.

INDEXES

Smith, William James, ed. GRANGER'S INDEX TO POETRY. 6th ed. New York and London: Columbia University Press, 1973.

A standard reference work which aims to help the reader identify and locate poems or selections of poems that have appeared in the most accessible anthologies. It contains title and first line index, author index, and subject index. Every entry in the title and first-line index is followed by alphabetical symbols of the anthologies in which the work appears. The key to the symbols is in the front of the book. The subject index itemizes poems under nearly five-thousand subject categories. The edition indexes a total of 514 volumes of anthologized poetry.

Part 2

BACKGROUND READINGS

Alvarez, Alfred. THE SHAPING SPIRIT. STUDIES IN MODERN ENGLISH AND AMERICAN POETS. London: Chatto and Windus, 1958.

> Alvarez discusses the essential differences between the English and American traditions in poetry and the reasons why the creative possibilities of modern poetry have come to so little. He devotes chapters to T.S. Eliot, W.B. Yeats, Ezra Pound, William Empson, W.H. Auden, Hart Crane, Wallace Stevens, and D.H. Lawrence.

Barnes, T.R. ENGLISH VERSE: VOICE AND MOVEMENT FROM WYATT TO YEATS. Cambridge, Engl.: Cambridge University Press, 1967.

> The book illustrates the most important characteristics of English verse and points out the contrasts between different periods and different modes of writing.

Batho, Edith, and Bonamy Dobree. THE VICTORIANS AND AFTER 1830-1914. Vol. 4 of INTRODUCTION TO ENGLISH AND AMERICAN LITERATURE. Ed. Bonamy Dobree. London: Cresset Press, 1962.

> An introduction to the literature of the period. Bibliography contains material for further study.

Bergonzi, Bernard. HEROES' TWILIGHT: A STUDY OF THE LITERATURE OF THE GREAT WAR. London: Constable, 1965.

> A brief and selective study of the poetry, novels, and autobiographical writings of men who fought in World War I. Literary analysis and assessment are Bergonzi's chief concern, although he takes great pains to present the writers as "victims and witnesses of a unique crisis in British civilization."

Blackburn, Thomas. THE PRICE OF AN EYE. Rev. ed. Westport, Conn.: Greenwood Press, 1974.

> Blackburn treats poetry as an attempt "to understand, clarify, and make articulate the dark processes of the human mind." This established, he presents chapters on the matter and form of the poems of W.B. Yeats, T.S. Eliot, Ezra Pound, Edwin Muir, Edith Sitwell, Robert Graves, W.H. Auden, Dylan Thomas, George Barker, Vernon Watkins and others.

Blackmur, Richard P. THE EXPENSE OF GREATNESS. New York: Arrow Editions, 1940.

> Blackmur includes in this series of essays on modern literature investigations of W.B. Yeats's later poetry, the shorter poems of Thomas Hardy, and methods of composition in A.E. Housman, Wallace Stevens, and Conrad Aiken, among others.

Blunden, Edmund. WAR POETS 1914-18. Rev. ed. London: Longmans, Green, 1964.

Blunden writes on the attitudes to war of Wilfred Owen, Sigfried Sassoon, and others. See Curry's companion volume for World War II, below.

Bowra, Cecil Maurice. THE BACKGROUND OF MODERN POETRY 1900-1950. London: Macmillan, 1951.

Bowra outlines the nature and history of new movements in the poetry of this period.

_____. THE CREATIVE EXPERIMENT. London: Macmillan, 1949.

Bowra sketches some main figures and characteristics of the poetry that succeeded post-symbolist poetry. He discusses the most significant works of the poets in order to clarify the problems and aims of movement.

_____. THE HERITAGE OF SYMBOLISM. London: Macmillan, 1943.

The author presents a survey of the symbolist movement in poetry that occurred during the first decades of the twentieth century.

Brooks, Cleanth. MODERN POETRY AND THE TRADITION. Chapel Hill: University of North Carolina Press, 1939.

Brooks relates the work of modern poets to traditional poetic practice and explains the nature of the modern critical revolution. He includes chapters on Robert Frost, W.H. Auden, T.S. Eliot, and W.B. Yeats.

Bullough, Geoffrey. THE TREND OF MODERN POETRY. London and Edinburgh: Oliver and Boyd, 1934.

Bullough presents "a brief summary of general tendencies and individual achievements which covers the last fifty years and shows how contemporary poetry has emerged from earlier English and French movements."

Bush, Douglas. ENGLISH POETRY: THE MAIN CURRENTS FROM CHAUCER TO THE PRESENT. New York: Oxford University Press, 1952.

An historical sketch of six centuries of English poetry. Bush concerns himself with "the individual poets and poems as they are in themselves rather than as products of their complex backgrounds."

Church, Richard. EIGHT FOR IMMORTALITY. Freeport, N.Y.: Books for Libraries Press, 1941.

Church presents essays on W.H. Davies, Walter de la Mare, Robert Frost, W.B. Yeats, Edmund Blunden, Victoria Sackville-West, T.S. Eliot, and Robert Graves.

Coffman, Stanley. IMAGISM: A CHAPTER FOR THE HISTORY OF MODERN POETRY. Norman: University of Oklahoma Press, 1951.

> A history of the imagist movement, which, from 1912-1917, acted as a reactionary force against "the careless technique and extra-poetic values of much nineteenth century verse."

Cronin, Anthony. A QUESTION OF MORALITY. London: Secker and Warburg, 1966.

> On the nature, causes, and history of the literary revolution known as "the modern movement."

Currey, R.N. POETS OF THE 1939-1945 WAR. London: Longmans, Green, 1907.

> A companion volume to Edmund Blunden's WAR POETS 1914-18 (see above), Curry's book shows how in the World War II, a new group of poets--Sidney Keys, Alun Lewis, Keith Douglas, and others--continued where the World War I poets left off.

Daiches, David. POETRY AND THE MODERN WORLD: A STUDY OF POETRY IN ENGLAND BETWEEN 1900 AND 1939. Chicago: University of Chicago Press, 1940.

> On the poetry of the first forty years of the twentieth century. Daiches presents chapters on the legacy of Victorianism, the poetry of Thomas Hardy, A.E. Housman, G.M. Hopkins, Georgian poetry, war poetry, the imagists and the Sitwells, T.E. Hulme, and T.S. Eliot.

_____. THE PRESENT AGE IN BRITISH LITERATURE AFTER 1920. Bloomington: Indiana University Press, 1959.

> A survey of British Literary history from 1920 to the late 1950s. Daiches presents, in Part 1, general background and discussions of poetry, fiction, critical and general prose, and drama. In part 2 he presents bibliographies of, among others, T.S. Eliot, W.B. Yeats, W.H. Auden, the Georgians, and bibliographies of selected authors of fiction, drama, and general prose.

Davidson, Mildred. THE POETRY IS THE PITY. London: Chatto and Windus, 1972.

> The book is historical survey that concentrates mainly on the poetry of the World War II.

Deutsch, Babette. POETRY IN OUR TIME. Rev. ed. New York: Columbia University Press, 1956.

> A survey of modern poetry, 1900-1950.

Dobree, Bonamy. THE BROKEN CISTERN. London: Cohen and West, 1954.

Dobree discusses the best poetry of the twentieth century as the re-statement of some universal theme to which a great majority of human beings immediately respond.

Drew, Elizabeth, and John L. Sweeney. DIRECTIONS IN MODERN POETRY. New York: W.W. Norton, 1940; rpt. New York: Holt, Rinehart and Winston, 1961.

The aim of the author is "to give some account of the variety and significance of the poetry of the last twenty-five years, by the method of supporting . . . generalizations by example and examination."

Durrell, Lawrence. A KEY TO MODERN BRITISH POETRY. Norman: University of Oklahoma Press, 1952.

Durrell attempts to untangle the complexities of modern poetry and give a brief account of the poets active during the time of the book's writing. He discusses, among other issues, the limits of criticism, space and time in poetry, the poetry of the nineties, the Georgians and imagists, and the poetry of the thirties; he devotes whole chapters to T.S. Eliot and G.M. Hopkins.

Ellmann, Richard. EMINENT DOMAIN: YEATS AMONG WILDE, JOYCE, POUND, ELIOT, AND AUDEN. New York: Oxford University Press, 1967.

Ellmann discusses the influence of W.B. Yeats upon writers mentioned in the title, and the influence of them upon Yeats.

Evans, Benjamin. ENGLISH LITERATURE BETWEEN THE WARS. 2nd ed. London: Methuen, 1949.

Evans treats the years between the wars as "an era in which the whole mind of man and his conception of his destiny changed in a fundamental way" and concentrates his study on those writers who most profoundly transformed into literature an awareness of these changes. He includes chapters on D.H. Lawrence, W.B. Yeats, and T.S. Eliot, among others.

Ford, Hugh D. A POET'S WAR: ENGLISH POETS AND THE SPANISH CIVIL WAR. Philadelphia: University of Pennsylvania Press, 1965.

Ford addresses himself to three questions: "What was the response of a large number of British poets to the war? How did their response affect the nature of, and their attitude toward, their work? What aesthetic, social or anti-social implications does this war poetry have in the pattern of recent British literature?"

Frankenburg, Lloyd. PLEASURE DOME: ON READING MODERN POETRY. Boston: Houghton Mifflin, 1949.

> Frankenburg discusses in detail the relationship between sound and meaning in the poems of James Stephens, T.S. Eliot, Marianne Moore, e.e. cummings, and Wallace Stevens, and examines the same relationship briefly in the poems of Ezra Pound, W.C. Williams, Ogden Nash, W.H. Auden, Dylan Thomas, Robert Lowell, and Elizabeth Bishop.

Fraser, G.S. THE MODERN WRITER AND HIS WORLD. New York: F.A. Praeger, 1964.

> Part 4 of Fraser's book deals with developments in British poetry from the 1890s to the 1950s.

Fussell, Paul. THE GREAT WAR IN MODERN MEMORY. New York and London: Oxford University Press, 1975.

> Fussell writes of the literary means by which the British experience on the western front has been "remembered, conventionalized, and mythologized." He concerns himself with "the literary dimensions of the trench experience itself," and with the manner in which "the dynamics and iconography of the Great War have proved crucial political, rhetorical, and artistic determinants on subsequent life." He suggests forms of the new myth that the war generated, and tries "to supply contexts, both actual and literary, for writers who have most effectively memorialized the Great War as a historical experience with conspicuous imaginative and artistic meaning." These writers are identified as Siegfried Sassoon, Robert Graves, and Edmund Blunden. Fussell also considers the poets David Jones, Isaac Rosenberg, and Wilfred Owen.

Hamburger, Michael. THE TRUTH OF POETRY: TENSIONS IN MODERN POETRY FROM BAUDELAIRE TO THE 1960S. New York: Harcourt, Brace, 1970.

> Hamburger attempts to understand the nature, assumptions, and functions of modern poetry.

Harmer, J.B. VICTORY IN LIMBO: IMAGISM 1908-1917. London: Secker and Warburg, 1975.

> In this history of the imagistic movement, Harmer characterizes imagism as "the one literary movement in Britain and America that reflected the energies of modernism" and goes on to discuss the work of Richard Aldington, Rupert Brooke, Joseph Campbell, Padraic Colum, H.D., J.G. Fletcher, F.S. Flint, T.E. Hulme, D.H. Lawrence, Harold Munro, and Ezra Pound.

Holroyd, Stuart. THE EMERGENCE FROM CHAOS. Boston: Houghton Mifflin; Cambridge, Mass.: Riverside Press, 1957.

Holroyd discusses the poets' responses to contemporary religious sensibility. The author describes the work as "an attack on humanism and a plea for the rediscovery of a religious standard of values."

Hough, Graham. REFLECTIONS ON A LITERARY REVOLUTION. Washington, D.C.: Catholic University of America Press, 1960.

Hough presents a series of lectures dealing with the nature of the poetic upheaval of the earlier part of the twentieth century.

Hughes, Glenn. IMAGISM AND THE IMAGISTS: A STUDY IN MODERN POETRY. Stanford, Calif.: Stanford University Press; London: H. Milford and Oxford University Press, 1931.

Hughes characterizes imagism as "the best-organized and most influential movement in English poetry since the activity of the pre-Raphaelites" and proceeds to outline its nature and development. Whole chapters are devoted to Richard Aldington, H.D., J.G. Fletcher, F.S. Flint, D.H. Lawrence, Amy Lowell, and Ezra Pound.

Isaacs, Jacob. THE BACKGROUND OF MODERN POETRY. New York: Dutton, 1952.

Isaacs discusses the nature and techniques of modern poetry and its impact on the contemporary reader. One chapter is devoted to T.S Eliot's achievement.

Johnston, J.H. ENGLISH POETRY OF THE FIRST WORLD WAR: A STUDY IN THE EVOLUTION OF LYRIC AND NARRATIVE FORM. Princeton, N.J.: Princeton University Press, 1964.

Johnston concerns himself with the work of ten British soldier-poets of World War I--Rupert Brooke, Siegfried Sassoon, Wilfred Owen, Isaac Rosenberg, Julian Grenfell, Robert Nicholes, Charles Sorley, Edmund Blunden, Herbert Read, and David Jones. Johnston feels these poets represent "the best or most characteristic poetry of the war."

Jones, Peter. IMAGIST POETRY. Harmondsworth, Engl.: Penguin Books, 1972.

In the introduction to this anthology of imagist poetry, Jones presents an historical account of the movement.

Kenner, Hugh. THE POUND ERA. Berkeley and Los Angeles: University of California Press, 1971.

Kenner's long study investigates how the modern epoch "was extricated from the fin de siecle." He discusses Pound as the leading

influence on twentieth-century literature, especially the work of Eliot,
Joyce, Lewis, and Williams. Kenner sees the literature of the era as
reflecting poetic conceptions of the physical and genetic laws of the
universe.

Kermode, Frank. THE ROMANTIC IMAGE. London: Routledge and Kegan
Paul, 1957.

Kermode's essay "is primarily concerned with the evolution of assumptions relating to the image of poetry; it is an attempt to
describe this image in a new way, and to suggest new ways of
looking at contingent issues in poetry and criticism."

Leavis, Frank Raymond. NEW BEARINGS IN ENGLISH POETRY. New York:
G.W. Stewart, 1950. Rpt. Ann Arbor: University of Michigan Press, 1960.

Leavis discusses what he considers the most important aspects of
contemporary poetry. He includes chapters on poetry and the
modern world, poetry at the end of World War I, T.S. Eliot,
Ezra Pound, and G.M. Hopkins.

Lehmann, John. THE OPEN NIGHT. New York: Harcourt, Brace, 1952.

Lehmann's essays concern themselves with "the search for the motives
and ideals that underlie the life pattern of men and women of
genius who have lived through the stresses of our age." He includes studies on W.B. Yeats, Edward Thomas, and the poet in
the modern world.

Lester, John A. JOURNEY THROUGH DESPAIR: 1800-1914: TRANSFORMA-
TIONS IN BRITISH LITERARY CULTURE. Princeton, N.J.: Princeton University Press, 1968.

In his description of the imaginative response to this epoch of
British history, Lester discusses the poetic achievement of W.B.
Yeats and D.H. Lawrence.

MacNeice, Louis. MODERN POETRY: A PERSONAL ESSAY. London: Oxford University Press, 1938.

The book is MacNeice's "plea for impure poetry, that is, for poetry conditioned by the poet's life and the world around him." He
urges poets to take the middle road between "pure entertainment
(escape poetry) and propaganda."

Maxwell, D.E.S. POETS OF THE THIRTIES. London: Routledge and Kegan
Paul, 1969.

Maxwell discusses the political and economic situation in England
during the 1930s and explores the nature, subject matter, and
technique of the poetry of the period. He includes chapters on

Christopher Caudwell and John Cornford, C. Day Lewis, W.H. Auden, Louis MacNeice, and Stephen Spender.

Muste, John M. SAY THAT WE SAW SPAIN DIE: LITERARY CONSEQUENCES OF THE SPANISH CIVIL WAR. Seattle: University of Washington Press, 1966.

Muste's book consists of a development of the idea that "the fundamental importance of the Spanish Civil War in the literature of the United States and Great Britain is in the fact that it was a major element in the almost complete destruction of one of the means by which modern writers have attempted to order their knowledge of a violent and chaotic world." The "means" here is Marxism.

O'Connor, William V. THE NEW UNIVERSITY WITS AND THE END OF MODERNISM. Carbondale: University of Southern Illinois Press, 1963.

O'Connor identifies a literary group that emerged after World War II as the "New University of Wits" and includes among them the poet Philip Larkin. Chapter 2 is devoted to Larkin's work and its place in the movement.

Paliwal, B.B. THE POETIC REVOLUTION OF THE NINETEEN TWENTIES. New Delhi: S. Chand, 1974.

Paliwal's inquiry concerns itself with "the poetic revolution led by Ezra Pound and T.S. Eliot in the twenties, and seeks to gather the results of their poetic theories and practice, specifically making an attempt to find out whether the movement was a renewal of contact with the main tradition of English poetry, or it was an aberration and was followed by a counter-revolution."

Pinto, Vivian de Sola. CRISIS IN ENGLISH POETRY 1880-1940. London: Hutchinson University Library, 1951.

This book discusses the crisis in English poetry that occurred between 1880 and 1940 and the relationship of this literary crisis to the social, political, and moral crises of modern England. Chapters are devoted to Thomas Hardy, A.E. Housman, G.M. Hopkins, Robert Bridges, W.B. Yeats and J.M. Synge, D.H. Lawrence, T.S. Eliot, and others.

Press, John. A MAP OF MODERN ENGLISH VERSE. London and Oxford: Oxford University Press, 1969.

Press's book has fourteen sections, each of which is concerned with a poet or group of poets and presents biographical and critical information, critical passages, selections of poems, and a bibliography. Press considers the study "a source book rather than a conspectus of the best critical opinion." A very good resource with which to begin investigations into twentieth-century English poetry. See also LITERARY RESEARCH GUIDE listed in part 1.

_____. RULE AND ENERGY: TRENDS IN BRITISH POETRY SINCE THE SECOND WORLD WAR. London and New York: Oxford University Press, 1963.

Rosenthal, M.L. THE MODERN POETS: A CRITICAL INTRODUCTION. New York: Oxford University Press, 1960.

Rosenthal presents a survey of modern poetry "with an aim to break down the formidable but quite unnecessary barriers between poetry and the general reader." Among others, he discusses W.B. Yeats, Ezra Pound, T.S. Eliot, D.H. Lawrence, W.H. Auden, and Dylan Thomas.

Ross, Alan. POETRY 1945-50. London and New York: Longmans, Green, 1951.

A discussion of several poets' artistic development in the five years after World War II. Ross attempts to describe the character of English poetry during these years. He relates it to the conditions in which the poetry was written and to the earlier work of the writers who produced this character. He concentrates on new developments in poetry.

Ross, Robert. THE GEORGIAN REVOLT, 1910-1922: THE RISE AND FALL OF A POETIC IDEAL. Carbondale: University of Southern Illinois, 1965.

An essentially historical study of the Georgians and their age. Ross explains rather than evaluates the literature of this age.

Scarfe, Francis. AUDEN AND AFTER: THE LIBERATION OF POETRY 1930-1941. London: George Routledge, 1942; rpt. New York: Kraus, 1969.

A series of essays devoted to the work of W.H. Auden, C. Day Lewis, Stephen Spender, Louis MacNeice, Geoffrey Grigson, Frederic Prokosch, Kenneth Allott, Dylan Thomas, George Barker, Julian Symons, the surrealists, and the apocalyptics.

Sergeant, Howard. TRADITION IN THE MAKING OF MODERN POETRY. London: Brittanicus Liber, 1951.

Sergeant's volume traces the development of English poetry from 1900 to 1950 and illutrates the belief that "the main stream of tradition flows continually, changing and being changed" from the nineteenth to the twentieth centuries.

Shivpuri, Jagdish. SIX MODERN ENGLISH POETS. New Delhi: S. Chand, 1973.

> Shivpuri presents essays on T.S. Eliot, W.H. Auden, Stephen Spender, C. Day Lewis, Louis MacNeice, and Dylan Thomas.

Silkin, Jon. THE POETRY OF THE GREAT WAR. London: Oxford University Press, 1972.

> Silkin includes in his study of World War I poetry chapters on Thomas Hardy, Rudyard Kipling, Rupert Brooke, Charles Sorley, Edward Thomas, Edmund Blunden and Ivor Gurney, Stephen Spender, Herbert Read, Richard Aldington, Ford Madox Ford, Wilfred Owen, Isaac Rosenberg, and David Jones.

Simon, Myron. THE GEORGIAN POETIC. Berkeley, Los Angeles, and London: University of California Press, 1975.

> Simon demonstrates the important contribution of the Georgians to the formation of twentieth-century English poetics. He considers the reputation of Georgian poetry, its intellectual background, the character of Georgian opposition, and the principles of Georgian poetry.

Sisson, C.H. ENGLISH POETRY 1900-1950. London: Rupert Hart-Davis, 1971.

> Sisson gives an account of "where the best English verse of the first half of the century is to be found . . . what its qualities are and . . . what sort of men wrote it." He discusses the work of thirty poets.

Sitwell, Edith. ASPECTS OF MODERN POETRY. London: Duckworth, 1934.

> Sitwell presents a survey of modern poetry that deals with some of its significant phases. She discusses the poetry of G.M. Hopkins, W.B. Yeats, T.S. Eliot, Sachaverell Sitwell, and Ezra Pound, among others.

Smith, Elton Edward. THE ANGRY YOUNG MEN OF THE THIRTIES. Carbondale: Southern Illinois University Press; London and Amsterdam: Feffer and Simons, 1975.

> Smith gives an account of the Auden-Spender-MacNeice group. He discusses their ideas and their modes of expression.

Southworth, James. SOWING THE SPRING: STUDIES IN BRITISH POETS FROM HOPKINS TO MacNEICE. Oxford: Basil Blackwell, 1940.

> Southworth concentrates mainly on the impact of political forces on G.M. Hopkins, W.B. Yeats, Lawrence Binyon, D.H. Lawrence, T.S. Eliot, C. Day Lewis, W.H. Auden, Stephen Spender, and Louis MacNeice.

Spear, Hilda. REMEMBERING, WE FORGET. A BACKGROUND STUDY TO THE POETRY OF THE FIRST WORLD WAR. London: Davis-Poynter, 1979.

> Spear's study "is concerned with the changing attitudes to war as they were manifested in contemporary writings, both personal and public, during the years 1914 to 1918; it attempts to demonstrate not only how the poetry of the period was a true reflection of men's thoughts and feelings, but how it finally crystallized the new awareness to war which developed in that era."

Spender, Stephen. POETRY SINCE 1939. London and New York: Longmans, Green, 1946.

> Spender discusses the impact of World War II on the poets who wrote after 1939.

_____. THE STRUGGLE OF THE MODERN. Berkeley: University of California Press, 1963.

> Spender's personal reflections on the modern qualities in twentieth-century literature and art. Much of the book is devoted to poetry.

Stanford, Derek. THE FREEDOM OF POETRY: STUDIES IN CONTEMPORARY VERSE. London: Falcon Press, 1947.

> Stanford writes on the artist's need to "be left to create those images and forms dictated by the inner needs of his nature." He discusses the work of Sidney Keyes, David Gascoyne, Alex Comfort, Lawrence Durrell, Nicholas Moore, Norman Nicholson, Wrey Gardiner, Kathleen Raine, Ruthven Todd, and Anne Ridler.

Stead, C.K. THE NEW POETIC: YEATS TO ELIOT. London: Hutchinson University Library, 1964.

> The aim of Stead's essay is "to define as nearly as possible what conception of the function of poetry is implied in the work of certain twentieth-century poets; and, in particular, to discern that function as it is implied in the work of Yeats and Eliot."

Stewart, J.I.M. OXFORD HISTORY OF ENGLISH LITERATURE. Vol. 12: EIGHT MODERN WRITERS. Oxford: Clarendon Press, 1963.

> Included in these studies of eight writers are essays on Thomas Hardy, W.B. Yeats, Rudyard Kipling, and D.H. Lawrence.

Swinnerton, Frank. THE GEORGIAN LITERARY SCENE 1910-1935. Rev. ed. London: Hutchinson, 1969.

> Swinnerton presents a detailed history of the British literary scene from 1910 to 1935.

Background Readings

Thurley, Geoffrey. THE IRONIC HARVEST: ENGLISH POETRY IN THE TWENTIETH CENTURY. London: Edward Arnold, 1974.

> Thurley perceives the employment of irony as the overdominant strategy of twentieth-century poetry.

Thwaite, Anthony. CONTEMPORARY ENGLISH POETRY: AN INTRODUCTION. Rev. ed. London: William Heinemann, 1964.

> Thwaite presents critical introductions to the major British poets of the twentieth century. He covers the poetry scene from G.M. Hopkins to the poets of the fifties and sixties.

Tindall, William York. FORCES IN MODERN BRITISH LITERATURE 1885-1946. New York: A.A. Knopf, 1947.

> Tindall explores contemporary British literature in order "to show its character as a whole and to emphasize books rather than authors." He discusses the work of many poets.

Tolley, A.T. THE POETRY OF THE THIRTIES. London: Victor Gollanz, 1975.

> Tolley employs the literary-historical approach in offering a critical account of the work of the British poets of the 1930s.

Treece, Henry. HOW I SEE APOCALYPSE. London: L. Drummond, 1946.

> Treece discusses the correlation between Romanticism and the form of anarchism forwarded by Herbert Read; the nature of poetry with emphasis on anarchic attitudes; and the work of such writers as Tennyson, Eliot, Sparrow, Hopkins, Thomas, and Read.

Tschumi, Raymond. THOUGHT IN 20TH CENTURY POETRY. London: Routledge and Kegan Paul, 1951.

> Tschumi explores the symbols, myths, and ideas behind the systems of thought of W.B. Yeats, Edwin Muir, T.S. Eliot, Herbert Read, C. Day Lewis, and others.

Williams, Charles. POETRY AT PRESENT. Oxford: Clarendon Press, 1931.

> Williams presents an introduction to the works of Thomas Hardy, Robert Bridges, A.E. Housman, W.B. Yeats, Walter de la Mare, John Masefield, T.S. Eliot, Edith, Osbert, and Socheverell Sitwell, Robert Graves, Edmund Blunden, and others.

Wilson, Edmund. AXEL'S CASTLE: A STUDY IN THE IMAGINATIVE LITERATURE OF 1870-1930. New York and London: C. Scribner, 1931.

> In Wilson's discussion of the origin and development of certain tendencies in contemporary literature, he considers the achievements of W.B. Yeats and T.S. Eliot.

Part 3

INDIVIDUAL AUTHORS

W[YSTAN] H[UGH] AUDEN (1907-73)

PRINCIPAL WORKS

Poetry

POEMS. N.p.: S.H. Spender, 1928.
POEMS. London: Faber, 1930.
THE ORATORS: AN ENGLISH STUDY. London: Faber, 1932.
LOOK, STRANGER! London: Faber, 1936.
SPAIN. London: Faber, 1937.
SELECTED POEMS. London: Faber, 1938.
ANOTHER TIME: POEMS. New York: Random House, 1940.
SOME POEMS. London: Faber, 1940.
NEW YEAR LETTER. London: Faber, 1941.
FOR THE TIME BEING. New York: Random House, 1944.
COLLECTED POETRY OF W.H. AUDEN. New York: Random House, 1945.
THE AGE OF ANXIETY: A BAROQUE ECLOGUE. New York: Random House, 1947.
COLLECTED SHORTER POEMS 1930-1944. London: Faber, 1950.
NONES. New York: Random House, 1951.
THE SHIELD OF ACHILLES. New York: Random House, 1955.
THE OLD MAN'S ROAD. New York: Voyages, 1956.
W.H. AUDEN: A SELECTION BY THE AUTHOR. London: Penguin-Faber, 1958.
HOMAGE TO CLIO. New York: Random House, 1960.
ABOUT THE HOUSE. New York: Random House, 1965.
COLLECTED SHORTER POEMS 1927-1957. London: Faber, 1966.
COLLECTED LONGER POEMS. London: Faber, 1968.
SELECTED POEMS. London: Faber, 1968.
CITY WITHOUT WALLS. London: Faber, 1969.
ACADEMIC GRAFFITI. London: Faber, 1969.
EPISTLE TO A GODSON AND OTHER POEMS. London: Faber, 1972.
AUDEN/MOORE: POEMS AND LITHOGRAPHS. London: British Museum, 1974.
POEMS, LITHOGRAPHS BY HENRY MOORE. London: Petersburg Press, 1974.
THANK YOU, FOG. London: Faber, 1974.

W[ystan] H[ugh] Auden

Other Works

THE DANCE OF DEATH (1933), drama.
THE DOG BENEATH THE SKIN, with Christopher Isherwood (1935), drama.
THE ASCENT OF F6, with Christopher Isherwood (1936), drama.
LETTERS FROM ICELAND, with Louis MacNeice (1937), prose, verse.
THE ENCHAFED FLOOD (1950), criticism.
THE DYER'S HAND (1962), criticism.
SELECTED ESSAYS (1964), criticism.
SECONDARY WORLDS (1968), criticism.
A CERTAIN WORLD: A COMMONPLACE BOOK (1970), prose.
FOREWORDS AND AFTERWORDS (1973), criticism.

BIBLIOGRAPHY

Bloomfield, B.C., and Edward Mendelson. W.H. AUDEN: A BIBLIOGRAPHY 1924-1969. 2nd ed. Charlottesville: University of Virginia, 1972.

> See also Spears, POETRY OF W.H. AUDEN, under "Criticism" below.

BIOGRAPHY

Osborne, Charles. W.H. AUDEN: THE LIFE OF A POET. London: Harcourt Brace Jovanovich, 1979.

> Osborne wrote this biography with the help of Stephen Spender who gave him memories of his life with Auden and also letters; John Lehman who supplied information about Auden in the thirties; and Ian Hamilton who suggested approaches and supplied criticism. The biography is thorough and detailed.

CRITICISM

Allen, Walter. "W.H. Auden: The Most Exciting Living Poet." LISTENER 47 (1952), 640-41.

> In 1930, with the first publication of a book of his verse, W.H. Auden changed the contemporary poetic landscape. This article investigates the manner in which Auden accomplished this.

Anderson, D.M. "Aspects of Auden." LANDFALL, 3 (1949), 270-79.

> Anderson studies the themes and techniques of NEW YEAR LETTER (1941) and of "The Sea and the Mirror" and "For the Time Being," both of which appeared in the volume FOR THE TIME BEING (1944).

Bahlke, G.W. THE LATER AUDEN: FROM "NEW YEAR LETTER" TO ABOUT THE HOUSE. New Brunswick, N.J.: Rutgers University Press, 1970.

> Bahlke presents an elucidation of Auden's later poetry and a refutation of "the contention that Auden's vision is frivolous, or ephemeral, or even dishonest." The focus is on four long poems, "New Year Letter," "The Sea and the Mirror," "For the Time Being," and THE AGE OF ANXIETY, and on the four volumes of poetry published in the fifties and sixties. The introduction considers Auden's poetry of the thirties; chapter 1 his relation to Christian thought; chapter 2 a reading of "New Year Letter"; chapter 3 a review of Auden's literary criticism; chapter 4 "The Sea and the Mirror"; chapter 5 FOR THE TIME BEING; chapter 6 THE AGE OF ANXIETY; chapter 7 "the dominant concern and mode of Auden's poetry" in volumes extending from NONES to ABOUT THE HOUSE.

Bayley, John. "Halcyon Structures." LISTENER, 80 (1969), 413-14.

> The best poems in CITY WITHOUT WALLS (1969) reveal, states Bayley, subtle metrics, technical excellence and sophistication concealed by an air of simplicity. Auden reveals an interest, not to himself, but in the world he turns into art.

_____. "Our Northern Manichee." ENCOUNTER 21 (1963), 74-81.

> In THE DYER'S HAND, states Bayley, Auden reveals himself as "a literary manichee," who continually "stresses the dualism between words as objects of play and craft." This stance "leads to firmness and clarity, never to confusion" and also to "forthrightness of moral judgment."

Beach, Joseph Warren. THE MAKING OF THE AUDEN CANON. Minneapolis: University of Minnesota Press, 1957.

> Beach describes his book as "a record of the facts in regard to W.H. Auden's procedure in making up the texts of the COLLECTED POEMS (1945) and the COLLECTED SHORTER POEMS (1950), in the following matters: textual alterations made in the poems as they appeared in earlier collections and/or in periodicals; excision of passages of some length in the poems reprinted; elimination of entire poems published in earlier collections and/or periodicals." The book attacks Auden for capriciousness in the selection and ordering of poems in the COLLECTED POEMS. The argument asserts that Auden refused to respect proper chronology and this lack manifests an absence of development as a poet, thus demonstrating the success of any individual poem to be an accident.

Bloom, Robert. "W.H. Auden's Bestiary of the Human." VIRGINIA QUARTERLY REVIEW 42 (1966), 207-33.

> This essay examines "one aspect of Auden's preoccupation with the

human condition and sees it in relation to the poetry that has
come of it and the poetry that has gone into it." The group of
poems dealing with the animal-man contrast, composed over a
period of almost thirty years, "constitutes a kind of human bestiary
in which Auden's constancy and variety are joined together as he
seeks to isolate, delineate, and render his sense of human nature."

Bradbury, John M. "Auden and the Tradition." WESTERN REVIEW 12 (1948),
223-29.

A study of Auden's "noticeable and far-reaching" break with the
intensely subjective poetic tradition which he inherited.

Braybrooke, Neville. "W.H. Auden: The Road from Marx." AMERICA 88
(1953), 680-81.

Braybrooke asserts that, despite the spiritual deepening of his poetry, Auden has not ceased to be an acute observer of society.

Brooke-Rose, Christine. "Notes on the Metre of Auden's 'The Age of Anxiety.'"
ESSAYS IN CRITICISM 13 (1963), 253-64.

A fanciful (the persona of the article is speaking in the year 2185
A.D. about the British poetry that survived two atomic wars) but
serious and detailed investigation of Auden's "deficient Anglo-Saxon
alliterative measure," his prosody, his syllabic verse forms, all of
which provide evidence for this futuristic persona that in her judgment "something had gone seriously awry with the noble epic line."

Brophy, James D. W.H. AUDEN: COLUMBIA ESSAYS ON MODERN WRITERS.
New York and London: Columbia University Press, 1970.

A brief survey of Auden's work which characterizes him, above
all, as a poet "with the temperament disposed toward balance."

Buell, Frederick. W.H. AUDEN AS A SOCIAL POET. Ithaca and London:
Cornell University Press, 1973.

This book is concerned with the social aspects of Auden's verse
and focuses on the years in which the poet's social vision was at
its stage of formation, the 1930s.

Burnham, James. "W.H. Auden." NATION, 8 August 1934, pp. 164-65.

Burnham sees Auden as the "most considerable" of the group of
young British poets pushing for a classless society. The article
discusses THE ORATORS (1932) as marking a change and reorienta-
tion in the poet: Auden is now "re-fusing his personality and his
art" in a way not previously evident.

Callan, Edward. "Auden's Ironic Masquerade: Criticism as Morality Play."
UNIVERSITY OF TORONTO QUARTERLY 35 (1966), 133-43.

> An investigation of the critical properties of FOR THE TIME
> BEING (1944). Callan sees the work as "both a criticism of litera-
> ture paving the way for the religious themes of the Christmas Ora-
> torio and a work of art in which the abstractions of theoretical
> criticism take flesh and prance on stage like the characters in
> morality plays."

_____. "Auden's 'New Year Letter': New Style of Architecture." RENAS-
CENCE 16 (1966), 13-19.

> Callan asserts that Auden believes it is one function of the artist
> to discover new forms to express man's situation: Jung's theories
> on the psyche and Kierkegaard's all-encompassing notional scheme
> of categories provided architectural models for NEW YEAR LETTER
> (1941), FOR THE TIME BEING (1944), and THE AGE OF ANXIETY
> (1947). NEW YEAR LETTER is constructed on a three-part scheme;
> the parts correspond to Kierkegaard's aesthetic, ethical, and reli-
> gious spheres. The problem of order is the subject matter and the
> work resembles Dante's DIVINE COMEDY in theme and method of
> structuring.

Close, H.M. "The Development of Auden's Poetry." CAMBRIDGE REVIEW
58 (1937), 478-79.

> An answer to F.R. Leavis' charge (SCRUTINY, December 1936)
> that Auden is "still without that with which a poet controls words,
> commands expression, writes poems. He has no organization."
> Close asserts that LOOK, STRANGER! (1936) and THE ASCENT
> OF F6 (1936) "display a maturing of talent even if it is not so
> noticeable as one might have hoped."

Cook, F.W. "Primordial Auden." ESSAYS IN CRITICISM 12 (1962), 402-12.

> An attempt by Cook to clarify the meaning of Auden's obscure
> "Paid on Both Sides." Cook gives an outline of the plot and ac-
> tion and discusses the techniques employed in the play.

_____. "The Wise Fool: W.H. Auden and the Management." TWENTIETH
CENTURY 168 (1960), 219-27.

> This article is an assertion that "Auden the Critic [in Auden's
> article "Balaam and the Ass," ENCOUNTER 2, July 1954] makes
> comments upon the role of the Fool which seem to provide clues
> to the function and methods of Auden the Poet, always a somewhat
> enigmatic figure." The later poetry is briefly analyzed in the light
> of Auden's perception of King Lear's Fool.

Daalder, Joost. "W.H. Auden." JOURNAL OF THE AUSTRALASIAN UNI-VERSITIES LANGUAGE AND LITERATURE ASSOCIATION, 42 (1974), 186-98.

A discussion of the sources that underlie Auden's poem, "The Shield of Achilles."

Duchêne, François. THE CASE OF THE HELMETED AIRMAN: A STUDY OF W.H. AUDEN'S POETRY. Totowa, N.J.: Rowman and Littlefield; London: Chatto and Windus, 1972.

A detailed study of Auden's poetry. Duchêne's investigation piv-ots on the assertion that "the unusual contract between Auden's universal terms of reference and his unattached manner, his 'old impersonality,' is the central puzzle of a very individual, even eccentric talent."

Duncan, Chester. "W.H. Auden." CANADIAN FORUM, 28 (1948), 131-32.

Duncan claims that Auden is dangerously inclined to one extreme of the poetic endeavor, for instance, he tries to deal at once with the "whole amazing panorama" of life; however, he is a successful poet "most of the time."

Eder, Doris L. "Auden's Eden." SOUTHERN HUMANITIES REVIEW, 12 (1978), 353-63.

Eder presents a study of Auden's landscape poetry. Most of the article deals with "Paysage moralisé," part of NEW YEAR LETTER (1941), "Bucolics" and "In Praise of Limestone," poems written between 1948 and 1957.

Engle, Paul. "New English Poets." ENGLISH JOURNAL, College Edition, 27 (1938), 89-101.

The article discusses Auden as belonging to the first generation of poets to reach maturity after the war. With C. Day Lewis and Stephen Spender, Auden restored to English poetry hope and "sub-ject matter beyond the personal."

Enright, D.J. "Reluctant Admiration: A Note on Auden and Rilke." ESSAYS IN CRITICISM, 2 (1952), 180-95.

Rilke is a poet who "immediately arrests attention by his lightning transitions between the most intangible abstract and the most vivid-ly concrete." This article traces Rilke's influence--"insidious but controlled"--on Auden's poetry.

Everett, Barbara. AUDEN. Writers and Critics Series, no. 042. Edinburgh and London: Oliver and Boyd, 1964.

The subject of this book is the unity of Auden's verse. Everett discusses its development in chronological fashion, utilizing the polemic and critical works of Auden where they illuminate the poetry.

Falck, Colin. "The Exposed Heart." ENCOUNTER, 27 (1966), 77-83.

An examination of Auden's poetry in the light of his theory that magic has no place in real life and therefore "there must always be two kinds of art--escape art, for man needs escape as he needs food and deep sleep, and parable art, that art which shall teach man to unlearn hatred and to learn love."

Fisher, A.S.T. "Auden's Juvenilia." NOTES AND QUERIES, 2 (1974), 370-73.

A presentation and brief examination of Auden's poems written before May 1926.

Foxall, Edgar. "The Politics of W.H. Auden." BOOKMAN, 85 (1934), 474-75.

A consideration of the young Auden as a Marxist poet.

Fraser, G.S. "Auden the Composite Giant." SHENANDOAH, 15 (1964), 46-59.

Fraser discusses Auden as a poet in whom two voices (English and American) and two rhythms (English and American) are fused.

Fuller, John. A READER'S GUIDE TO W.H. AUDEN. New York: Farrar, Straus, and Giroux, 1970.

This book is primarily a commentary on Auden's poetry and drama. Fuller examines the works in chronological order, tracing sources and allusions in the more difficult passages. The study falls chiefly into four well-defined periods: 1927-32, 1933-38, 1939-47, 1948-57. There is, however, a chapter at the end devoted to poems written after 1957.

Grant, Damian. "Tones of Voice." CRITICAL QUARTERLY, 11 (1969), 195-98.

Grant investigates Auden's belief that the "intimate tone of voice" constitutes the characteristic style of "modern" poetry. This intimate tone appears as a deliberate gesture in the volume ABOUT THE HOUSE (1965) and manifests itself again, though in a less pronounced manner, in CITY WITHOUT WALLS (1969).

_____. "Verbal Elements." CRITICAL QUARTERLY, 16 (1974), 81-86.

EPISTLE TO A GODSON AND OTHER POEMS (1972), according

to Grant, evidences Auden's "mistrust of romanticism, rhetoric, and all the habits of thought or expression we have invented to flatter and deceive ourselves." In EPISTLE, the earlier poets are praised for their modesty and simplicity; the silent language of animals and plants is allowed new respect; the "verbal event" whose root in reality has "rotted away" is disparaged. Auden's "studied irreverence" and bravado in the face of death is in striking contrast to the traditional sober stance.

Greenberg, Herbert. QUEST FOR THE NECESSARY: W.H. AUDEN AND THE DILEMMA OF DIVIDED CONSCIOUSNESS. Cambridge, Mass.: Harvard University Press, 1968.

The purpose of this book is to investigate Auden's poetry as it focuses on the thesis that "Divided consciousness . . . is more than a controlling idea in Auden's thought; it is the principal subject matter of his poetry, and provides the conceptual foundation for his way of looking at things." The secondary aim of the book is to defend Auden as a moral and philosophical poet of the great tradition whose vision penetrates "the nature of human nature." This defense is largely in answer to Randall Jarrell's charge in PARTISAN REVIEW (12 [Fall 1945], 437-57) that Auden writes from an inner state of permanent guilt, anxiety, and isolation "adhered to with unchanging firmness in every stage of his development, justified for different reasons in every stage." See Jarrell, below.

Grigson, Geoffrey. "Notes on Contemporary Poetry." BOOKMAN, 72 (1932), 287-89.

Grigson discusses Auden's role in the on-going poetry revolution, begun in the early 1900s by Eliot, Pound, and Hopkins.

Hardy, Barbara. "W.H. Auden, Thirties to Sixties: A Face and a Map." SOUTHERN REVIEW, 5 (1969), 655-72.

A study of Auden's "imaginative effort to look at private and public worlds at the same time, overlapping, blurred, mutually determining, or interlocked, their distinctiveness often diffused, dissolved, and dissipated." The discussion covers the poetry from the thirties to the sixties.

Hazard, Forrest E. "The Father Christmas Passage in Auden's 'Paid on Both Sides.'" MODERN DRAMA, 12 (1969), 155-64.

An article that examines the Father Christmas passage as a warning dream that makes up "the call" (voice of God, the life force, the unconscious, destiny) common to the quest pattern. Hazard also asserts that Auden's purpose in this reworking of a mummer's play is to prove the relevance of its theme to modern times.

Hoggart, Richard. AUDEN: AN INTRODUCTORY ESSAY. London: Chatto and Windus, 1951.

> This book, an introductory survey of Auden's poetry from the thirties to 1950, includes chapters on the poet's use of symbolic landscape, his stylistic techniques and early themes, his American sojourn, and his later themes.

_____. W.H. AUDEN. British Council and the National Book League. London: Longmans, Green, 1957.

> An essay devoted to Auden's development from the thirties to the late fifties.

Hyde, Virginia M. "The Pastoral Formula of W.H. Auden and Piero di Cosimo." CONTEMPORARY LITERATURE 14 (1974), 332-46.

> Hyde states that Auden turned to the Italian Renaissance painter di Cosimo for the "artifice proper to the pastoral" and in so doing "arrived at anti-idyllic realism through a faithful description of art."

Janet, Sr. M., S.C.L. "W.H. Auden: Two Poems in Sequence." RENASCENCE, 13 (1961), 115-18.

> Sr. Janet discusses Auden's work since 1939 as characterized by symbolic and thematic unity. This unity is most obvious in THE SEA AND THE MIRROR and FOR THE TIME BEING, semidramatic poems published in 1944. Both poems investigate the anxiety, guilt, despair, and isolation resulting from modernity. Both are concerned with the problem of reality. FOR THE TIME BEING is a sequel to THE SEA AND THE MIRROR, inasmuch as the latter "follows man through that isolation of the artist from reality which brings him ultimately and inevitably to the 'unabiding void,'" and the former finds man "at that eternal intrusion of the Timeless into time, of the infinite into the finite that is the Incarnation."

Jarrell, Randall. "From Freud to Paul: The Stages of Auden's Ideology." PARTISAN REVIEW, 12 (Fall 1945), 437-57.

> Jarrell claims that Auden's views are determined by the presence of obvious psychological determinants. Auden turned his back on the need for social and political action by becoming a Christian. "A complex of ideas, emotions and unconscious attitudes about anxiety, guilt, and isolation" constitutes the "permanent causal core" of Auden's thought.

Johnson, Richard. MAN'S PLACE: AN ESSAY ON AUDEN. Ithaca and London: Cornell University Press, 1973.

> Johnson views Auden's poems written after 1940 as "presenting models of existence that involve the reader in the process of ex-

ploration," and states that the "patterns of sound, imagery, syntax, rhyme, diction, metaphor, perspective, stanza, and argument are the means by which Auden assays his fundamental subject: man in the world."

Johnson, Wendell S. "Auden, Hopkins, and the Poetry of Reticence." TWEN-TIETH CENTURY LITERATURE, 20 (1974), 165-71.

The article traces the influence of G.M. Hopkins on Auden's poetry, in regard to its matter and manner.

Kermode, Frank. "The Theme of Auden's Poetry: Part I." RIVISTA DI LET-TERATURE MODERNE E COMPARATE, 3 (1948), 1-14.

This essay was written in English and appeared before the publication, in America, of Auden's AGE OF ANXIETY (1947). Part 2 did not appear.

Macbeth, George. "A Myth of Menace." LISTENER, 76 (1966), 579.

Macbeth believes that the Fascist flavor of THE ORATORS (1932), which is a manifestation of the book's "total involvement with the psychology of glamorous action," is the reason behind its "power to provide stimulus and food for thought in the 1960s." The work is a "landmark" in the history of experimental writing inasmuch as "its power to move from prose to verse form--and even into pictures--provides a method for a new kind of rough-edged intermedial structure hitherto only intermittently attempted by Zukofsky and Nabokov."

McDiarmid, Lucy S. "Poetry's Landscape in Auden's Elegy for Yeats." MOD-ERN LANGUAGE QUARTERLY, 38 (1977), 167-77.

McDiarmid discusses Auden's commemoration of "dead parts of himself" in the elegy. He considers the pessimism Auden experienced in the years preceding 1932, the new flow of creative power he felt in the thirties, and the final period of "tension balancing opposing forces" of hate and affirmation of life.

McDowell, Frederick P.W. "Subtle, Various, Ornamental, Clever: Auden in His Recent Poetry." WISCONSIN STUDIES IN CONTEMPORARY LITERATURE, 3 (1962), 29-44.

McDowell asserts that Auden's volumes, NONES (1951), THE SHIELD OF ACHILLES (1955), and HOMAGE TO CLIO (1960), manifest a serenity of tone and "firm and sure voice" not evident in earlier works. He discusses what he considers the best poems in each of the volumes: "In Praise of Limestone" in NONES; "Winds," "Islands," and "The Shield of Achilles" in THE SHIELD OF ACHILLES; and "Goodbye to the Mezzogiornio" in HOMAGE TO CLIO.

Moore, Gerald. "Luck in Auden." ESSAYS IN CRITICISM, 7 (1951), 103-08.

The article examines Auden's use of the word "luck" in eighteen different poems.

Nelson, Gerald. CHANGES OF HEART: A STUDY OF THE POETRY OF W.H. AUDEN. Perspectives in Criticism, no. 21. Berkeley and Los Angeles: University of California Press, 1969.

This study traces Auden's attempt, in the forties, "to adjust his art to a new metaphysical point of view," to "rebuild his images upon a new metaphoric base." Nelson focuses directly on the poems themselves and examines the ideas and attitudes of the various characters in the longer works. In the shorter pieces he investigates the poetic voice or persona.

Ohmann, Richard. "Auden's Sacred Awe." COMMONWEAL, 78 (1963), 279-81.

The article investigates Auden's position on literature, art, and politics, as expressed in THE DYER'S HAND (1962), a collection of essays described by Ohmann as "fifteen years worth of major comments on literature, which serves as a gloss on his early poetry no less than on his later."

Ostroff, Anthony, ed. "A Symposium on W.H. Auden's 'A Change of Air.'" KENYON REVIEW, 26 (1964), 190-208.

A series of short investigations of the poem by George P. Elliott, Karl Shapiro, and Stephen Spender. At the end, Auden replies to the critics.

Peschmann, Hermann. "W.H. Auden (1907-1973)." ENGLISH, 23 (1974), 3-4.

A brief general survey of Auden's poetic achievement. A memorial article.

Quinn, M. Bernetts. "Persona and Places in Auden." RENASCENCE, 12 (1960), 115-24, 148.

Quinn's argument is essentially that "Each of Auden's persons and places . . . borrowed by him as all poets borrow such things, is to make the abstract concrete, acts as a kind of synechdoche to bring wider realms of thought home to the other reflective citizens who share his planet, with all its problems. His images fit one inside the other, like Japanese boxes: the individual with his private landscape at the centre; next, the limestone regions of his boyhood; then England and/or Spain, a larger 'symbol of us all,' and enclosing the rest, the symbol of the 'Just City.'"

Replogle, Justin. "Auden's Homage to Thalia." BUCKNELL REVIEW, 11 (1963), 98–117.

Replogle investigates Auden's poetry as comic.

_____. AUDEN'S POETRY. Seattle and London: University of Washington Press, 1969.

Replogle writes of Auden's poetry in three different ways: as "a storehouse of ideas," as "the dwelling place of speakers," and as "a verbal contraption." The examination traces the pattern of Auden's development from the thirties through the sixties, showing how "his ideas, personae, and style move forward toward . . . his greatest achievement, the later comic poetry."

_____. "Auden's Religious Leap." WISCONSIN STUDIES IN CONTEMPORARY LITERATURE, 7 (1966), 47–75.

An investigation of the later appearance of the thread of existentialism in Auden's poetry. The article demonstrates "the philosophical continuity in the poet's transition from Marx-Engels to Kierkegaard" and then "traces the development of his religious thought through its great blossoming in the forties."

_____. "Social Philosophy in Auden's Early Poetry." CRITICISM, 2 (1960), 351–61.

The aim of the essay is "to show the nature of Auden's early non-Marxist views, and to record how and when the philosophical principles guiding his poetry change from those of his psychological sources to those of the Marxists."

Roberts, David. "W.H. Auden's Mountain." HORIZON, 22 (1979), 56–61.

Roberts discusses Auden's love of mountaineering, asserting that his feelings "as he grew older shifted from the automatic acceptance of the sport one might expect from a lifelong devotee of its literature. Taken in perspective, his view of mountaineering amounts to a moral critique of the sort no active climber . . . has ever engaged in."

Rosenheim, Edward W., Jr. "The Elegiac Act: Auden's 'In Memory of W.B. Yeats.'" COLLEGE ENGLISH, 27 (1966), 422–25.

Some works of art, asserts Rosenheim, are satisfying because the viewer or reader recognizes them as "achievements." At the same time that one responds to the "timeless, anonymous qualities" traditionally seen as at the root of aesthetic pleasure, one can also respond to a work as a "human accomplishment." Auden's "In Memory of W.B. Yeats" is one such work of art. This article presents an analysis of the poem applying the given proposition.

Roth, Robert. "The Sophistication of W.H. Auden: A Sketch in Longinian Method." MODERN PHILOLOGY, 48 (1951), 193-204.

> An application of the Longinian methodology and terminology to W.H. Auden's poetry.

Savage, D.S. "The Poet's Perspectives." POETRY (Chicago), 64 (1944), 148-58.

> Savage states that W.H. Auden established himself as a gifted writer on the basis of his early achievement; however, there has been a notable process of deterioration in his work due in part to Auden's touching the surface of life rather than penetrating the ultimate of existence.

Schwartz, Delmore. "The Two Audens." KENYON REVIEW, 1 (1939), 34-45.

> An exploration of Auden's two voices, the first being that of "the clever guy, the Noel Coward, of literary Marxism" who is "at once the popular entertainer, propagandist and satirist," and the second being that of the id, which generates "images of the greatest impact and power" and is "a kind of sibyl who utters the telltale symbols in a psychoanalytic trance."

Scott, Nathan A., Jr. "The Poetry of Auden." LONDON MAGAZINE, 8 (1961), 44-63.

> An examination of NEW YEAR LETTER (1941) as a summary of "all that Auden had learned in the 1930s and of how he had come to conceive not only his personal vocation as a poet but the status of art in general within the life of the human community."

"Sixteen Comments on Auden." NEW VERSE, Nos. 26-27 (1937), pp. 1-30.

> Christopher Isherwood on the early verse; Stephen Spender's "Oxford to Communism"; Geoffrey Grigson's "Auden as a Monster"; Kenneth Alcott's "Auden in the Theatre"; Edgell Rickword's "Auden and Politics." Shorter comments on Auden by Edwin Muir, George Barker, Frederick Prokosch, Allen Tate, C. Day Lewis, Graham Greene, Dylan Thomas, and others.

Spears, Monroe K. "Auden in the Fifties: Rites of Homage." SEWANEE REVIEW, 69 (1961), 375-98.

> Auden's poems, claims Spears, are "rarely self-sufficient and isolated entities: their full significance becomes apparent only when they are seen as part of a pattern." This article devotes itself to elucidating the dominant patterns in the poetry from 1950 to 1960.

_____. THE POETRY OF W.H. AUDEN: THE DISENCHANTED ISLAND. Rev. ed. London, Oxford, and New York: Oxford University Press, 1968.

Spears's basic aim is "to set the facts in order, clear away the obstacles to understanding, and provide the background and context required for a full appreciation of Auden's poetry." The revised edition covers the poetry up to the late sixties. The investigation is done in chronological order, and the emphasis throughout is on the poetry rather than on the ideas behind the poetry. A bibliography of Auden's major works is included, as well as title and first line indexes.

Spender, Stephen. "The Importance of Auden." LONDON MERCURY, 34 (1939), 613-18.

An attempt to ascertain the importance of Auden's poetry in relation to the whole tradition of English poetry.

_____, ed. W.H. AUDEN: A TRIBUTE. London: Weidenfeld and Nicolson, 1974.

With few exceptions, everything in this collection, which constitutes a loving memoir of the poet, is new. The essays, meant to cover the different periods of Auden's life, include contributions by Geoffrey Grigson, Sir John Betjeman, Cyril Connolly, Christopher Isherwood, Ann Freemantle, Ursula Nieburh, Robert Craft, Hannah Arendt, John Hollander, John Bayley, and Stephen Spender.

Stoll, John E. W.H. AUDEN: A READING. Ball State University Monograph, n.p. 18. Muncie, Ind.: Ball State University Press, 1970.

This essay takes as its subject the role of psychological duality in Auden's work, the development of the work, and the relationship between this duality and religion.

Thomson, John. "Auden at the Sheldonian." TRUTH, 15 (1956), 690.

An account of Auden's address, at the Sheldonian Theatre, on the event of his becoming the thirty-third professor of poetry at Oxford.

Weatherhead, A. Kingsley. "The Good Place in the Latest Poems of W.H. Auden." TWENTIETH CENTURY LITERATURE, 10 (1964), 99-107.

Weatherhead investigates the "pastoralizing" of Auden's latest poetry. He contrasts the poet's new creation of "a state of innocence within the familiar world" to his earlier Kierkegaardian approach to poetry, wherein he avoided the guilt from attachment to everyday esthetic and ethical views by a leap to the religious level. Weatherhead claims Auden now "creates an Eden out of the materials of ordinary or nearly ordinary living," a "consciously fictional innocence" that constitutes the pastoral.

Wright, George S. W.H. AUDEN. Twayne United States Authors Series, no. 144. New York: Twayne Publishers, 1969.

The objective of this study is "to make more intelligible the bewildering changes in thought, style, and feeling that mark Auden's poetry." Wright "takes Auden's major works in turn, to show their relation to his fundamental artistic (and intellectual) concerns, so that the development of his poetry can be seen not as bizarre or perverse but as perfectly consistent." Wright's second aim is to describe the basic elements of each important title in order to provide a discussion of the "kind" of work it is with all its "special qualities of form or feeling, especially its combinations and changes of tone, its structural innovations, its ways of presenting and arranging its human subjects."

SIR JOHN BETJEMAN (1906-)

PRINCIPAL WORKS

Poetry

MOUNT ZION; OR, IN TOUCH WITH THE INFINITE. London: James Press, 1931.

CONTINUAL DEW: A LITTLE BOOK OF BOURGEOIS VERSE. London: John Murray, 1937.

OLD LIGHTS FOR NEW CHANCELS: VERSES TOPOGRAPHICAL AND AMA-TORY. London: John Murray, 1940.

NEW BATS IN OLD BELFRIES. London: John Murray, 1945.

SLICK BUT NOT STREAMLINED. Garden City, N.Y.: Doubleday, 1947.

SELECTED POEMS. London: John Murray, 1948.

A FEW LATE CHRYSANTHEMUMS: NEW POEMS. London: John Murray, 1954.

POEMS IN THE PORCH. London: S.P.C.K., 1954.

COLLECTED POEMS. London: John Murray, 1958.

POEMS. London: Hulton, 1959.

SUMMONED BY BELLS. London: John Murray, 1960.

A RING OF BELLS. London: John Murray, 1962.

HIGH AND LOW. London: John Murray, 1966.

A WEMBLEY LAD, AND THE CREM. London: Poem-of-the-Month-Club, 1971.

A NIP IN THE AIR. London: John Murray, 1974.

Other Works

GHASTLY GOOD TASTE: OR, A DEPRESSING STORY OF THE RISE AND FALL OF ENGLISH ARCHITECTURE (1933), prose.

ANTIQUARIAN PREJUDICE (1939), prose.

ENGLISH CITIES AND SMALL TOWNS (1943), prose.

MURRAY'S SHROPSHIRE ARCHITECTURAL GUIDE, with John Piper (1951), prose.

FIRST AND LAST LOVES (1952), prose.

THE ENGLISH TOWN IN THE LAST HUNDRED YEARS (1956), prose.

ENGLISH CHURCHES, with Basil Clarke (1964), prose.

CORNWALL (1965), prose.
TEN WREN CHURCHES (1970), prose.
LONDON'S HISTORIC RAILWAY STATIONS (1972), prose.
A PICTORIAL HISTORY OF ENGLISH ARCHITECTURE (1972), prose.
WEST COUNTRY CHURCHES (1973), prose.

BIBLIOGRAPHIES

Carter, J. "Betjemania." BOOK COLLECTOR, 9 (1960), 199, 452.

Stapleton, Margaret. SIR JOHN BETJEMAN: A BIBLIOGRAPHY OF THE WRITINGS BY AND ABOUT HIM. Metuchen, N.J.: Scarecrow, 1974.

AUTOBIOGRAPHY

SUMMONED BY BELLS. London: John Murray, 1960.

> Betjeman's autobiography in blank verse recalls the poet's Georgian boyhood in London and Cornwall, and culminates in an account of his experience at Oxford in the twenties.

BIOGRAPHIES

Stanford, Derek. JOHN BETJEMAN: A STUDY. London: Neville Spearman, 1961.

> Stanford devotes a chapter to the poet's biography as a lead-in to the world of his art. See "Criticism" below.

Brooke, Jocelyn. "John Betjeman." In her RONALD FIRBANK AND JOHN BETJEMAN. Writers and Their Work Series, no. 153. London: Longmans, Green, 1962, pp. 25-43.

> See "Criticism" below.

Press, John. JOHN BETJEMAN. Writers and Their Work Series, no. 237. London: Longmans, Green, 1974.

> See "Criticism" below.

CRITICISM

Alvarez, A. "London Letter: Exile's Return." PARTISAN REVIEW, 26 (1959), 284-89.

> Alvarez characterizes Betjeman as "a skillful, harmless, minor writer

of light verse" who has "stuck to his reactionary guns through all
the great revolutions of modern poetry." His verse is depressing
in its "scale, its literary and political implication"; and its very
large sales indicate that the poetry revolution "never took place
for a huge portion of the English poetry reading public."

Bergonzi, Bernard. "Culture and Mr. Betjeman: 'That's a Surrey Sunset.'"
TWENTIETH CENTURY, 165 (1959), 130-37.

"Betjeman's sense of social fact is his principal strength, but it
leads directly to his major weakness, which is best described as
a lack of intellectual grasp or conviction. This is by no means
essential equipment for a poet, but the lack of it in Betjeman
means that his satirical impulses are directed only by a sense of
social--or cultural--habit." Bergonzi's article is an exploration
of this assertion.

Bogan, Louise. "John Betjeman." In SELECTED CRITICISM: PROSE AND
POETRY. New York: Noonday Press, 1955, pp. 343-45.

Bogan claims that Betjeman's contribution to the modern lyric is
his use of pathos, defined as "an emotion derived from contemporary objects or contemporary experience; it is not a yearning for
the past."

Brooke, Jocelyn. "John Betjeman." In her RONALD FIRBANK AND JOHN
BETJEMAN. Writers and Their Work Series, no. 153. London: Longmans,
Green, 1962, pp. 25-43.

Brooke characterizes Betjeman as a poet "who has written light
verse in a manner which transcends the limitations of his medium."
He is "conservative by temperament," "extremely patriotic," and
"totally independent of the avant garde." The essay contains some
biographical material.

Fraser, G.S. THE MODERN WRITER IN HIS WORLD. London: Verschoyel,
1953.

Fraser says that in order to appreciate Betjeman's poetry, readers
must be able to take for granted the background of experience
that displays itself in the poems in the form of precise local allusions and/or specialized and exact social settings, as well as his
"profound conservatism." Brief comments are offered on Betjeman's
humorous light verse.

Gunn, Thom. "Poets, English and American." YALE REVIEW, 48 (1959),
617-20.

Gunn identifies Betjeman as "a popular poet" and says, in reference to the huge sales of SUMMONED BY BELLS (1960), that we
have here a familiar and, therefore, not surprising pattern: that

"nine thousand bourgeois adore a poet whose principal occupation is to devastate the bourgeoisie." Gunn observes further, "But it is too easy an occupation, because Betjeman has no understanding of the middle class. All he tells about it in this book is entirely superficial," and finds the cause of Betjeman's superficiality in the fact that his poetry is "founded so completely on snobbery rather than on observation." Among what Gunn describes as "a small number of astonishingly good poems" are "An Impoverished Irish Peer," "The Death of King George V," "House of Rest," "A Child III," and "On the Portrait of a Deaf Man."

Kermode, Frank. "Henry Miller and John Betjeman." ENCOUNTER, 16 (1961), 69-75.

Kermode brings together Betjeman and Miller as "laudatores temporis acti, seeking to free themselves from the hated present and establish contact . . . with das Heilage." Kermode criticizes the blank verse of SUMMONED BY BELLS (1960) as "too easy" and claims that the best passages are those on Oxford, "The dear, private giggles," and "the Kolkhorst Sunday morning routs." Betjeman and Miller are also viewed as dealing similarly with love and fear.

Kunitz, Stanley. "SUMMONED BY BELLS." HARPER'S MAGAZINE, 223 (1961), 88.

Kunitz calls Betjeman's autobiography in verse "a Wordsworthian Prelude without the philosophic weight or the Orphic intensity." The book is "sometimes poignant, frequently comic, always readable."

Larkin, Philip. "The Blending of Betjeman." SPECTATOR, 205 (1960), 913.

Larkin presents a survey of the content, style, and techniques of SUMMONED BY BELLS (1960). He concludes that Betjeman's poetic success is due to "an astonishing command of detail, both visual and circumstantial" and "his palpably greater interest in things other than himself."

_____. "It Could Only Happen in England: A Study of John Betjeman's Poems for American Readers." CORNHILL, No. 1069 (1971), pp. 21-36.

A study of Betjeman's poems designed for the American reader.

Neame, Alan. "Poet of Anglicanism." COMMONWEAL, 71 (1959), 282-84.

Neame investigates Betjeman's relationship to the Anglican tradition. He says of the poet: "he seems to be the first poet to celebrate the Church of England as institution. . . . Betjeman writes consciously within the Anglican schism."

"Poet on Stopover." NEW YORKER, 33 (1957), 22-24.

> The author's recollection of a meeting with Betjeman in New
> York, the occasion of which was the poet's first visit to America.
> It contains interesting material supplied by Betjeman.

Press, John. JOHN BETJEMAN. Writers and Their Work Series, no. 237.
London: Longmans, Green, 1974.

> In this brief essay, Press "traces Betjeman's progress as a writer
> in prose and in verse, and illustrates the range and variety of
> his work." Includes a select bibliography.

"The Reticent Faith, The British Imagination." TIMES LITERARY SUPPLEMENT,
special supplement, 9 September 1960, p. iv.

> The author comments on some occasional poetry written by Betje-
> man and considers what the author dubs the double response to
> Betjeman--a response from the English people without faith and
> the English people with faith.

Ross, Alan. "Satires and Suburbs." In his POETRY 1945-1950. London:
Longmans, Green, 1951, pp. 50-53.

> Ross compares William Plomer and Betjeman: "their similarities are
> great technical skill, a sensitivity to visual beauty, and an aware-
> ness of the 'period' aspect of their time"; they "observe and re-
> produce, photographically but without comment, characters, situa-
> tions or environments commonly regarded as comic in themselves."
> He notes that "it is a measure of Betjeman's skill that the 'second
> rate' is given by his poetic vision a newfound beauty. Betjeman's
> poems in fact accomplish a minor aesthetic revolution." Ross also
> comments on the poets' themes and subject matter.

Ross, Theodore J. "Life in Betjeman-Land." NEW REPUBLIC, 141 (1959),
18-19.

> The article describes and comments on the ingredients of Betjeman's
> landscape, such as moments of anticipation, evening scenes, eves
> of important events, solitary meditation, sudden death, upperclass
> "Insiders," lower class "Outsiders," and nomenclature.

Smith, Janet Adam. "--And Betjeman's Verses." NEW STATESMAN, 56
(1958), 819-20.

> The author claims that Lord Birkenhead, who compiled COLLECTED
> POEMS (1958), does Betjeman a disservice "by claiming too much
> for him." Betjeman is a poet of church architecture, but his
> church "seems more of a shelter where he can shut the door on
> science, mass production and other uncomfortable things than a
> place which has something to say to a world where the uncomfort-
> able things have to be dealt with."

Sir John Betjeman

Spender, Stephen. "Poetry for Poetry's Sake and Poetry Beyond Poetry." HORIZON (London), 13 (1946), 221-38.

> Spender says that Betjeman's appeal is "not that he is satirizing the things he satirizes but himself for liking them. His poetry has the charm of the double bluff."

Stanford, Derek. JOHN BETJEMAN: A STUDY. London: Neville Spearman, 1961.

> Stanford attempts "to locate the various courses, social, psychological, and artistic, for the success of Betjeman's poems, and asks what intrinsic literary merit this substantially successful work contains." Stanford asserts that "Merit and fashion are the two main cares in the examination of Betjeman's work."

_____. "Mr. Betjeman's Satire." CONTEMPORARY REVIEW, 197 (1960), 286-87.

> Stanford's article is a defense of Betjeman against the assertions of Lord Birkenhead (introduction to COLLECTED POEMS, 1958) and Bernard Bergonzi (cited above) that the poet has failed as a satirist.

Wain, John. "Four Observer Pieces: John Betjeman." In his ESSAYS ON LITERATURE AND IDEAS. London: Macmillan; New York: St. Martin's Press, 1963, pp. 168-71.

> Wain attempts "to sum up Betjeman's work as a poet" and tries "to account for its vast popularity." He concludes that the success of the poetry lies in the fact that it is "warmly sympathetic," "nostalgic," "free of any wish to be smart," and indecisive as to whether "the way of life he describes is damnable or admirable." This latter feature is most dear to the hearts of the English, he thinks, because they, too, are perpetually perplexed by the same inability to decide this issue.

Wiehe, R.E. "Summoned by Nostalgia: John Betjeman's Poetry." ARIZONA QUARTERLY, 19 (1963), 37-49.

> Wiehe discusses the subjects of Betjeman's poetry--class and ecclesiastical architecture and city life and manners--as well as his use of blank verse, diction, imagery, and phrasing. Specific comments are made on several poems including "How to Get On in Society," "Beside the Seaside," "Slough," "A Lincolnshire Church," "The Old Liberals," and others. The article ends with a consideration of SUMMONED BY BELLS (1960) in the light of Betjeman's poetic development.

ROBERT SEYMOUR BRIDGES (1844-1930)

PRINCIPAL WORKS

Poetry

POEMS. London: Basil Montague Pickering, 1873.
CARMEN ELEGIACUM. London: Edward Bumpus, 1876.
THE GROWTH OF LOVE: A POEM IN 24 SONNETS. London: Edward
    Bumpus, 1876.
POEMS. Second Series. London: Edward Bumpus, 1879.
POEMS. Third Series. London: Edward Bumpus, 1880.
PROMETHEUS THE FIREGIVER. Oxford: H. Daniel Press, 1883.
POEMS. Oxford: H. Daniel Press, 1884.
EIGHT PLAYS: NERO, PARTS I & II, PALICIO, ULYSSES, CAPTIVES, ACHIL-
    LES, HUMOURS, FEAST OF BACCHUS. London: George Bell, 1885-94.
EROS AND PSYCHE: A POEM IN TWELVE MEASURES. London: George
    Bell, 1885.
THE GROWTH OF LOVE: 79 SONNETS. Oxford: H. Daniel Press, 1889.
THE SHORTER POEMS. 5 vols. London: George Bell, 1890.
POETICAL WORKS. 6 vols. London: Smith, Elder, 1898-1905.
NOW IN WINTRY DELIGHTS. Oxford: H. Daniel Press, 1903.
POETICAL WORKS. London: Oxford University Press, 1912. Excluding the
    eight dramas.
POEMS WRITTEN IN THE YEAR MXCIII. Chelsea: Ashendene Press, 1914.
OCTOBER, AND OTHER POEMS. With Occasional Verses on the War. Lon-
    don: William Heinemann, 1920.
NEW VERSE WRITTEN IN 1921. Oxford: Clarendon Press, 1925.
THE TAPESTRY: POEMS. London: F. Warde and S. Morison, 1925.
THE TESTAMENT OF BEAUTY. A POEM IN FOUR BOOKS. Oxford: Claren-
    don Press, 1929.

Other Works

MILTON'S PROSODY: ON THE PROSODY OF PARADISE REGAINED AND
    SAMSON AGONISTES. Being a supplement to the paper on the Elements
    of Milton's Blank Verse in Paradise Lost, etc. (1889), criticism.

MILTON'S PROSODY BY R. BRIDGES AND CLASSICAL METRES IN ENGLISH VERSE BY WILLIAM JOHNSON STONE (1901), criticism.
ON THE PRESENT STATE OF ENGLISH PRONOUNS (1910), prose.
THE NECESSITY OF POETRY: AN ADDRESS (1918), prose.
ON ENGLISH HOMOPHONES (1919), prose.

BIBLIOGRAPHIES

Chaundry, Leslie, and E.H.M. Cox. ROBERT BRIDGES: A BIBLIOGRAPHY. London: Leslie Chaundry, 1921.

McKay, George L. A BIBLIOGRAPHY OF ROBERT BRIDGES. New York: Columbia University Press, 1933.

AUTOBIOGRAPHY

COLLECTED ESSAYS, PAPERS, ETC. 10 vols. London: Oxford University Press, 1927-36.

BIOGRAPHIES

Thompson, Edward. ROBERT BRIDGES: 1844-1930. London: Oxford University Press, 1944.

In his introduction, Thompson provides a personal narrative to "bring out the background of an art which was of exceptional integrity, with nothing of schism between the man and his work."

Ritz, Jean Georges. ROBERT BRIDGES AND GERARD MANLEY HOPKINS 1863-1889: A LITERARY FRIENDSHIP. London: Oxford University Press, 1960.

Ritz presents a close examination of the two poets' friendship and analyzes the influence of one on the other in the area of poetic achievements.

Sparrow, John. ROBERT BRIDGES. Writers and Their Work Series. London: Longmans, Green, 1963.

Sparrow presents a brief biographical essay. See "Criticism" below.

Kelshall, T.M. ROBERT BRIDGES. Folcroft, Pa.: Folcroft Library Editions, 1976.

Kelshall presents a short biographical-critical essay.

LETTERS

THE CORRESPONDENCE OF ROBERT BRIDGES AND HENRY BRADLEY 1900-1923. Oxford: Clarendon Press, 1940.
XXI LETTERS: CORRESPONDENCE BETWEEN ROBERT BRIDGES AND R.C. TREVELYAN ON "NEW VERSE" AND "THE TESTAMENT OF BEAUTY." Stanford Dingley, Engl.: Mill House Press, 1955.
CORRESPONDENCE OF ROBERT BRIDGES AND W.B. YEATS. Ed. Richard J. Finneran. London: Macmillan, 1977.

CRITICISM

Baines, Arnold H.J. "Robert Bridges: A Source." NOTES AND QUERIES, 195 (1950), 478.

> Baines claims a stanza in SIX SELECT SONGS AND ONE CANTATA, set to music by James Newton, M.A. (London: John Jonston, 1775), is the source for Bridges' lyric "Anniversary."

Baker, J. Gordon. "Robert Bridges' Concept of Nature." PUBLICATIONS OF THE MODERN LANGUAGE ASSOCIATION OF AMERICA, 54 (1939), 1181-97.

> Baker discusses in detail the concept of nature as it appears in THE TESTAMENT OF BEAUTY (1929). The concept, stated simply, is that Nature impresses on the spiritually responsive human psyche, ideas of beauty, and these ideas draw men upward toward God's love.

Beaum, R. "Profundity Revisited: Bridges and His Critics." DALHOUSIE REVIEW, 44 (1965), 172-79.

> Beum defends Bridges against Kunitz' and Haycroft's comment in their TWENTIETH CENTURY AUTHORS (See General Aids: "Biographies," above) as "a curious combination of consumate style, pure formal beauty, and a complete lack of profundity of thought."

Brown, T.J. "English Literary Autographs XX: Robert Bridges, 1844-1930." BOOK COLLECTOR, 5 (1956), 369.

> On Bridges both as a poet and as a connoisseur of handwriting.

Dumbleton, William A. "Bridges and the Hopkins MSS: 1889-1930." THOUGHT, 47 (1972), 428-46.

> It speaks well of Bridges' judgment, Dumbleton states, that he recognized the value of Hopkins' work, but that he had only a superficial appreciation of Hopkins' poetry "betrays Bridges's spiritual, emotional, and critical limitations."

Elton, Oliver. ROBERT BRIDGES AND "THE TESTAMENT OF BEAUTY."
English Association Pamphlet, no. 83. Oxford: Oxford University Press, 1932.

Elton treats the poem as a bequest to the world of beauty. The topic of THE TESTAMENT, Elton asserts, "is the historical growth of an idea and the place of that idea in the final outlook of the writer. It is the last fruit of a life given to art--musical as well as poetic art--and to philosophic thought."

Green, Andrew J. "Robert Bridges and the Spiritual Animal." PHILOSOPHICAL REVIEW, 53 (1944), 286-95.

Guerard, Albert J. "Robert Bridges." VIRGINIA QUARTERLY REVIEW, 12 (1936), 354-67.

_____. ROBERT BRIDGES: A STUDY OF TRADITIONALISM IN POETRY. New York: Russell and Russell, 1965.

Guerard aims in this book to establish Bridges as "one of the most impressive as well as one of the most serious poets of the last hundred years." He attempts an exhaustive critical study of Bridges' poetry and a defense of his traditionalism. The book is divided into investigations of the lyric, dramatic, and philosophical poetry, and includes material on the sources and analogues of Bridges' poems.

Jack, Peter Monro. "The Poetical Works." NEW YORK TIMES BOOK REVIEW, 28 June 1936, p. 2.

The poems that hold the reader's interest in POETICAL WORKS (6 vols., 1898-1905) most surely are those written in classical prosody. They are characterized as "intimate and conversational, yet thoroughly disciplined."

Kellog, George A. "Bridges' 'Milton's Prosody' and Renaissance Metrical Theory." PUBLICATIONS OF THE MODERN LANGUAGE ASSOCIATION OF AMERICA, 68 (1953), 268-85.

In this essay Kellog summarizes and interprets the section in MILTON'S PROSODY (1901) entitled "Chapter on Accentual Verse and Notes." He compares Bridges' study with Milton's notions of prosody and meter and contemporary concepts with precepts of prosody and meter from Renaissance verse manuals, grammars, and rhetorics. Kellog stresses the powerful influence of Italian and classical works on Milton.

Nowell-Smith, Simon. "Bridges, Hopkins and Dr. Daniel." TIMES LITERARY SUPPLEMENT, 13 December 1957, p. 764.

Discusses the evidence that twice before publication in bulk of Hopkins' verse in 1918, once before and once immediately after

Hopkins' death, Bridges planned to print at least some of his poems. The evidence is found in Bridges' unpublished letters to C.H.O. Daniel that Nowell-Smith examines.

_____. "A Poet on Walton Street." In ESSAYS MAINLY ON THE NINE-TEENTH CENTURY PRESENTED TO SIR HUMPHREY MILFORD. Ed. Geoffrey Cumberlege. Oxford: Oxford University Press, 1948, pp. 58-71.

This essay is devoted to the publishing history of Bridges' works.

Patmore, Derek. "Three Poets Discuss New Verse Forms: The Correspondence of Gerard Manley Hopkins, Robert Bridges, and Coventry Patmore." MONTH, 6 (1951), 69-78.

Ritz, Jean Georges. ROBERT BRIDGES AND GERARD MANLEY HOPKINS 1863-1889: A LITERARY FRIENDSHIP. London: Oxford University Press, 1960.

A close examination of the influence of the two poets on one another's poetic achievement.

Sparrow, John. "Introduction." In his ROBERT BRIDGES: POETRY AND PROSE. Oxford: Clarendon Press, 1955, pp. vii-xvii.

Sparrow characterizes Bridges as a link between two ages, the Victorian and the modern, and sees his poetry as unpopular be-cause it is the fruit of "self seclusion for the sake of concentra-tion." Bridges' true gift was lyrical, Sparrow states: "To write a perfect lyric is a rare achievement, and Bridges repeated the miracle perhaps more than any other English poet."

_____. ROBERT BRIDGES. Writers and Their Work Series. London: Long-mans, Green, 1962.

Sparrow's brief study considers Bridges' poetry as a union of stylis-tic and technical control and the emotional expression of spiritual beauty.

Stanford, Donald E. IN THE CLASSIC MODE: THE ACHIEVEMENT OF ROBERT BRIDGES. Newark: University of Delaware Press, 1978.

Stanford offers "a survey and attempt to evaluate the major achieve-ments of an important poet, scholar, and man of letters whose work in recent years has been neglected." He provides insight into Bridges' use of accentual and syllabic metres, into quantity in English verse and into the legitimacy of free verse.

_____. "Introduction." In his ROBERT BRIDGES: SELECTED POEMS. Che-shire: Caracenet Press, 1974, pp. 9-23.

Stanford points out the recurring themes and attitudes in Bridges' poetry: "praise of the secluded, rural, cultured and intellectual life," "a kind of robust hedonism consisting of a balanced enjoyment of animal pleasures, the beauty of nature and of the arts, a skepticism concerning religious dogma (particularly Roman Catholic), but ultimately a belief in a benevolent deity, the experience of love both human and divine."

Thompson, Edward. ROBERT BRIDGES 1844-1930. Oxford: University Press; London: Milford, 1944.

Thompson presents a survey of Bridges' literary contribution, devoting several chapters to analyses of poems.

Wright, Elizabeth Cox. METAPHOR, SOUND, AND MEANING IN BRIDGES' 'THE TESTAMENT OF BEAUTY.' Philadelphia: University of Pennsylvania Press, 1951.

In what she terms an attempt at a new critical theory of aesthetic integrity, Cox undertakes a technical examination of the metre in THE TESTAMENT OF BEAUTY and analyzes its "extraordinary unity of tone and arrangement."

ALEXANDER COMFORT (1920-)

PRINCIPAL WORKS

Poetry

FRANCE AND OTHER POEMS. London: Favil Press, 1941.
A WREATH FOR THE LIVING. London: George Routledge, 1942.
ELEGIES. London: George Routledge, 1944.
THE SONG OF LAZARUS. New York: Viking, 1945.
THE SIGNAL TO ENGAGE. London: George Routledge, 1947.
AND ALL BUT HE DEPARTED. London: Routledge and Kegan Paul, 1951.
HASTE TO THE WEDDING. London: Eyre and Spottiswoode, 1962.
POEMS FOR JANE. New York: Crown, 1979.

Other Works

THE ALMOND TREE (1942), fiction.
INTO EGYPT: A MIRACLE PLAY (1942), drama.
CITIES OF THE PLAIN (1943), verse drama.
ART AND SOCIAL RESPONSIBILITY (1946), criticism.
Charles Ferdinand Ramuz' PRESENCE DE LA MORT, with Allan R. MacDougall
    (1946), translation.
LETTERS FROM AN OUTPOST (1947), fiction.
THE NOVEL IN OUR TIME (1948), criticism.
DARWIN AND THE NAKED LADY (1961), criticism.
THE PROCESS OF AGING (1964), prose.
THE KOKA SHASTRA (1965), translation.
THE JOY OF SEX (2 vols., 1974-76), prose.

BIBLIOGRAPHY

Callahan, Robert D. "Alex Comfort: A Bibliography in Progress." WEST
COAST REVIEW, 4 (1969), 48-67.

CRITICISM

Abrahams, William. "Without Irony." NEW REPUBLIC, 26 November 1945, p. 723.

> Abrahams discusses THE SONG OF LAZARUS (1945) and concludes that Comfort "suffers from a kind of cosmic simplemindedness; his poetry is all so simple--no irony, no ambiguity, no counterpoint." He concludes that "his is at best a meager talent."

Davie, Donald. "Reason Reversed." NEW STATESMAN, 63 (1962), 640.

> Davie compares Comfort to Graves and says of the former, "animal aplomb is very much Alex Comfort's business--not so much to have it and express it, as continually to recommend it, with elegance, impropriety and wit."

Jarrell, Randall. "Verse Chronicle." In his POETRY AND THE AGE. New York: Vintage, 1953, pp. 154-56.

> Jarrell states that in THE SONGS OF LAZARUS (1945), Comfort manifests himself as "potentially and in diffusion an interesting poet. Unfortunately, neither organization nor economy is natural to him, and the extensive, rather clumsy energy of his best prose is tenuous in his verse."

Rexroth, Kenneth. "Introduction." In his THE NEW BRITISH POETS. Norfolk, Conn.: New Directions, 1949, p. xxvii.

> Rexroth classifies Comfort as "a systematic Romantic who has made the concern of death, or the mechanization of the State, and all the other institutions of irresponsibility and spiritual sloth central to the philosophy of life he holds." He states that "Comfort, Woodcock, and Savage are the most remarkable of the young men who came first to prominence during the War, and it is significant that they are all anarchists, personalists and pacifists."

Ross, Alan. POETRY 1945-1950. London: Longmans, Green, 1951, pp. 25-26.

> Ross comments on the propagandistic nature of Comfort's poetry, concluding that "too often the strength of feeling is not supported by any comparable poetic skill."

Salmon, Arthur E. ALEX COMFORT. Twayne English Authors Series, no. 237. New York: Twayne, 1978.

> Salmon provides "an analysis of Comfort's art and thought and focuses on his treatment of death and power, two closely related themes in his works." Chapter 4 is on the poetry. A selected bibliography appears on pages 159-62.

Skelton, Robin. "Reviews and Comment." CRITICAL QUARTERLY, 3-4 (1962), 274.

> Skelton praises the "lucidity, wit and subtlety" in HASTE TO THE WEDDING (1962) and calls the poems on sexual enjoyment "some of the most pleasing and healthy" that he has read "for a very long time." He adds that Comfort's poetry is sometimes "slight, but fun," and wonders if perhaps "we are all really as hell-bent upon the Significant, the Serious, the Moral" as we are wont to believe.

Stanford, Derek. "Alex Comfort." In his THE FREEDOM OF POETRY: STUDIES IN CONTEMPORARY VERSE. London: Falcon Press, 1947, pp. 74-122.

> In the first part of his study, Stanford places Comfort among the neo-Romantics, and proceeds in part 2 to investigate the themes and techniques of A WREATH FOR THE LIVING (1942), ELEGIES (1944), and THE SIGNAL TO ENGAGE (1947), presenting a prolonged comparison between Comfort and Kenneth Patchen. Part 3 is devoted to Comfort's novel THE ALMOND TREE (1942), and part 4 to the plays, INTO EGYPT (1942) and CITIES OF THE PLAIN (1942). Part 5 explores Comfort's essay ART AND SOCIAL RESPONSIBILITY (1946). Stanford concludes with the statement: "Along with Gascoyne, Comfort appears, after the poets of the thirties proper--Spender, MacNeice, and denaturalized Auden--as the most virile figure in recent verse."

Thwaite, Anthony. "HASTE TO THE WEDDING." ENCOUNTER, 19 (1962), 81.

> Of the poems devoted to sex in HASTE TO THE WEDDING (1962), Thwaite says "the result is a sniggering jollity in the cause of straight speaking, high class dirt with lots of fashionable literary references, not unlike Aldous Huxley's poems of the 1920's. The Alex Comfort who wrote a handful of moving, sensual poems in the early 1940's seems to have degenerated into middle-aged prurience."

Treece, Henry. "Bird's Eye View of a Romantic Revival." In his HOW I SEE APOCALYPSE. London: Lindsay Drummond, 1946, pp. 173-82.

> Treece identifies Comfort as "a sympathizer of the Apocalyptic Movement" and calls him "one of the most accomplished poets of the younger generation." He comments on the sensuousness of Comfort's lines and on his "great and varied use of a liquid, musical language."

WALTER JOHN DE LA MARE (1873-1956)

PRINCIPAL WORKS

Poetry

SONGS OF CHILDHOOD. London: Longmans, Green, 1902.
POEMS. London: John Murray, 1906.
THE LISTENERS AND OTHER POEMS. London: Constable, 1912.
A CHILD'S DAY. A BOOK OF RHYMES. London: Constable, 1912.
PEACOCK PIE: A BOOK OF RHYMES. London: Constable, 1913.
MOTLEY AND OTHER POEMS. London: Constable, 1918.
POEMS 1901 TO 1918. London: Constable, 1920.
DOWN-ADOWN-DERRY: A BOOK OF FAIRY POEMS. London: Constable, 1922.
STUFF AND NONSENSE AND SO ON. London: Constable, 1927.
POEMS FOR CHILDREN. London: Constable, 1930.
THE FLEETING AND OTHER POEMS. London: Constable, 1933.
POEMS 1919 TO 1934. London: Constable, 1935.
THIS YEAR, NEXT YEAR. London: Faber, 1937.
MEMORY AND OTHER POEMS. London: Constable, 1938.
BELLS AND GRASS: A BOOK OF RHYMES. London: Faber, 1941.
COLLECTED POEMS. New York: Viking, 1941.
COLLECTED RHYMES AND VERSES. London: Faber, 1944.
THE BURNING GLASS AND OTHER POEMS INCLUDING THE TRAVELER. New York: Viking, 1945.
WINGED CHARIOT. London: Faber, 1951.
O LOVELY ENGLAND AND OTHER POEMS. London: Faber, 1953.
A CHOICE OF DE LA MARE'S VERSE. London: Faber, 1963.
COMPLETE POEMS. London: Faber, 1969.

Other Works

THE THREE MULLA-MULGARS (1910), fiction.
CROSSINGS (1921), drama.
THE RIDDLE AND OTHER STORIES (1923), fiction.
DING DONG BELL (1924), fiction.

BROOMSTICKS AND OTHER TALES (1925), fiction.
MISS JEMIMA (1925), fiction.
THE BEST STORIES OF WALTER DE LA MARE SELECTED BY THE AUTHOR
  (1942), fiction.
THE MAGIC JACKET AND OTHER STORIES (1943), fiction.
THE SCARECROW AND OTHER STORIES (1945), fiction.
A BEGINNING AND OTHER STORIES (1955), fiction.
GHOST STORIES (1956), fiction.
SOME STORIES (1962), fiction.

BIBLIOGRAPHIES

Clark, Leonard. "A Handlist of the Writings in Book Form (1902-53) of Walter de la Mare." STUDIES IN BIBLIOGRAPHY, 1953, pp. 197-217.

WALTER DE LA MARE: A CHECKLIST PREPARED ON THE OCCASION OF AN EXHIBITION OF HIS BOOKS AND MANUSCRIPTS AT THE NATIONAL BOOK LEAGUE, APRIL 20 TO MAY 19, 1956. Cambridge, Engl.: Cambridge University Press, 1956.

McCrosson, Doris Ross. "Selected Bibliography." In her WALTER DE LA MARE. New York: Twayne, 1966, pp. 161-67.

BIOGRAPHIES

Megroz, Ralph. WALTER DE LA MARE: A BIOGRAPHICAL AND CRITICAL STUDY. New York: Geo. H. Doran, 19-- .

> One of the first books dealing with de la Mare's work, Megroz' study contains the chapters "Personal Impressions," "Biography," "Poetry of Childhood," "Poetry as Dream," "Psychology of Dream," "Poetry of Life," "De la Mare's Ghosts," "The Language of Poetry," "De la Mare's Style and Content," and "The Poet and His Environment." There are three appendixes dealing with bibliography, de la Mare's blood relationship to Robert Browning, and an analysis of "The Listeners."

Bett, R.W., ed. TRIBUTE TO WALTER DE LA MARE ON HIS 75TH BIRTHDAY. London: Faber, 1948.

> This tribute includes essays and memoirs by C. Day Lewis, Graham Greene, Edmund Blunden, Christopher Morley and others.

Clark, Leonard. WALTER DE LA MARE. New York: H.Z. Walck, 1961.

> Clark devotes two chapters of his book to biographical information.

McCrosson, Doris Ross. WALTER DE LA MARE. New York: Twayne, 1966.

McCrosson devotes a chapter to biographical information.

CRITICISM

Atkins, John. WALTER DE LA MARE: AN EXPLORATION. London: Temple, 1947. Reissue. Folcroft, Pa.: Folcroft Library Editions, 1972.

Atkins contends that de la Mare's fame will ultimately rest on his stories and novels, not on his "accomplished minor verse."

Auden, W.H., ed. "Introduction." In A CHOICE OF DE LA MARE'S VERSE. London: Faber, 1963, pp. 13-26.

In his introduction, Auden comments on the poet's style, his children's poems, and his lyric poems. He identifies the poetry's most valuable element as its ability to call forth in the reader a "sense of wonder, awe, and reference for the beauty and strangeness of creation."

Bett, R.W., ed. TRIBUTE TO WALTER DE LA MARE ON HIS 75TH BIRTHDAY. London: Faber, 1948.

This tribute includes both biographical and critical information. Among its contributors are J.B. Priestley, V. Sackville West, J. Middleton Murry, Graham Greene, John Masefield, T.S. Eliot, C. Day Lewis, Siegfried Sassoon, and Edmund Blunden.

Blackmur, R.P. "POEMS 1919 TO 1934." POETRY (Chicago), 48 (1936), 334-37.

Blackmur asserts in this review that "it is in the archaic, specious, haunting realm of the consciousness, where every flight of fancy is final, disarming, and on the verge of the profound" that de la Mare belongs. Walter de la Mare, he explains, "is not a major poet, and you have the sense in reading him that he extracts much of his meaning from the separable devices of form which he employs, which is working in the wrong direction. Hence in his ambitious poems his verse is formal where it ought to be final, waste when it should brim; he loses his subject matter by finding only a form for it."

Brain, Russell. TEA WITH WALTER DE LA MARE. London: Faber, 1957.

A loving account of the author's friendship with de la Mare. It consists of a record of informal conversations between himself and the poet during the years 1951-56.

Walter John de la Mare

Brown, E.K. "The Epilogue to Mr. de la Mare's Poetry." POETRY (Chicago), 68 (1948), 90-96.

> In reviewing de la Mare's THE BURNING GLASS (1948), Brown claims that the value of this collection lies in its "supplying clues for a somewhat fuller understanding of the themes which were so elusively and subtly wrought out in earlier times."

Cecil, Lord David. WALTER DE LA MARE. English Association Presidential Address. London and New York: Oxford University Press, 1973.

> Cecil identifies de la Mare as "our last great writer in the original romantic tradition" and finds his poetry rooted in "the inner life, the inner dream of rapture or sadness or terror." He compares the poet with Keats, Wordsworth, Coleridge, Poe, and Christina Rossetti.

Child, Harold. "Mr. de la Mare's World." In his ESSAYS AND REFLECTIONS. Cambridge: Cambridge University Press, 1948, pp. 20-29.

> A brief survey of de la Mare's poetic achievement. Child directs his attention chiefly to those elements which create the "mystery" in the poems.

Church, Richard. "Walter de la Mare." In his EIGHT FOR IMMORTALITY. London: J.M. Dent, 1941, pp. 13-26.

> Church sees as the keynote of de la Mare's poetry "an inner conflict of clarity in near objects against an ever receding horizon."

Clark, Leonard. "Portrait of Walter de la Mare." LISTENER, 58 (1957), 619-20.

> Recollections of Clark's conversations with de la Mare at the poet's home in Twickenham, England.

_____. WALTER DE LA MARE. New York: H.Z. Walck, 1961.

> Among the chapters in Clark's book are two of a biographical nature and one devoted to poetry. Clark asserts, in regard to the poetry, "the secrets of Walter de la Mare's craftsmanship are quaint fancy vowel melody and cunning rhythm, all combining to give haunting overtones, strangeness and spellbinding dreams. The strongest influences on his poetry were Shakespeare . . . , Christina Rossetti, and to a lesser degree, Robert Louis Stevenson."

Duffen, Henry Charles. WALTER DE LA MARE: A STUDY OF HIS POETRY. London: Sedgwick and Jackson, 1949.

> Duffen considers, in some detail, the themes, imagery, and techniques employed in de la Mare's poetry.

Dyson, A.E. "Walter de la Mare's 'The Listeners.'" CRITICAL QUARTERLY, 2 (1960), 150-54.

A detailed discussion of the imagery and theme of the poem. Dyson concludes de la Mare's "odd, but impressive achievement has been to make the strange, the non-existent even, almost tangible, with the tangibility that language and poetry can confer."

Eberhart, Richard. "A Human Good." POETRY (Chicago), 58 (1941), 146-48.

Eberhart attempts to estimate de la Mare's place in the history of poetry.

Ferguson, De Lancey. "De la Mare's 'The Listeners' and Housman's 'On Wenlock Edge.'" EXPLICATOR, 4 (1945), item 15.

Ferguson says that the theme of de la Mare's poem is not the voice of God speaking to man but rather "that of 'Childe Roland to the Dark Tower Came'--a man keeping his pledge word in the face of all the powers of darkness."

Gregory, Horace. "The Nocturnal Traveller: Walter de la Mare." POETRY (Chicago), 80 (1952), 222-30.

Gregory describes de la Mare as "a traditional lyric poet 'with a difference.'" The "difference" consists in the "quality of wit which is revealed and is central to the character of his imagination."

Hopkins, Kenneth. WALTER DE LA MARE. London: Longmans, Green, 1957.

Hopkins characterizes de la Mare as "a poet of sustained power, and a prose writer of originality and grace." He devotes sections of the book to biography and to a critical survey of the prose works, essays, and poetry.

Larkin, Philip. "Big Victims: Emily Dickinson and Walter de la Mare." NEW STATESMAN, 79 (1970), 367-68.

Larkin compares Dickinson and de la Mare on the basis of "an odd linking aberration of childhood." "The difference between them," Larkin observes, is that "whereas Emily Dickinson built up her childishness into a theatrical hat and cloak to be worn day in and day out, de la Mare tamed his obsession to a point at which, although it remained the key to his writing, he could pass at will backwards and forwards from childhood to maturity."

Love, Glen. "Frost's 'The Census-Taker' and de la Mare's 'The Listeners.'" PAPERS ON LANGUAGE AND LITERATURE, 4 (1968), 198-200.

Love attempts to establish de la Mare's poem as the source for the Robert Frost poem (1923).

McCrosson, Doris Ross. WALTER DE LA MARE. Twayne English Authors Series, no. 33. New York: Twayne, 1966.

> McCrosson devotes her fourth chapter to de la Mare's poetry. She considers its themes, its preoccupation with death, its supernatural elements, and the "Impossible She," or spirit, whom the poet constantly evokes.

Megroz, R.L. "Walter de la Mare." In his FIVE NOVELIST POETS OF TO-DAY. London: Joiner and Steele, 1933, pp. 19-58.

> Megroz' discussion of de la Mare's poetry emphasizes its evocation of a dream atmosphere. He compares the qualities of the poet's "Child poems" with those of the adult poems.

"Mr. de la Mare in Epitome." TIMES LITERARY SUPPLEMENT, 28 December 1935, p. 895.

> This review characterizes POEMS 1919 TO 1934 as "strongly characteristic of the poet's mind." The author discusses reasons behind the poet's sometimes lukewarm reception by the critics of the 1930s.

"Mr. de la Mare's World. The Reality and the Dream." TIMES LITERARY SUPPLEMENT, 6 June 1942, pp. 282, 286.

> The unidentified critic defends de la Mare against those critics who accuse him of escapism.

Peschmann, Hermann. "The Poetry of Walter de la Mare." ENGLISH, 11 (1957), 129-33.

> Peschmann discusses the technical excellence of de la Mare's verse.

Pierson, Robert M. "The Meter of 'The Listeners.'" ENGLISH STUDIES, 45 (1964), 373-81.

> Pierson presents a detailed discussion.

"A Poet of Two Worlds: The Imagery of Mr. de la Mare." TIMES LITERARY SUPPLEMENT, 1 August 1936, p. 620.

> The author presents a cursory survey of de la Mare's images and ideas, calling particular attention to the nature of the poet's mythology, which he describes as "taken partly from fairy-tales, partly from the Bible and partly from 'The Pilgrim's Progress.'" The use of such familiar mythologies, he concludes, allows the poet to project an "acquiescent, receptive and alert mood" in the reader, which once done, allows him to lead the reader "unresisting and unsuspicious, through very strange company."

Purcell, J.M. "De la Mare's 'The Listeners.'" EXPLICATOR, 3 (1945), item 42.

Purcell charges de la Mare with using symbols in a vague way, stating that "It may be that he himself did not think clearly in verse."

Press, John. "The Poetry of Walter de la Mare." ARIEL, 1 (1970), 29-38.

Press's article surveys the whole of de la Mare's poetic achivement. He uses as his guide Luce Bonnerot's as yet untranslated L'OEUVRE DE WALTER DE LA MARE (1969).

Reeves, James. "Walter de la Mare: 1873-1956." LISTENER, 56 (1956), 24-25.

Reeves compares de la Mare's life and work with that of Charles Lamb.

Reid, Forrest. WALTER DE LA MARE: A CRITICAL STUDY. London: Faber, 1929.

This early work contains studies of SONGS OF CHILDHOOD (1902), POEMS (1906), THE LISTENERS (1912), and PEACOCK PIE (1913).

Sackville-West, Victoria. "Walter de la Mare and 'The Traveller.'" PROCEEDINGS OF THE BRITISH ACADEMY, 39 (1953), 23-26.

Sackville-West finds this poem an "affirmation of faith." The discovery is based on the fact that the Traveller prays, as Sackville-West expresses it, "to a mysterious, but in the last resort, a pitiful God."

Williams, Charles. "Walter de la Mare." In his POETRY AT PRESENT. Oxford: Clarendon Press, 1930, pp. 82-97.

Williams defines "pure poetry" as "that in which from the common facts, the most general associations, is produced the most concentrated and piercing effect" and then discusses de la Mare's verse as an example of "pure poetry."

WILLIAM EMPSON (1906-)

PRINCIPAL WORKS

Poetry

POEMS. London: Chatto and Windus, 1935.
THE GATHERING STORM. London: Faber, 1940.
COLLECTED POEMS. New York: Harcourt, Brace, 1949.
COLLECTED POEMS. London: Chatto and Windus, 1955.

Other Works

SEVEN TYPES OF AMBIGUITY (1930), criticism.
SOME VERSIONS OF THE PASTORAL (1935), criticism.
THE STRUCTURE OF COMPLEX WORDS (1951), criticism.
MILTON'S GOD (1961), criticism.

BIBLIOGRAPHY

Lowbridge, Peter. "An Empson Bibliography." REVIEW, nos. 6 and 7 (June 1963), 64-74.

See Gill, Roma, below.

BIOGRAPHY

See Gill, Roma, and "Special Number on William Empson," below.

CRITICISM

Adams, Robert Martin. "Empson and Bentley: Something About Milton Too." PARTISAN REVIEW, 21 (1954), 178-89.

Adams gives an account of the mistakes that Empson made in his revival of the debate that resulted from criticism by Zachary Pearce on Richard Bentley's criticism of John Milton that appears in Empson's SOME VERSIONS OF THE PASTORAL (1935).

Alpers, Paul. "Empson on Pastoral." NEW LITERARY HISTORY 10 (1978), 102-23.

Alpers' main purpose in this essay is to clarify Empson's ideas "not only about style and its relation to social convention, but also about language itself; about the nature of the reader and the way in which works imply their readers; about the relation of literature to popular arts and modes of expression; about the modes of existence of literary works and their claims to our reverence or attention."

Alvarez, A. "A Style from Despair: William Empson." TWENTIETH CENTURY, 161 (1957), 344-53.

This is something in Empson's work, Alvarez states, that encourages other writers to use it for their own ends. Probably it is his essential objectivity. His earlier poems especially are created out of an emotional response to something he comprehends intellectually, not from circumstances and feelings related to personal situation. They succeed because of a perfectly established manner and tone, not because of any particularly personal involvement or intensity. "To An Old Lady," which appears in COLLECTED POEMS (1955), is an example of such a poem. THE GATHERING STORM (1940), as a whole admits to a style of clear tone, with a previous tendency toward verbal elaborateness replaced by bare statements that fix attention on "weightless little words one can hardly otherwise notice" and more self involvement in the poet. One of this volume's poems, "The Teasers," demonstrates this change in style that brought with it an effort to work from and state personal experience and generalize it into ideas. These later poems have a static quality that more than anything else distinguishes them from the earlier verse. "What the later poems have gained in general truth, Alvarez concludes, "they have lost in stylish and inquiring originality. And it is as a stylist of poetry and ideas that Empson is most important."

Breitkreuz, Harmut. "Empson's 'The Beautiful Train.'" EXPLICATOR, 31 (1972), item 9.

Breitkreuz asserts that the different levels of human experience reflected in Empson's poem are "presented in a poetic synthesis by telescoping three forms of movement and change: the rhythm of dancing, the rhythm of the train, and the rhythm of thought. The artistic devices of achieving this end are the functional use of the title metaphor, and, above all, the imagery of dancing which is maintained throughout 'The Beautiful Train,' expressing the incongruity between man and a world in conflict."

Brooks, Cleanth. "Empson's Criticism." ACCENT, 4 (1944), 208-16.

On SEVEN TYPES OF AMBIGUITY (1930). The significance of
Empson's criticism lies, Brooks believes, in its attempt "to deal
with what the poem 'means' in terms of its structure <u>as a poem.</u>"
Critics in the past attempted to find the goodness in a poem in
terms of its prose argument, or they tried to find the poetry in
the delight of its embellishments, or they tried to combine the
two. Empson fights this crippling division of approach by showing
how the poem actually "works" within a complex of meanings.
He demonstrates how metaphor, metrics, and connotations are all
active forces in the development of the multiple meanings that is
the poem. The poem is thus seen as dynamic, the product of the
development of a whole process.

One of the difficulties of SEVEN TYPES OF AMBIGUITY stems,
says Brooks, from Empson's being forced to combat somewhat con-
fusedly the romantic and magical conception of poetry in order to
state his case at all. He therefore made concessions to the "enemy" in trying to be fair and the result was that he seems to con-
tradict his own theory. Another difficulty comes from his attempt
to adapt the viewpoint of the "imperfect reader" rather than forcing such a reader to comply to his theory. The most serious
charge, however, that can be leveled at Empson is that he forces
upon a poem his own personal associations, idiosyncratic readings,
and strained analogies. Brooks asserts that SEVEN TYPES OF AM-
BIGUITY is full of subjective criteria leading to a relativistic im-
broglio caused by Empson's allowing his desire for complete objectivity to rule over common sense. Empson's work is nevertheless "fraught with revolutionary consequences for the teaching of
all literature and for the future of literary history."

Corke, Hilary. "Empson's Poems." LISTENER, 54 (1956), 565.

"Empson's poems are as much criticisms of his criticism as his
criticisms are in another sense poems about his poems," states
Corke. He contends that Empson's "unit of creation" is not the
poem but the poem in addition to the note upon it.

Danby, John F. "William Empson." CRITICAL QUARTERLY, 1 (1959), 99-104.

Danby claims that Empson's elliptic, cryptic, acrostic style leaves
the impression that a lot is going on in his poems. However, it
is questionable whether real articulation of thought is possible in
such conditions. Empson's notes of clarification are necessary because the prose explains to us what the poem failed to communicate.

Eberhart, Richard. "Empson's Poetry." ACCENT, 4 (1944), 195-207.

The article, written in four parts, first recalls Empson's student
years at Cambridge and considers his poetic contribution to EXPERI-

MENT and CAMBRIDGE REVIEW. The second part is devoted to
general comments on Empson's early poetry. A detailed analysis
of the poem "This Last Pain" constitutes the third part. Part 4
investigates the later poetry, particularly the poems "Your Teeth
are Ivory Towers," "Aubade," and "Four Legs, Two Legs, Three
Legs."

Ford, Newell. "Empson's and Ransom's Mutilations of Texts." PHILOLOGICAL
QUARTERLY, 29 (1950), 18-84.

Ford contends that Empson, in SEVEN TYPES OF AMBIGUITY
(1930), predicates aesthetic judgments that mutilate the texts from
Wordsworth and Keats that he treats.

Forrest-Thomson, Veronica. "Rational Artifice: Some Remarks on the Poetry
of William Empson." YEARBOOK OF ENGLISH STUDIES, 4 (1974), 225-38.

Forrest-Thomson presents an examination of Empson's stand against
"the 'lethal theory' that poetry may be, in rational terms, sheer
nonsense" and also of "his accompanying insight into the complexity
of poetry's relation to our other modes of discourse and primarily
to the critical language that integrates a poem into the network
of our experience."

Fraser, G.S. "On the Interpretation of a Difficult Poem." In INTERPRETA-
TIONS. Ed. John Wain. London and Boston: Routledge and Kegan Paul,
1972, pp. 211-37.

Fraser tests on Empson's poem "The Teasers" some of the tactics
he has learned from Empson's critical methods. He defends Empson against the accusation, by John Wain, of "formal carelessness"
(NEW WRITINGS, Penguin 40, 1950). Fraser asserts also that the
exclusion of background information by the "New Critics" in the
examination of this or any other poem, prevents the reader from
"enjoying the full social, or aesthetic sense of the statement."

Gardner, Philip, and Averil Gardner. THE GOD APPROACHED: A COM-
MENTARY ON THE POEMS OF WILLIAM EMPSON. Totowa, N.J.: Rowman
and Littlefield, 1978.

The Gardners' study consists of short commentaries on the poems
in COLLECTED POEMS (1955). The introduction includes a bibliographical sketch of Empson.

Gill, Roma, ed. WILLIAM EMPSON: THE MAN AND HIS WORK. London:
Routledge and Kegan Paul, 1974.

Gill's book contains articles by M.C. Bradbrook, Kathleen Raine,
Ronald Bottral, G.S. Fraser, Graham Hough, I.A. Richards, L.C.
Knight, John Wain, and Christopher Ricks. Contains a bibliog-
raphy by M. Megaw on pp. 213-34.

Glicksberg, Charles I. "William Empson: Genius of Ambiguity." DAL-
HOUSIE REVIEW, 29 (1950), 366-77.

> Glicksberg presents a clarification of Empson's method of "disen-
> tangling the ambiguities of meaning in the skein of poetic context."

Hedges, William M. "The Empson Treatment." ACCENT, 17 (1957), 231-41.

> Hedges presents a detailed analysis of Empson's poem "Four Legs,
> Two Legs, Three Legs." Includes a lengthy discussion of the poet's
> notes on the poem.

Jensen, James. "Some Ambiguous Preliminaries: Empson in THE GRANTA."
CRITICISM, 8 (1966), 349-61.

> Jenson presents a consideration of the reviews contributed by Emp-
> son to the Cambridge undergraduate magazine, GRANTA, that
> show significant relation to the theory of ambiguity as it was later
> developed in SEVEN TYPES OF AMBIGUITY (1930).

Kenner, Hugh. "Alice in Empsonland." HUDSON REVIEW, 5 (1952), 144.

> On THE STRUCTURE OF COMPLEX WORDS (1951). The chapters
> in this work are dull, Kenner asserts, because the method is not
> right for discussing poetry. Long poems cannot be reduced to the
> intricacies of their key words. The method only succeeds well in
> showing off the analytic machinery. Empson's most enlightening
> performance is with Pope's "wit." His move to push discussion of
> complex poetic work back into a discussion of writer-audience rela-
> tions is indicative of his general attitude to poetry: its language
> is a "kind of heliographic signalling, a faint and desperate attempt
> to stretch filaments from monad to monad." Kenner concludes, "His
> style is narcissistic . . . , a kind of pathetic elegance in manip-
> ulating the inconsequential."

Mason, H.A. "Some Versions of the Pastoral." SCRUTINY, 4 (1936), 431-
34.

> SOME VERSIONS OF THE PASTORAL (1935) is interesting, Mason
> allows, but it lacks the vigor and exhuberance of SEVEN TYPES
> OF AMBIGUITY (1930). He claims that the pastoral theme fails
> to bind the eight essays together and that the author pursues di-
> gressions too often. The first chapter, "Proletarian Literature,"
> is the best in the book.

Maxwell-Mahon, W.D. "The Early Poetry of William Empson." UNISA EN-
GLISH STUDIES, 10 (1972), 12-22.

> This article is an investigation of Empson's early poetry as reveal-
> ing a concern for the moral health of society. Much attention is
> given to the nature of Empson's imagery.

_____. "William Empson: The Development of an Idiom." UNISA ENGLISH STUDIES, 8 (1970), 24-26.

Maxwell-Mahon presents an examination of the six poems that Empson as an undergraduate contributed to CAMBRIDGE POETRY: 1929 as examples of a poetic style arising from the combination of elliptical syntax and compressed thought.

Norris, Christopher. WILLIAM EMPSON AND THE PHILOSOPHY OF LITERARY CRITICISM. London: Althone Press, 1978.

Norris relates Empson's work as a consistent whole to his philosophy of humanistic rationalism. Particular attention is given to THE STRUCTURE OF COMPLEX WORDS (1951).

Olson, Elder. "William Empson: Contemporary Criticism and Poetic Diction." MODERN PHILOLOGY, 47 (1950), 222-52.

Olson presents a detailed critique of Empson's theory of ambiguity. He claims that Empson's method of interpretation reduces all poetic considerations of poetic diction, and reduces all discussion of diction to problems of ambiguities. Empson, he states, misses the governance of "diction by thought, of thought by character, of character by action" and that his theory deals only with a single part of poetry and that part is not even the most important one. Olson claims that this mistake of Empson's abounds everywhere in the "New Criticism" and that other faults Empson and his method propound include an attempt to establish principles of art "without any clear, widely, accepted metaphysics, epistomology, philosophy of science, an attempt to allow definitions to operate as bases of proof, as principles of demonstration, thus making them sources of misreading and error (e.g., the assertion that poetry is language characterized by ambiguity, and an inability to recognize distinctions within the genre of poetry itself)." The article ends with a lengthy and detailed discussion of poetic diction and its place in critical theory.

"Pastoral and Proletarian: In Search of All Possible Meanings." TIMES LITERARY SUPPLEMENT, 30 November 1935, p. 798.

SOME VERSIONS OF THE PASTORAL (1935) is an exciting and stimulating book that "runs disappointingly to seed," claims the critic. He asserts that half of its pages could have been cut with advantage and what was left expanded "under a normative influence of some kind into something quite different for the intellectual gymnastics which ought to have been sacrificed." The first chapter is brilliant, he asserts, but thereafter Empson gets lost in vast mountains of "possible meanings." The critic adds that Empson's comments on Bentley's criticism of Milton are fresh and original.

Sleight, Richard. "Mr. Empson's Complex Words." ESSAYS IN CRITICISM, 2 (1952), 325-37.

On THE STRUCTURE OF COMPLEX WORDS (1951). This critique takes issue with Empson's methods of verbal analysis, especially his treatment of "wit" as used by Pope. In his chapter on "mesopo-tamia" Empson traces the suasive method of the false argument connected to the statement "Grammar is usage." Sleight asserts that "His elucidation is brilliant and close but that he neglects the more subconscious processes involved in its imposition—one supposes these exist and make the argument plausible." It is ne-cessary, Sleight insists, to have more respect for the irrational side of human thought, especially in the interpretation of fiction-al characters or poetic modes of thought. He believes that Emp-son's chapter on Wordsworth's THE PRELUDE removes any doubts about the possibilities of applying the new critical method to the Romantics.

"Special Number on William Empson." REVIEW, 6 and 7 (June 1963), entire issue.

This issue, devoted entirely to William Empson, contains the follow-ing essays: Martin Dodsworth's "Empson at Cambridge"; Philip Hobsbaum's "Empson as Critical Practitioner"; John Fuller's "Emp-son's Tone"; Christopher Rick's "In Conversation with Christopher Ricks"; Ian Hamilton's "A Girl Can't Go On Laughing All the Time"; Saul Tousler's "Legal Fiction"; Colin Falck's "This Deep Blankness"; Peter Lowbridge's "An Empson Bibliography"; L.E. Sissman's poem "Just a Whack at Empson."

ROBERT VON RANKE GRAVES (1895-)

PRINCIPAL WORKS

Poetry

OVER THE BRAZIER: POEMS. London: Poetry Bookshop, 1916.
GOLIATH AND DAVID: POEMS. London: Charles Whittingham, 1917.
FAERIES AND FUSILIERS: POEMS. London: William Heinemann, 1917.
COUNTRY SENTIMENT: POEMS. London: Martin Secker, 1920.
THE PIER-GLASS. London: Martin Secker, 1921.
THE FEATHER BED: A POEM. Richmond, Engl.: Leonard and Virginia Woolf, 1923.
WHIPPERGINNY. London: William Heinemann, 1923.
MOCK BEGGAR HALL: SKETCHES IN PROSE AND VERSE. London: Hogarth Press, 1924.
WELSHMAN'S HOSE. London: Fleuron, 1925.
THE MARMOSITE'S MISCELLANY. [By] John Doyle [pseud]. London: Leonard and Virginia Woolf, 1925.
POEMS 1914-1926. London: William Heinemann, 1927.
POEMS 1929. London: Seizin Press, 1929.
TEN POEMS MORE. Paris: Hours Press, 1930.
POEMS 1926-1930. London: William Heinemann, 1931.
TO WHOM ELSE?: POEMS. Deya, Spain: Seizin Press, 1931.
COLLECTED POEMS 1938. London: Cassell, 1938.
NO MORE GHOSTS. SELECTED POEMS. London: Faber, 1940.
WORK IN HAND: EIGHTEEN POEMS: BY ALAN HODGE, NORMAN CAMERON, ROBERT GRAVES. New Hogarth Library, vol. 6. London: Hogarth Press, 1942.
POEMS 1938-1945. London: Cassell, 1946.
COLLECTED POEMS 1914-1947. London: Cassell, 1948.
POEMS AND SATIRES. London: Cassell, 1951.
POEMS 1953. London: Cassell, 1953.
COLLECTED POEMS. London: Cassell, 1955.
POEMS SELECTED BY HIMSELF. Harmondsworth, Engl.: Penguin Books, 1957.
COLLECTED POEMS 1959. London: Cassell, 1959.
THE PENNY FIDDLE: POEMS FOR CHILDREN. London: Cassell, 1960.
MORE POEMS 1961. London: Cassell, 1961.

NEW POEMS 1962. London: Cassell, 1962.

THE MORE DESERVING CASES: 18 OLD POEMS FOR RECONSIDERATION. Marlborough, Engl.: Marlborough College Press, 1962.

ANN AT HIGHWOOD HALL: POEMS FOR CHILDREN. London: Cassell, 1964.

MAN DOES, WOMAN IS. London: Cassell, 1964.

COLLECTED POEMS 1965. London: Cassell, 1965.

LOVE RESPELT. London: Cassell, 1965.

SEVENTEEN POEMS MISSING FROM "LOVE RESPELT." London: Cassell, 1966.

POEMS 1965-1968. London: Cassell, 1968.

THE NEW COLLECTED POEMS OF ROBERT GRAVES. New York: Doubleday, 1978.

Other Works

ON ENGLISH POETRY (1922), criticism.

A SURVEY OF MODERNIST POETRY, with Laura Riding (1927), criticism.

I, CLAUDIUS (1934), fiction.

ANTIGUA PENNY PUCE (1936), fiction.

COUNT BELISARIUS (1938), fiction.

THE LONG WEEK-END: A SOCIAL HISTORY OF GREAT BRITAIN, 1918-1939. With Alan Hodge (1940), history.

SERGEANT LAMB OF THE NINTH (1940), fiction.

PROCEED SERGEANT LAMB (1941), fiction.

THE STORY OF MARIE POWELL, WIFE TO MR. MILTON (1943), fiction.

THE GOLDEN FLEECE (1944), fiction.

KING JESUS (1946), fiction.

THE WHITE GODDESS (1948), criticism.

THE COMMON ASPHODEL (1949), criticism.

SEVEN DAYS IN NEW CRETE (1949), fiction.

THE ISLANDS OF UNWISDOM (1949), fiction.

OCCUPATION WRITER (1950), fiction, criticism.

HOMER'S DAUGHTER (1955), fiction.

THE GREEK MYTHS (2 vols., 1955), translation.

THE CROWNING PRIVILEGE (1955), criticism.

5 PENS IN HAND (1958), fiction, essays, poems.

STEPS (1958), miscellaneous.

CATACROK! (1959), fiction.

FOOD FOR CENTAURS (1960), fiction, essays, poems.

THE ANGER OF ACHILLES (1960), translation.

OXFORD ADDRESSES ON POETRY (1962), criticism.

COLLECTED SHORT STORIES (1965), fiction.

MAMMON AND THE BLACK GODDESS (1965), criticism.

POETIC CRAFT AND PRINCIPLE (1967), criticism.

RUBAIYAT OF OMAR KHAYAAM, with O. Ali-Shah (1967), translation.

THE CRANE BAG AND OTHER DISPUTED SUBJECTS (1969), criticism.

ON POETRY: COLLECTED TALKS AND ESSAYS (1969), criticism.

BIBLIOGRAPHY

Higginson, F.H. A BIBLIOGRAPHY OF THE WORKS OF ROBERT GRAVES. Hamden, Conn.: Archon Books, 1966.

AUTOBIOGRAPHY

GOODBYE TO ALL THAT. New York: J. Cape and H. Smith, 1929.

> The first section of the book is devoted to Graves's memories of his school days at Charterhouse. This is followed by a narrative of his marriage to Nancy Nicholson and a detailed account of life at the front during the First World War. The book contains anecdotes of people prominent in English letters.

BIOGRAPHIES

See Quennell, "The Multiple Robert Graves," under "Criticism" below.

Snipes, Katherine. ROBERT GRAVES. New York: Frederick Ungar, 1979.

> Snipes devotes her first chapter to a biographical study.

CRITICISM

Auden, W.H., et al. "A Symposium on Robert Graves." SHENANDOAH, 13 (1962), 5-62.

> Auden presents a series of essays designed to present Graves as England's "greatest living poet." Critical contributions include W.H. Auden's "A Poet of Honor," Donald Davie's "Impersonal and Emblematic," D.J. Enright's "The Example of Robert Graves," G.S. Fraser's "The Reputation of Robert Graves," Thom Gunn's "In Nobody's Pantheon," Allan Sillitoe's "I Reminded Him of Muggleton," and Colin Wilson's "Some Notes on Graves's Prose."

Blackburn, Thomas. "Ezra Pound, Edwin Muir, Edith Sitwell, Robert Graves, Kathleen Raine." In his THE PRICE OF AN EYE. London: Longmans, 1960, pp. 73-78.

> Blackburn asserts that Graves's sense of reality increases steadily from the early poems. The poet is unequaled in his talent for expressing with understanding and immediacy the meeting between man and woman.

Church, Richard. "Robert Graves: A Traveler in the Desert." In his EIGHT FOR IMMORTALITY. London: J.M. Dent, 1941, pp. 93-113.

Church asserts that Graves's development as one of the best poets
of the times is rooted in his series of spiritual and emotional
"suicides": "The more violent these deaths, the more agonizing
the rebirths, the firmer is the poet's technique and the more personal and original his idiom."

Day, Douglas. SWIFTER THAN REASON: THE POETRY AND CRITICISM OF
ROBERT GRAVES. London: Oxford University Press, 1963.

Day presents the first systematic assessment of the poetry and
critical writings of Graves. He traces Graves's progress as a
poet from 1916 on, utilizing the poet's critical writings as a key
to understanding this progress. Sees Graves's career as falling
into four major phases: Georgian juvenilia, a self-styled "ano-
dynic" period of therapeutic writing, a period of detached and
abstract poetry, and finally, the most successful phase, when
Graves worked under the influence of Laura Riding, a period
during which he discovered the mythological image of his muse,
the White Goddess.

Dudek, Louis. "The Case of Robert Graves." CANADIAN FORUM, 40 (1960),
199-201.

According to Dudek, the thin and retrograde tradition presented
by Robert Graves in this decade is a sign of the "nerveless and
tottering condition" of English literary culture. Graves writes
unoriginal poetry in a cold and mechanical fashion and receives
praise from a conservative and directionless generation who are
afraid of losing the little culture they have. Graves's "is a very
small, conventional voice in a period of great and exciting poetry.
In his practice he is against the best spirit of his time." It is to
his own loss that he set his back against modernism early in his
career.

Enright, D.J. ROBERT GRAVES AND THE DECLINE OF MODERNISM. Singapore: University of Malaya, 1960; rpt. in ESSAYS IN CRITICISM, 11 (1961),
319-36.

This sermon on the spontaneity of art takes as its text Graves's
poems and the liberal attitude they express. Enright's argument
is directed at two targets: the officials who, at the price of
human freedom, set out to remove what they regard as unhealthy
influences from our common cultural life; and the academic critics
who feel that good poems can be written only by those who have
absorbed the best work of the past. The former target finds its
embodiment in the Singapore government, the latter in poet and
critic John Wain.

Fletcher, J.G. "Collected Poems." KENYON REVIEW, 2 (1939-40), 100.

Fletcher believes that the later poems of Graves as exhibited in

COLLECTED POEMS (1938) are not poems but exercises in the poetic form. They speak of warfare, love, friendship, human pride, and humility, but only in an abstract manner. Logic and reason are Graves's guides and are necessarily false ones because his subjects need the underpinnings of the Christian faith as a frame of reference. Graves has totally rejected this faith, not realizing that Christian distrust of reason is the best excuse for a poet's existence.

Fraser, G.S. "The Universal Man." LITERARY GUIDE, 70 (1955), 6-8.

Fraser states that Robert Graves's versatility distracts attention from his poetry. This article contains a survey of the poet's work, attitudes, and style.

Fuller, Roy. "Some Vintages of Graves." LONDON MAGAZINE, 5 (1958), 56-59.

Fuller presents a brief account of Graves's stages of development as evidenced in POEMS SELECTED BY HIMSELF (1951). Fuller discusses the "innocent origins, independence of ideology, and isolated literary position" of Graves's work, yet another of the rigorously dissident artistic figures of the century.

Gaskell, Ronald. "The Poetry of Robert Graves." CRITICAL QUARTERLY, 3 (1961), 213-22.

Gaskell presents a discussion of Graves's autobiography, the irrational and nightmarish character of the poems up to 1940, the poet's handling of lust as a poetic theme, his distancing of emotion through use of a single image or legendary situation realized in vivid detail, and, finally, his employment of the natural unexpected rhythms of speech played off against regular meter.

"Graves, 1965." TIMES LITERARY SUPPLEMENT, 7 October 1968, p. 898.

In the main, a comparison of COLLECTED POEMS 1959 with COLLECTED POEMS 1965. The volumes, the article asserts, produce different effects. The later one shows no falling off of craftsmanship or "spontaneous directness of feeling," but, compared to the earlier one, lacks "weight and tension, the sense of pain and struggle, and also, perhaps, a certain freshness, rawness, directness." The later volume is mannerist, showing a stylized attitude toward life and love. A comparison of two earlier poems from Graves's discarded work, with a sample from his most recent work, illustrates this opinion. The article ends with a perceptive comparison and contrast between Graves and Yeats.

Gregory, Horace. "Faithful to a Goddess and a Queen." NEW YORK TIMES BOOK REVIEW, 16 July 1961, pp. 1, 20.

With the publication of COLLECTED POEMS (1959), the time has become ripe, Gregory claims, for a re-evaluation of Graves as a poet because of his strength of character as well as the merits of his verse. The early poems, though too "soft and clumsy" and tied to Georgian sentimentalities, have hidden merits of candor and roughness and a "flash of coarsegrained violence." Imposing strong criticism on himself over the years, Graves remade himself as a poet. His style is soldierly and formal, and his devotion is directed to a goddess related to his Celtic Roman paganism and to Queen Elizabeth II. The contrast results in the elements of conflict that constitute the essential vigor of Graves's poetry. He is a modern poet with no alliances, and his individual approach has given him the freedom to produce poetry that is mature, firm, vigorous, and courtly.

Grigson, Geoffrey. "Romanticism Boiled Dry." BOOKMAN (London), 79 (1931), 351.

Grigson claims that POEMS 1926-1930 shows the development in Graves of an aim at "pure poetry." This "pure poetry," Grigson asserts, is "non-literary" and "integral" in the sense that it records the total poetic experience, unrestricted by rigid literary form, traditions, and language. Grigson goes on to say that the poetry insists not on logical inference but intuition. The danger of this kind of poetry is that the purer one's verse becomes the less value it holds for anyone other than the writer, and in this case, could just as well remain in the poet's head, unwritten. Graves's approach, thus, represents a "fag end of Romanticism and is as barren as the extreme of classicism where the opposite phenomenon occurred."

Hadas, Moses. "5 Pens at Hand." SATURDAY REVIEW OF LITERATURE, 29 March 1958, pp. 28-30.

Graves's prime material is in this collection, Hadas asserts. The "full-blooded personality" it reveals is a phenomenon in the world of letters today. The best of the book is not in the poems but in the lecture "Legitimate Criticism of Poetry," a demonstration of the proper techniques of literary study.

Hayman, Ronald. "Robert Graves." ESSAYS IN CRITICISM, 5 (1955), 32-43.

Hayman identifies and discusses a small corpus of Graves's poems that are "neither metaphysical nor romantic" and whose strength lies in their complete freedom from either of the two "weaknesses." This corpus is compared to a number of Graves's poems which are considered too "metaphysical," too detached from the particularities of emotional experience to be truly successful.

Hijmans, Ben L. "Robert Graves, the White Goddess and Virgil." MOSAIC, 2 (1969), 58-73.

Hijmans states that Graves contends in "The Virgil Cult" (VIRGINIA

QUARTERLY REVIEW, 38 [1962], 13-35) that Virgil did not respond
to the muse in a sexual way and therefore could not be a good
poet. Hijmans, in some detail, refutes this and other reasons
Graves forwards to substantiate his opinion that Virgil was an inferior poet.

Hoffman, Daniel. BARBAROUS KNOWLEDGE: MYTH IN THE POETRY OF
YEATS, GRAVES, MUIR. London: Oxford University Press, 1970.

Hoffman sees Yeats, Graves, and Muir as the "last romantics,"
each identifying with the older cultures of Ireland, the Orkneys,
and Wales. Each of these poets relies on folk beliefs and ballad
tradition and in his own way believes that man redeemed, that is,
man transcending circumstances, comes about, not by his willful
and conscious discovery, but by a myth of his own shaping.
Graves's myth, of course, centers on that of the White Goddess,
his "historic grammar encouraging the rule of intuition over reason
and submission of the poet to the muse." The book contains
analyses of Graves's ballads, lyrics, reflective pieces, and investigates his reverence for the logic of language whereby the truth
of unreason is exposed.

Janeway, Elizabeth. "An Evaluation of Robert Graves, a Neglected Writer."
NEW YORK TIMES BOOK REVIEW, 18 September 1949, p. 5.

Janeway sees Graves as a romantic writer (as opposed to a classicist) who creates worlds of intuition, dynamism, and disruption
instead of logic, formalism, and order.

Jarrell, Randall. "Graves and the White Goddess, Parts I and II." YALE
REVIEW, 45 (1956), 302-14, 467-78.

Jarrell claims that Graves's poems divide into six types: mythical-
archaic poems; poems about extreme situations; magical landscapes;
grotesques; observations of types of behavior, attitude, situation,
of the processes and categories of existence; love poems, ballads
or nursery rhymes. Part 1 of this article discusses each of these
types using specific poems for demonstration. Part 2 discusses
"Graves's theoretical picture of what life necessarily must be" and
how this picture related actually to his life.

Kirkham, Michael. THE POETRY OF ROBERT GRAVES. New York: Oxford
University Press, 1969.

Kirkham presents a detailed historical and critical examination devoted to the poetry of Graves. Kirkham deals with the canon
poem by poem and chronologically. He explores the early poems
as products of a poet suffering from neurasthenia and illustrates the
profound influence of Laura Riding on Graves's technique, criticism,
and intellectual, ethical, and religious views. He presents a critique of the Black Goddess of the more recent poetry, seeing her

as a representative of a miraculous certitude of love discovered by the poet who passes through all the ordeals to which the White Goddess subjects him. The Black Goddess is a source of "new wisdom" and "spiritual understanding."

Mehoke, James S. ROBERT GRAVES: PEACE WEAVER. Paris: Mouton, 1975.

Mehoke's book attempts to "summarize attitudes relative to Graves's Goddess and Myth and to underlie the nature of the debate going on in this regard." Chapter 5 is devoted to the poetry as related to the myth.

"Modern Riddles." TIMES LITERARY SUPPLEMENT, 1 January 1931, p. 8.

The critic describes Graves as one of the modern poets who takes the more intricate workings of the mind as a subject of his verse, and who expresses this subject by connecting "wildly dissimilar thoughts by the frailest possible bridge of association" and by jumping from one image or idea to another. The "idea" of the poem can be derived only from the poem taken as a whole. Graves's poems are often obscure.

Moran, James. "The Seizin Press of Laura Riding and Robert Graves." BLACK ART, 2 (1963), 34-39.

The article presents the facts about the Seizin Press that was founded by the two poets in 1921.

"Mr. Graves's New Poems." TIMES LITERARY SUPPLEMENT, 1 June 1933, p. 377.

The author places Graves halfway between the Georgian poets and the Modernist poets. He claims that Graves is concerned with general ideas rather than the outward world and is most successful when he fuses old poetic symbols with a modernist approach.

"Mr. Graves's Poems." TIMES LITERARY SUPPLEMENT, 23 July 1931, p. 578.

The critic claims that the merriment in POEMS 1926-1930 is hollow. Graves's intentional echo of John Skelton's wit is weak, and there is only an echo of an earlier enthusiasm. The gaiety that is present weakens the thrust of the poetry, and the metaphysical compositions do not hit the mark. TO WHOM ELSE? (1931) as a collection leaves much to be desired. It lacks evidence of development, is lethargic in tone, and identifies the poet's detachment from common persons and common things.

Muir, Edwin. "Robert Graves." In his TRANSITION. London: Hogarth Press, 1926, pp. 163-76.

Muir regrets Graves's "pseudopsychological poetry," which he describes as unoriginal, lacking in immediacy, and failing in an organic correspondence between internal conflict and external images.

"Obscurity in Poetry." TIMES LITERARY SUPPLEMENT, 16 January 1959, p. 33.

The critic identifies true "Georgians" as those poets who accepted Thomas Hardy as their living master. The young Graves was one of those who shared Hardy's interest in "country life, human quirks and oddities." He also had, like Hardy, "a sharp eye for material detail." Graves directed attention, in Hardy fashion, to a subdued and natural style, and was reluctant to define any general attitudes.

"A Personal Mythology." TIMES LITERARY SUPPLEMENT, 5 June 1959, p. 336.

A summary of Graves's poetic achievement up to 1959. Graves is considered as a young Romantic, writing in the pattern of Georgian verse, who looked to John Skelton's traditional ballads, and Welsh poetry for freshness of approach. He flowered as a serious, mature poet under Laura Riding's influence, producing pieces of delicately blended ingenuities and subtleties by way of myth: "His work is an object lesson in the construction of a personal mythology which has no apparent religious or political connections; or, as he puts it himself in speaking of his fifth poetic stage, 'in the struggle to be a poet in the more literary sense,' [I have achieved] a sense of poetic liberation--not by mysticism, but by practical persistence.'"

Pettet, E.C. "The Poetry of Robert Graves." ENGLISH, 3 (1940-43), 216-20.

Pettet considers Graves's work as an example of "one of the most revealing cross-sections of twentieth-century poetry to be found." He is adept at writing Georgian poetry, war poetry, introspective poetry, metaphysical poetry, and characteristically modern poetry.

Pick, J.B. "The Poet as Cynic." OUTPOSTS, 14 (1949), 23-25.

Pick presents a discussion of Graves's skepticism and its effect on his poetry.

Quennell, Peter. "The Multiple Robert Graves." HORIZON, 4 (1962), 50-55.

Quennell presents a biographical-critical survey on Graves that covers the poet's family background and childhood, the war years, the years with Laura Riding, and those that followed, ending in 1961. Quennell sees Graves as the only writer among his contemporaries who has held to a steady onward literary course. He survived his Georgian period, rid himself gradually of his many ghosts, and became obsessed with love as a poetic theme. In overcoming the trauma of his World War I experiences, he gained the strength and direction he needed for the rest of his life.

Robert Von Ranke Graves

Seymour-Smith, Martin. ROBERT GRAVES. Writers and Their Work Series, no. 78. London: Longmans, Green, 1956.

> Seymour-Smith presents an early survey of Graves's work that concerns itself with the poet's personal history and offers brief discussions of his novels, pamphlets, critical works, and poetry.

Simon, John. "Nowhere is Washing So Well Done." MID-CENTURY, 16 (1960), 11-18.

> Simon claims that Graves is not recognized as the literary giant he is, and offers several reasons: he is often difficult to read, literary snobs have decided that anyone who writes as much as he does cannot possibly be a good writer, and there is the disconcerting feature of his individualism. Graves's FOOD FOR CENTAURS (1960) provides direction through his controversial, multifaceted material. It is a "perfect introduction" to his work.

Snipes, Katherine. ROBERT GRAVES. New York: Frederick Ungar, 1979.

> Snipes devotes her first chapter to a biographical study. The second, third, and fourth chapters discuss the author's poetical theory and the poetry itself. The remaining chapters deal with aspects of his novels, satirical writings, and other prose.

Spears, Monroe K. "The Latest Graves: Poet and Private Eye." SEWANEE REVIEW, 73 (1965), 660-78.

> Spears is highly critical of Graves's position regarding the interpretation of the past and his attitude toward the Modernist movement in poetry. He also takes exception to Graves's private myth. He sees him as a highly accomplished poet but as "a limited and dubious exemplar."

Stade, George. ROBERT GRAVES. Columbia Essays on Modern Writers Series, no. 25. New York and London: Columbia University Press, 1967.

> Stade presents a brief general survey of Graves's work with most of the attention given to his poetry and preoccupation with the goddess myth.

Steiner, George. "The Genius of Robert Graves." KENYON REVIEW, 22 (1960), 340-65.

> Steiner's article is a mixture of a romantic portrayal and a consideration of Graves's work in all its forms: poetry ("it is not the summit of his achievement"), fiction ("it is in the historical novel that he stands supreme"), and scholarly works ("what counts most heavily in the final analysis is whether or not the given account of an historical event or the particular reading of a myth 'feels right' to Graves's sensibility and to his image of human experience").

Tolley, A.T. "Rhetoric and the Moderns." SOUTHERN REVIEW, 6 (1970), 380-97.

> Tolley concludes, after an inquiry into alternative views of modern poetry, that Graves (as well as Edward Thomas, Robert Frost, Laura Riding, and William Carlos Williams) practiced a "direct unrhetorical style that asserted itself, rightly, as revolutionary."

Ussher, Arland. "Robert Graves: The Philoctetes of Majorca." DUBLIN MAGAZINE, 32 (1957), 18-21.

> Ussher's visit with Graves in Majorca yielded this estimate of the poet: "Robert Graves is the English aristocrat of the high tradition, preserved like a trout in aspic: eager, adventurous, voracious of information, eccentrically erudite, interested in all things foreign though perhaps least in the foreigners, his mind a jostling theatre of huge historical realities like the Platonic form. He is the most unspoilt of acclaimed great wits, the least patronizing of kindly men."

Vickery, John. ROBERT GRAVES AND THE WHITE GODDESS. Lincoln: University of Nebraska Press, 1972.

> Vickery presents a detailed study of Graves's "mythopoeic thought, its genesis, nature, and contours." The book contains chapters on "The Origins of the Myth," "The White Goddess and King Jesus," "The White Goddess and the Beloved Victim," "Rituals of Nature," and "The Rituals of Dream and Language."

Williams, Charles. "Robert Graves." In his POETRY AT PRESENT. Oxford: Oxford University Press, 1930, pp. 194-206.

> Williams investigates POEMS 1914-1926 and concludes that Graves is one of the most interesting of the younger established poets. His success is due to a working mixture of old and new poetic themes and devices. The poet is adept at combining poetic rage and poetic commonplaces and a subdued monstrosity tempered with beauty.

THOMAS HARDY (1840-1928)

PRINCIPAL WORKS

Poetry

WESSEX POEMS AND OTHER VERSES. London and New York: Harper, 1898.

POEMS OF THE PAST AND PRESENT. London: Harper, 1902.

THE DYNASTS: A DRAMA OF THE NAPOLEONIC WARS. 3 vols. London: Macmillan, 1903-08.

TIME'S LAUGHINGSTOCK AND OTHER VERSES. London: Macmillan, 1909.

THE WORKS OF THOMAS HARDY IN PROSE AND VERSE. 24 vols. London: Macmillan, 1912-31.

SATIRES OF CIRCUMSTANCE. London: Macmillan, 1914.

MOMENTS OF VISION AND MISCELLANEOUS VERSES. London: Macmillan, 1917.

THE POETICAL WORKS. 2 vols. London: Macmillan, 1919-21.

THE WORKS OF THOMAS HARDY. 37 vols. Mellstock Edition. London: Macmillan, 1919-20.

SELECTED POEMS. London: Riccardi Press Books, 1921.

LATE LYRICS AND EARLIER WITH MANY OTHER VERSES. London: Macmillan, 1925.

HUMAN SHOWS, FAR PHANTASIES, SONGS, AND TRIFLES. London: Macmillan, 1925.

COLLECTED POEMS. London: Macmillan, 1926.

WINTER WORDS: VARIOUS MOODS AND METRES. London: Macmillan, 1928.

CHOSEN POEMS. School Edition. London: Macmillan, 1929.

COLLECTED POEMS. London: Macmillan, 1938.

SELECTED POEMS. London: Macmillan, 1940.

SELECTED POEMS. London: Macmillan, 1954.

LOVE POEMS. London: Macmillan, 1954.

COLLECTED POEMS. London: Macmillan, 1960.

THOMAS HARDY: A SELECTION OF POEMS. Harmondsworth, Engl.: Penguin Books, 1960.

SELECTED POEMS. London: Macmillan, 1961.

HARDY'S LOVE POEMS. London: Macmillan, 1963.

SELECTED POEMS. London: Macmillan, 1964.

Other Works

UNDER THE GREENWOOD TREE (1872), fiction.
FAR FROM THE MADDING CROWD (1874), fiction.
THE RETURN OF THE NATIVE (1878), fiction.
THE MAYOR OF CASTERBRIDGE (1886), fiction.
TESS OF THE D'URBERVILLES (1891), fiction.
LIFE'S LITTLE IRONIES (1894), fiction.
JUDE THE OBSCURE (1896), fiction.
THE FAMOUS TRAGEDY OF THE QUEEN OF CORNWALL (1923), drama.
THE SHORT STORIES OF THOMAS HARDY (1928), fiction.

BIBLIOGRAPHIES

Webb, A.P., ed. A BIBLIOGRAPHY OF THE WORKS OF THOMAS HARDY
1865-1915. London: F. Hullings, 1916.

Weber, Carl J., ed. THE FIRST HUNDRED YEARS OF THOMAS HARDY 1840-
1940: A CENTENARY BIBLIOGRAPHY OF HARDIANA. New York: Russell
and Russell, 1942.

Purdy, Richard L., ed. THOMAS HARDY: A BIBLIOGRAPHICAL STUDY.
London and New York: Oxford University Press, 1954.

Cox, R.G., ed. THOMAS HARDY: THE CRITICAL HERITAGE. New York:
Barnes and Noble, 1970.

    See "Criticism" below.

Gerber, Helmut E., ed. THOMAS HARDY: AN ANNOTATED BIBLIOGRAPHY
OF WRITINGS ABOUT HIM. DeKalb: Northern Illinois University Press, 1973.

THOMAS HARDY CATALOGUE: A LIST OF THE BOOKS BY AND ABOUT
THOMAS HARDY, O.M. (1840-1928) IN DORSET COUNTY LIBRARY. 2nd
ed. Comp. Dorset County Library, ed. Kenneth Carter and June M. Whether-
ly. Introd. Dorset, Engl.: Dorset County Council, 1973.

AUTOBIOGRAPHIES

THOMAS HARDY'S WRITINGS: PREFACES, LITERARY OPINIONS, REMINIS-
CENCES. Ed. Harold Orel. London and Melbourne: Macmillan, 1967.

    Orel's book contains prefaces Hardy wrote for his own books of
    poetry and for eight books by other writers. There are seventeen
    pieces of literary criticism; three statements on THE DYNASTS;
    biographical comments on writers including R.L. Stevenson and

George Meredith; comments on poetry writing; and eleven reminiscences and personal views. There is an appendix of paraphrases and brief quotations from sixty-nine items. All pieces have bibliographical headnotes and explanatory afternotes. Orel provides commentary and notes.

Brennecke, Ernest, Jr., ed. LIFE AND ART: ESSAYS, NOTES AND LETTERS COLLECTED FOR THE FIRST TIME WITH INTRODUCTION BY ERNEST BRENNEKE, JR. New York: Greenburg, 1925.

BIOGRAPHIES

Hardy, Florence Emily. THE EARLY LIFE OF THOMAS HARDY: 1840-1891. London: Macmillan, 1928.

_____. THE LATER YEARS OF THOMAS HARDY 1892-1928. London: Macmillan, 1940.

Both these books are essentially autobiographies that Hardy dictated to his wife. They contain essential primary material.

Nevinson, H.W. THOMAS HARDY. London: George Allen and Unwin, 1941.

Nevinson's study is divided into four chapters--on personal memories, the novels RETURN OF THE NATIVE (1878), FAR FROM THE MADDING CROWD (1874), TESS OF THE D'URBERVILLES (1891), JUDE THE OBSCURE (1896), the poems, and THE DYNASTS (1903-08).

Blunden, Edmund. THOMAS HARDY. London: Macmillan, 1942.

Blunden outlines the factors and influences of Hardy's origin and upbringing which he believes are essential to know if one is to understand the place the novelist-poet holds in English literature.

Hardy, Evelyn. THOMAS HARDY: A CRITICAL BIOGRAPHY. New York: St. Martin's Press, 1954.

Hardy reviews what has been said, but goes on to present new material. She examines Hardy's reading of the experiences and observations that he turned into poetry and fiction, and offers a detailed discussion of his language. She provides an investigation of Hardy's method based on a previously inaccessible "rough draft in its tangled form" of THE DYNASTS (1903-08).

Weber, Carl. HARDY OF WESSEX: HIS LIFE AND LITERARY CAREER. Rev. ed. New York: Columbia University Press, 1965.

Weber devotes chapters 1 and 3 to the poet's boyhood and archi-

tectural apprenticeship; chapter 4 to his efforts to teach himself
to write fiction; chapter 5 to his courtship with and marriage to
Emma Gifford; chapters 6, 7, and 8 to the publication of the novels
up to THE RETURN OF THE NATIVE; chapter 9 to his writing of
the early short stories, his interest in drama, the controversy over
the source of FAR FROM THE MADDING CROWD and the publication of "Two on a Tower"; chapter 10 to the MAYOR OF CASTER-
BRIDGE; chapter 11 to THE WOODLANDERS; chapter 12 to TESS
OF THE D'URBERVILLES; chapter 13 to copyright problems, American piracies, the writing of THE WELL-BELOVED; chapter 14 to
JUDE THE OBSCURE; and the last six chapters to his marital problems, poetry writing, and second marriage. There are thirteen
appendixes in the first edition that provide valuable material.

Stewart, J.I.M. THOMAS HARDY: A CRITICAL BIOGRAPHY. New York:
Dodd and Mead, 1971.

Stewart's work discusses Hardy's autobiography, his private life
and intellectual background, the early writing, and several novels
including A PAIR OF BLUE EYES, FAR FROM THE MADDING
CROWD, THE RETURN OF THE NATIVE, and TESS OF THE D'
URBERVILLES. He devotes chapters to the minor fiction, the
major poetry, and THE DYNASTS. The study includes a chronology and a bibliography.

Hardy, Emma. SOME RECOLLECTIONS. Notes by Evelyn Hardy. Together
with Some Relevant Poems by Thomas Hardy. Notes by Robert Gittings. Ed.
Evelyn Hardy and Robert Gittings. Freeport, N.Y.: Books for Libraries Press,
1972.

Emma Hardy's recollections cover the years between her birth in
1840 to her engagement to Hardy in 1874. It was Hardy's discovery of these recollections in 1911 that led to his writing of
the love poems contained in POEMS OF 1912-13, which form part
of his collection SATIRES OF CIRCUMSTANCE (1914). Fourteen
of these poems that show the direct influence of SOME RECOL-
LECTIONS are appended to the transcript. The appendix includes
"A Note on Emma Hardy's Novel, THE MAID ON THE SHORE."

Gittings, Robert. YOUNG THOMAS HARDY. London: William Heinemann,
1975.

Gittings claims to have "started from the facts of life itself" in
his presentation of Hardy's early years. His study depends on personal memories and knowledge of those related to Hardy, as well
as on documents from the Dorset County Museum, the County of
Dorset Library, and the Dorset County Council Record Office. He
includes chapters on Hardy's architect apprenticeship, his attitudes
toward religion, loss of faith, first novel, friendship with Horace
Moule, and first marriage.

O'Sullivan, Timothy. THOMAS HARDY: AN ILLUSTRATED BIOGRAPHY.
London: Macmillan, 1975.

> O'Sullivan presents a lavish photographic and prose account of
> Hardy's life.

Orel, Harold. THE FINAL YEARS OF THOMAS HARDY 1912-1928. Lawrence:
University of Kansas Press, 1976.

> Orel's concern is with five volumes of poetry published after the ap-
> pearance of THE DYNASTS, PART THIRD, in 1908: SATIRES OF
> CIRCUMSTANCE and LYRICS AND REVERIES in 1914, MOMENTS
> OF VISION in 1917, LATE LYRICS AND EARLIER in 1922, HU-
> MAN SHOWS in 1925, and WINTER WOODS in 1928. He in-
> vestigates categories of subject matter and textures of attitudes in
> these poems. The book's primary concern is to study "the ways
> in which Hardy wrote about his continuing concerns in poetical
> form, and it attempts to use biographical information whenever
> possible to distinguish and define the boundary lines between
> lyrical and dramatic expression."

Gittings, Robert. THE OLDER HARDY. London: Heinemann, 1978.

> A sequel to Gittings's YOUNG THOMAS HARDY, which covers
> Hardy's life from birth to his mid-thirties, this volume concentrates
> on Hardy's last fifty years. Gittings' focus is on the "stress"
> factors in Hardy's life and "their intimate connection with his
> novels and poems."

Gittings, Robert, and Jo Manton. THE SECOND MRS. HARDY. London:
Heinemann; Seattle: University of Washington Press, 1979.

> Gittings and Manton present a fully documented biography of
> Florence Hardy. Part 1, "Florence Dugdale," is an account of
> her first thirty years, before she became Hardy's wife; part 2,
> "Florence Hardy," is an account of her life in Dorchester with
> Hardy.

Kay-Robinson, Denys. THE FIRST MRS. THOMAS HARDY. New York: St.
Martin's Press, 1979.

> Kay-Robinson presents an appraisal of Hardy's unhappy first mar-
> riage to Emma Gifford. He includes some new material.

LETTERS

THE LETTERS OF THOMAS HARDY. Ed. Carl J. Weber. Waterville, Maine:
Colby College Press, 1954.

THOMAS HARDY'S NOTEBOOKS AND SOME LETTERS FROM JULIA AUGUSTA
MARTIN. Ed. Evelyn Hardy. London: Hogarth Press, 1955.

FORTY YEARS IN AN AUTHOR'S LIFE: A DOZEN LETTERS (1876-1915) FROM HARDY. Annotated by Carl J. Weber. COLBY LIBRARY QUARTERLY, 4 (1956), 108-09.

'DEAREST EMMIE': HARDY'S LETTERS TO HIS FIRST WIFE. Ed. Carl Weber. New York: Columbia University Press, 1963.

Parker, W.M. "Hardy's Letters to Sir George Douglas." ENGLISH, 14 (1963), 218-24.

THOMAS HARDY'S CORRESPONDENCE AT MAX GATE: A DESCRIPTIVE CHECKLIST. Ed. Carl J. Weber and Clara Carter Weber. Waterville, Maine: Colby College Press, 1968.

ONE RARE WOMAN: THOMAS HARDY'S LETTERS TO FLORENCE HENNIKER 1893-1922. Ed. Evelyn Hardy and F.B. Pinion. London: Macmillan, 1972.

THE COLLECTED LETTERS OF THOMAS HARDY 1840-1892. Eds. Richard L. Pardy and Michael Millgate. Vol. 1. Oxford: Clarendon Press, 1978.

DICTIONARY

Saxelby, F. Outwin. A THOMAS HARDY DICTIONARY: THE CHARACTERS AND SCENES OF THE NOVELS AND POEMS ARRANGED AND DESCRIBED. London: George Routledge; New York: E.P. Dutton, 1911.

COMPANIONS

Pinion, F.B. A HARDY COMPANION: A GUIDE TO THE WORKS OF THOMAS HARDY AND THEIR BACKGROUND. London and Melbourne: Macmillan; New York: St. Martin's Press, 1968.

See "Criticism" below.

Bailey, J.O. THE POETRY OF THOMAS HARDY: A HANDBOOK AND COMPANION. Chapel Hill: University of North Carolina Press, 1970.

See "Criticism" below.

HANDBOOK

THE THOMAS HARDY YEARBOOK. Ed. J.S. Cox and G. Stevens Cox. St. Peter Port, Engl.: Toucan Press, 1970-- .

NOTEBOOKS

THOMAS HARDY'S NOTEBOOKS AND SOME LETTERS FROM JULIA AUGUSTA MARTIN. Ed. Evelyn Hardy. London: Hogarth Press, 1955.

THOMAS HARDY'S PERSONAL WRITINGS: LITERARY OPINIONS, REMINIS-CENCES. Ed. Harold Orel. London and Melbourne: Macmillan, 1967.

THE LITERARY NOTES OF THOMAS HARDY. Ed. Lennart A. Bjork. Gothe-berg Studies in English. Gotheberg, Sweden: Acta Universitatis Gothobur-gensis, 1974-- .

CRITICISM

Arkans, Norman. "Hardy's Poetic Landscapes." COLBY LIBRARY QUARTERLY 15 (1979), 19-35.

> Arkans discusses Hardy's belief that man perceives the world in a
> manner that is intensely personal and as existing starkly and anony-
> mously apart from himself and how this belief manifests itself in
> his poetry.

Auden, W.H. "A Literary Transference." SOUTHERN REVIEW, 6 (1940), 78-86.

> During his own adolescence Auden claims, Hardy was for him "the
> archetype of the Poetic," as well as "the expression of the con-
> temporary scene," "his Keats and Carl Sandburg."

Bailey, J.O. "Evolutionary Meliorism in the Poetry of Thomas Hardy." STUDIES IN PHILOLOGY, 60 (1963), 569-87.

> This essay traces Hardy's growth from an early pessimistic stand to
> a later one of "evolutionary meliorism," described as "a hope"
> that human action can make the circumstances of life and life it-
> self better in ethical quality and in happiness than they have
> been" over a long period of time. Bailey presents selected poems
> to "illustrate three phases in this growth--the first that of the in-
> fluence of Charles Darwin, Aldous Huxley, Herbert Spenser, and
> John Stuart Mill on Hardy; the second that of Schopenhauer's in-
> fluence on Hardy; and the third that of Hardy's reaching "evolu-
> tionary meliorism."

_____. "Fact and Fiction in Hardy's Poetry." CEA CRITIC, 30 (1968), 10-11.

> Bailey asserts that most of Hardy's poems are based on fact. Ex-
> amples given include "After the Last Breath," "I Watched a Black-
> bird," "The Inscription," "Squire Hooper," and "The War-Wife of
> Catknoll."

_____. "Hardy's Poems of Pilgrimage." ENGLISH LITERATURE IN TRANSI-
TION, 9 (1966), 190-96.

> The poems from Hardy's visit to Italy are discussed chronologically
> in relation to Baedeker's HANDBOOK FOR TRAVELERS (1895-1909)
> and the fifteenth chapter of Florence Hardy's THE EARLY LIFE OF
> THOMAS HARDY (1928).

_____. THE POETRY OF THOMAS HARDY: A HANDBOOK AND COM-
MENTARY. Chapel Hill: University of North Carolina Press, 1970.

> Bailey's study provides background for the understanding of Hardy's
> poems. He provides analyses for over one thousand poems, relat-
> ing many to other poems and also to passages in Hardy's fiction.
> In the second part of the book, Bailey presents, with notes, poems
> not previously published. The book contains, in addition, a
> chronology of the important events in Hardy's life, keys to the
> significant persons and places prominent in the poems, and a bib-
> liography.

Baker, Howard. "Hardy's Poetic Certitude." SOUTHERN REVIEW, 6 (1940),
49-63.

> Baker claims that "Central in any estimate of Hardy must be an
> appreciation of his tendency to find greatest values in the homely
> relationships of people, finally in the life-loyalties which now
> and then appear. . . . These concerns provide Hardy with his
> principal materials." The article explores this assertion.

Barzun, Jacques. "Truth and Poetry in Thomas Hardy." SOUTHERN REVIEW,
6 (1940), 179-92.

> Barzun defends Hardy against the charge that the conflict within
> him between poet and realist rendered him an "obstinate and per-
> verse genius." Barzun asserts that in Hardy's world "Truth and
> Poetry do not fight a Manichean fight which will leave Science
> or Ignorance master of the field; they merge into each other by
> degrees and constitute together the sum total of mind-measured
> reality."

Blackmur, Richard P. "The Shorter Poems of Thomas Hardy." SOUTHERN RE-
VIEW, 6 (1940), 20-48; rpt. in his LANGUAGE AS GESTURE, pp. 51-79.
New York: Harcourt, Brace, 1952.

> We see in Hardy, Blackmur says, "the consummate double ruin of
> an extraordinary sensibility that had been deprived of both emo-
> tional discipline and the structural support of a received imagina-
> tion." He wrote poems of ideas ("to which there is no primary
> objection") but he failed "to absorb them by craft into representa-
> tive effect of his verse." In spite of this problem, Blackmur con-
> cludes, Hardy produced some astonishing poetry.

Bowra, Cecil Maurice. THE LYRICAL POETRY OF THOMAS HARDY. Nottingham: Nottingham University Press, 1946; rpt. in his INSPIRATION AND POETRY, pp. 220–41. London: Macmillan; New York: St. Martin's Press, 1955.

> Bowra sees Hardy as "the most representative British poet between Tennyson and Yeats." His poetry, though not specifically designed to do so, exhibits a scheme of the universe "in concrete instances where the individual can raise questions of vast import beyond itself and becomes an example and a symbol of universal laws." Hardy wrote like the country man that he was, not like the Victorians with their refined and sensitive manner. His poetry is akin to prose and the dramatic situation. It is realistic and journalistic. Pessimism is, however, not the key to the nature of the poetry.

Brennecke, Ernest, Jr. THOMAS HARDY'S UNIVERSE: A STUDY OF A POET'S MIND. Boston: Small, Maynard; London: T. Fisher Unwin, 1924; rpt. New York: Russell and Russell, 1966.

> Brennecke demonstrates in detail the impact on Hardy's poetry and fiction of the philosophy of Schopenhauer.

Brooks, Cleanth. "The Language of Poetry: Some Problem Cases." ARCHIV FÜR DAS STUDIUM DER NEUEREN SPRACHEN UND LITERATUREN, 203 (1967), 401-14.

> Hardy's mixture of traditional and unusual diction often does not work, but when it does, the poetry comes near the sublime, states Brooks. The poem "The Convergence of the Twain" which appeared in SATIRES OF CIRCUMSTANCE (1914), provides an example of a combination of Victorian poetic diction and Dorset words that operates to make a great lyric.

———. "A Note on Thomas Hardy, with Six Poems by Thomas Hardy." HOPKINS REVIEW, 5 (1952), 68-79.

> Brooks believes that Hardy and Robert Browning prepared the way for the imagists. THE COLLECTED POEMS (1930) contains about sixty poems of superb quality. The poems in the volume produce effects that remind one of an 1840s country newspaper and contain "blendings" of Dorset dialect, odd coinages, Latinisms, and awkward inversions. Brooks comments on the poems "Wessex Heights," "Death Divided," and "The Glory."

Brooks, Jean R. THOMAS HARDY: THE POETIC STRUCTURE. Ithaca: Cornell University Press, 1972.

> Brooks devotes the opening essay to a discussion of the meanings, themes, and structure of Hardy's novels and poems. Four chapters are then given to an examination of the poetry. The remainder of the book consists of a chapter on the minor fiction and chapters on each of the six major novels.

Carpenter, Richard. "Hardy's Dramatic Narrative Poems." ENGLISH LITERA-
TURE IN TRANSITION, 9 (1966), 185-86.

> The elements of dramatic narrative show up in only one-tenth of
> the COLLECTED POEMS (1930), Carpenter says. They manifest
> the spirit and method of the traditional ballad, and the theme is
> often that of sardonic irony toward love and marriage. Examples
> of the best of these poems are "A Trampwoman's Tragedy" and
> "Conversation at Dawn."

Chakravarty, Amiya. THE DYNASTS AND THE POST-WAR AGE IN POETRY.
London: Oxford University Press, 1938.

> THE DYNASTS, Chakravarty claims, connects Hardy to the modern
> poets inasmuch as it expresses the intricacies and complexities of
> modern mentality.

Church, Richard. "Thomas Hardy as Revealed in THE DYNASTS." ETUDES
ANGLAISES, 7 (1954), 70-79; rpt. in ESSAYS BY DIVERS HANDS: BEING
THE TRANSACTIONS OF THE ROYAL SOCIETY OF LITERATURE, 29 (1958),
1-17.

> Church claims that THE DYNASTS is on a plane of poetic excel-
> lence with works of Dante and Milton, has the "epic simplicity of
> WAR AND PEACE, and is a religious Aeschylean drama."

Clifford, Emma. "The Impressionistic View of Hardy in THE DYNASTS."
MODERN LANGUAGE QUARTERLY, 22 (1961), 21-31.

> The essay attempts to "establish something of the importance of
> Hardy's well-known 'anti-realism' in the achievement of THE DY-
> NASTS." Hardy's philosophy is "vague and inconsistent" in its
> many expressions, leading a reader to believe he formed impres-
> sions rather than asserted a dogma. THE DYNASTS is considered
> here in relation to what is seen as the impressionism Hardy exer-
> cised.

Cox, R.G., ed. THOMAS HARDY: THE CRITICAL HERITAGE. New York:
Barnes and Noble, 1970.

> This collection contains reviews and discussions of Hardy's poetry
> and fiction. The extracts end with the First World War. The re-
> views of the poems are grouped together.

Collins, V.H. "The Love Poetry of Thomas Hardy." ESSAYS AND STUDIES
BY MEMBERS OF THE ENGLISH ASSOCIATION, 28 (1942), 69-83.

> The article investigates in detail "the supremacy of the love inter-
> est" in Hardy's poetry.

Daiches, David. "Hardy and the Avant-Garde." NEW STATESMAN, 20 October 1961, pp. 560-61.

Daiches believes that contrary to the popular belief that Hardy's poetry escaped being influenced by the avant-garde movement, he wrote some poems the meaning of which lies in the image arrangement, making them akin to those of Eliot and Pound. "During Wind and Rain," which appeared in MOMENTS OF VISION (1917), is an example. Hardy's decision to use rhythm as a means of helping the reader move through the images is the only factor that differentiates it from THE WASTE LAND. However, "During Wind and Rain" "feels different" from avant-garde pieces because of the peculiarity of some of its details. Hardy's art consists in the choice and arrangement of images drawn from literary works just as Pound's art depended upon images he took from Arnault Daniel, T.S. Eliot, or Charles Baudelaire.

_____. POETRY AND THE MODERN WORLD: A STUDY OF POETRY IN ENGLAND BETWEEN 1900 AND 1939. Chicago: University of Chicago Press, 1940, pp. 17-19.

Hardy's perception of the social values of the Victorian world are at the root of his pessimism. Hardy saw this world as wicked and transferred this vision into an assertion of cosmic evil.

Davie, Donald. THOMAS HARDY AND BRITISH POETRY. New York: Oxford University Press, 1972.

Davie asserts that in the British poetry of the last fifty years, the "most far reaching influence" has been Hardy's. Davie examines Hardy's place in poetic history and offers technical criticism and observations on many of the poems. He sees Hardy as a "scientific humanist" who "deals with life on its own terms." He traces the influence of Hardy on British poets from Auden to Roy Fisher.

Dean, Susan. HARDY'S POETIC VISION IN THE DYNASTS. Princeton, N.J.: Princeton University Press, 1977.

Dean looks at THE DYNASTS (1903-08) "primarily as a vision as tho it were a diorama." In chapter 1 she attempts to prove that it is "first of all a poem: an expressive structure that uses prose and verse to create a rounded image." In chapter 2 she describes the poem's "dioramic system of lighting." In chapters 3 and 4 she explores the poem's image "that creates a unified network connecting the poem's various surfaces."

Dove, John Roland. "Thomas Hardy and the Dilemma of Naturalism (A Study of Hardy's Lyric Poetry)." NEUEREN SPRACHEN, 16 (1967), 253-68.

In Hardy's lyric poetry, Dove states, we are confronted with "the dilemma of an ethical consciousness that is scandalized by its na-

tural source." Hardy protests the victimization of man by the
natural order and anguishes that the very source of condemnation
is itself a part of nature. His poetry "is an ironic gloss on man's
claim that he is master of nature." The very opposite is the case.
This is his central theme. The dialectic that produces Hardy's
lyric poetry consists of "an invocation to nescience at one extreme;
an apocalyptic longing at the other."

Drabble, Margaret, ed. THE GENIUS OF THOMAS HARDY. London: Wei-
denfield and Nicolson, 1976.

Drabble presents a collection of essays by "scholars and critics,
novelists and poets, experts in Hardy history and topography,
British and Americans." The essays focus on Hardy's life, various
aspects of his work and thought, and his relations with his critics.
Among the contributors are Terry Coleman, Sheila Sullivan, J.I.M.
Stewart, Elizabeth Hardwick, Geoffrey Grigson, Harold Orel,
A.L. Rowse, Sir John Betjeman, Lord David Cecil, and Margaret
Drabble.

Eliot, T.S. "Poetry and Propaganda." BOOKMAN (New York), 70 (1930),
595–602.

Eliot believes that Hardy rooted his work in a bad philosophy—the
mechanistic philosophy of science. Hardy's work could have been
"better for a better philosophy or none at all."

Fairchild, Hoxie N. "The Immediate Source of THE DYNASTS." PUBLICA-
TIONS OF THE MODERN LANGUAGE ASSOCIATION OF AMERICA, 67 (1952),
43–64.

The article demonstrates in detail the assertion that THE DYNASTS
was most powerfully influenced by Robert Buchanan's THE DRAMA
OF KINGS (1871). The works share a common theme, make use
of choruses, and have as their subject matter the downfall of Bona-
parte. Hardy's notes contain a reference to Buchanan's title, which
is only one of many clues revealing a connection between the two
authors.

Gibson, James, and Trevor Johnson. THOMAS HARDY. POEMS. A SELEC-
TION OF CRITICAL ESSAYS. Casebook Series. London: Macmillan, 1979.

Part 1 of this study presents extracts from Hardy's notebooks, biography, correspondence, and prefaces to the collections of verse.
Part 2 considers critical comment up to 1928. Part 3 considers
critical comment since 1928.

Grundy, Joan. HARDY AND THE SISTER ARTS. New York: Barnes and
Noble, 1979.

Grundy discusses Hardy's employment of the other arts in his writing. She connects THE DYNASTS (1903-08) to the early cinema epic BIRTH OF A NATION.

Guerard, Albert J. "The Illusion of Simplicity: The Shorter Poems of Thomas Hardy." SEWANEE REVIEW, 72 (1964), 363-88.

The major question, Guerard believes, is why Hardy's simple poetry has such considerable appeal for readers used to paradox and ambiguity. The answer lies, he says, in its sincerity, lucidity of expression, the spoken quality of the verse. Other aspects of his art worthy of note are his ironic use of poetic form, his experiments in metrics, his disavowal of a correspondence between spoken phrase and written line. His poems, claim Guerard, fall into various categories: occasionals, ballads, ballad-tragedies, personal lyrics, and poems of pessimism and disillusioned wisdom.

Hardy, Evelyn. THOMAS HARDY: A CRITICAL BIOGRAPHY. London: Hogarth Press; New York: St. Martin's Press, 1954.

This study links individual poems with the events of Hardy's life and passages in his novels. It includes a discussion of imagery. See "Biographies," above.

Hawkins, Desmond. HARDY: NOVELIST AND POET. New York: Barnes and Noble, 1976.

Hawkins attempts "to bring within a critical and interpretative framework the whole of Hardy's formidable creation in prose and verse, and to associate with it as much biographical and historical material as the reader may need to give depth and context to what he hopes will be a comprehensive appraisal." An appendix provides brief synopses and notes of the principal characters for readers who need information on the novels. A second appendix provides a checklist of the principal adaptations that have been made of Hardy's work for theatre, cinema, radio and television. Hawkins provides a bibliography and list of sources.

Hickson, Elizabeth. VERSIFICATION OF THOMAS HARDY. Philadelphia: Privately printed, 1931.

Hickson classifies Hardy's poems according to subjects, settings, rhythmical variations, and stanzaic forms, and analyzes the diction, versification, and style of THE DYNASTS.

Hollander, John. "The Metrical Emblem." KENYON REVIEW, 21 (1959), 279-96.

This essay attempts "to justify prosodic analysis in terms of its success in confirming and accounting for the almost magical effects upon a reader of the 'musical' or non-semantic patterns of poetic structure," and includes in the discussion an account of Hardy as the last major poet to write in the Ben Jonson tradition.

Hopcutt, G.C.S. "Religion as Poetry and Ritual." LITERARY GUIDE AND RATIONALIST REVIEW, 68 (1963), 161-62.

In spite of his stoical disbelief, Hardy still appreciated the aesthetics of religion. This is manifested in his use of spirits in THE DYNASTS.

Howe, Irving. THOMAS HARDY. New York: Macmillan, 1967.

Howe asserts that Hardy's poetry and fiction are the result of "the formative experience of Dorset" and "the pressure of nineteenth century thought." Chapters 7 and 8 contain examinations of THE DYNASTS and lyric poems respectively.

King, R.W. "Verse and Prose Parallels in the Work of Thomas Hardy." REVIEW OF ENGLISH STUDIES (London), 12 (1962), 52-61.

By examining parallels in Hardy's novels and poems, King shows that, in the absence of further external evidence, it cannot be determined whether the poem passage or the novel passage was written first. The article offers a detailed analysis of the similarities between chapter 35 of TESS OF THE D'URBERVILLES and "Beyond the Last Lamp" (1911).

Leavis, Frank Raymond. "Hardy the Poet." SOUTHERN REVIEW, 6 (1940), 87-98.

Most of Hardy's poetry is inferior, asserts Lewis. The exceptions include "Friends Beyond" (1898), "Julie-Jones" (1909), "The Darkling Thrush" (1901), "Neutral Tones" (1867), "A Broken Appointment" (1901), "The Voice" (1912), "After a Journey" (1912), and "During Wind and Rain" (1917). John Middleton Murry's advocacy of Hardy is responsible for the "gross overestimate" of his poetic works.

Lewis, C. Day. "The Lyrical Poetry of Thomas Hardy." PROCEEDINGS OF THE BRITISH ACADEMY, 37 (1951), 155-74; rpt. as THE LYRIC POETRY OF THOMAS HARDY. London: Cumberledge, 1957.

Lewis discusses Hardy's "great personal poetry."

_____. "The Shorter Poems of Thomas Hardy." BELL (Dublin), 8 (1944), 513-25.

Hardy's poems, states Lewis, manifest the struggle between the peasant and the genius, between a man operating on both orthodoxy and unorthodoxy of imagination.

Lowes, John Livingston. "Two Readings of Earth." YALE REVIEW, 15 (1926), 515-39; rpt. in his ESSAYS IN APPRECIATION. Boston: Houghton Mifflin, 1936, pp. 119-56.

The article contrasts Hardy's attitude toward nature with George Meredith's.

McDowall, Arthur. THOMAS HARDY: A CRITICAL STUDY. London: Faber, 1931.

McDowall's study includes two chapters on the conception and execution of THE DYNASTS and others on general aspects of the poems, Hardy's poetic technique, and the love poems.

Marsden, Kenneth. THE POEMS OF THOMAS HARDY: A CRITICAL INTRO-DUCTION. London: Athlone; New York: Oxford University Press, 1969.

Marsden claims that Hardy's verse is not as appreciated as it should be for two reasons: he labored under peculiar pressures and assumptions from the critics when he first started publishing poems, and his verse is very irregular and eccentric. A sympathy toward the persona increases the pleasure derived from the poems and also increases one's tolerance of eccentricities in composition and diction. Hardy was not an innovator in his use of poetic forms; he created, however, a very effective "personal living language." Marsden traces Hardy's development from the conventional early verse, to a personal and philosophical idiom in the early 1900s, to a detached (although still personal) descriptive manner in the later verse.

Mayers, D.E. "Dialectical Structures in Hardy's Poems." VICTORIAN NEWS-LETTER, 27 (1965), 15–18.

The article is an attack on Samuel Hynes's position in THE PATTERN OF HARDY'S POETRY (1956). Hynes's assertion that Hardy's formalized pattern is antinomical is incorrect. The opposition of thesis to antithesis results in a synthesis for the ironist. The synthesis in Hardy springs from the Immanent Will. The success or failure of Hardy's poems is determined by the degree to which Hardy's formula is integrated into the total structure of the poems. Mayers demonstrates his position by an examination of the "operation of Hardy's transcendent and universal principle of accident" in "The Convergence of the Twain," where it is successful, and in "The Torn Letter," where it is not successful.

Miller, J. Hillis. THOMAS HARDY: DISTANCE AND DESIRE. Boston: Belknap Press of Harvard University Press, 1970.

This study concentrates mainly on the novels; however, Miller does investigate the reasons for Hardy's turning from novels to poetry and his outpouring of love poetry after his wife's death. He examines the role of the Immanent Will and Hardy's "pessimism" in the poetry.

_____. "Wessex Heights: The Persistance of Past in Thomas Hardy's Poetry." CRITICAL QUARTERLY, 10 (1968), 336–59.

Hardy's persona has intense visual power, and this results in geography becoming a collective present experience. Present time and the past are linked in a painful flow in the lyric poetry. Miller demonstrates this thesis in a detailed analysis of "Wessex Heights."

Morgan, William M. "The Partial Vision: Hardy's Idea of Dramatic Poetry." TENNESSEE STUDIES IN LITERATURE, 20 (1975), 100-108.

Morgan contends that Hardy's use of the word "dramatic" to describe his poetry extends the common usage to include a "partial" personal vision, and that a reader's understanding of this will clarify his reading of the poems.

Murfin, Ross C. SWINBURNE, HARDY, AND LAWRENCE. Chicago: University of Chicago Press, 1978.

Murfin writes on the poetic influence of Algernon Swinburne on Thomas Hardy, and on Swinburne and Hardy's influence on D.H. Lawrence.

Paulin, Tom. THOMAS HARDY. London: Macmillan, 1975.

Paulin's approach is through Hardy's "stress on sight and the numerous issues which are implicit in it." He gives a full account of the poetry. Notes at the back of the study include sources of the less accessible quotations.

Perkins, David. "Hardy and the Poetry of Isolation." JOURNAL OF ENGLISH LITERARY HISTORY, 26 (1959), 253-70.

Perkins presents an investigation of Hardy's poetry as "an exploration of the isolation theme" and the means of escaping such isolation. One way out is unawareness (of the isolation), achieved by concentration on the present moment and all that it entails; another way out is acquiring a knowledge of "transcendental things" through visionary imagination. Hardy chose neither of these. He found unawareness intolerable and the imagination untrustworthy. However, he possessed a "tentative openness," a humility, and an honesty which militated against his measuring life only against programmatic ideas.

Peters, Eric. "Thomas Hardy as Poet." POETRY REVIEW, 38 (1947), 503-07.

Peters states that Hardy managed a cosmic vision even though his fiction and poetry are situated in Wessex. The unique quality of his verse is due to an "innate honesty and straightforwardness, freedom from cant," a "keen and bitter sense of humor," "a sense of the pathetic dignity of human existence," and a delightful coinage of "odd and bastard words."

Pinion, F.B. A COMMENTARY ON THE POEMS OF THOMAS HARDY. London: Macmillan, 1976.

In this study Pinion occasionally comments on Hardy's style and craftsmanship, but the principal aim throughout is to "provide as far as possible information and background which will assist in the interpretation of the poems." The book contains chapters on each of Hardy's most significant verse publications and includes a chronology, supplementary notes, and a glossary on Wessex place names.

———. A HARDY COMPANION: A GUIDE TO THE WORKS OF THOMAS HARDY AND THEIR BACKGROUND. London and Melbourne: Macmillan; New York: St. Martin's Press, 1968.

Chapter 4 of Pinion's book deals with the composition, publication, sources, and critical reception of the poems. The remainder of the book deals, in the same manner, with the novels, short stories, and plays, and with special problems in Hardy's works. It includes a "Dictionary of People and Places in Hardy's Works," a glossary of "dialect, literary . . . and words of foreign derivation," a manuscript location list, and a select bibliography.

Pipkin, Charles, ed. SOUTHERN REVIEW, 6 (1940), entire issue.

A number of the articles in this Thomas Hardy Centennial Issue are annotated, above, under author entries for individual critics: W.H. Auden's "A Literary Transference," Howard Baker's "Hardy's Poetic Certitude," Jacques Barzun's "Truth and Poetry in Thomas Hardy," R.P. Blackmur's "The Shorter Poems of Thomas Hardy," F.R. Leavis' "Hardy the Poet," John Crowe Ransom's "Honey and Gall," and Delmore Schwartz's "Poetry and Belief in Thomas Hardy."

Ransom, John Crowe. "Hardy--Old Poet." NEW REPUBLIC, 126 (1952), 16, 30-31.

The usual metric line for Hardy is the iambic or iambic-anapestic; however, occasionally the dipodic line, much evident in the hymn books of Hardy's youth, appears. The agony the poet suffered during the disintegration of his faith during the 1860s in London is reflected in the poems "Friends Beyond" and "Neutral Tones." The pattern here is terza rima and indicates "the coalescence of high and low in Hardy's poetry."

———. "Honey and Gall." SOUTHERN REVIEW, 6 (1940), 1-19.

The essay contains commentary on Hardy's irony, using as its starting point LATE LYRICS AND EARLIER (1922) since the poems in this volume show "overwhelmingly Hardy's preoccupation with the irony of life, and ideologically as well as technically furnish authorization" for such commentary. Hardy is the best of the ironic poets--better than Housman and Swinburne. The short lyrics show off his best effort, THE DYNASTS his least successful.

_____. "The Poetry of Hardy 1900-1950." KENYON REVIEW, 13 (1951), 445-54.

> Ransom claims that Hardy is one of the five major poets of 1900-1950. When he began to write poetry in the 1860s the theme of the conflict between indifferent universe and the human spirit with its decencies and affections was timely. By the time he had returned to poetry in the 1900s, this conflict was stale. However, Hardy's is "the best record, the classic" of the experience of a person's painful adaptation to the "brute universe."

_____. "Thomas Hardy's Poems and the Religious Difficulties of a Naturalist." KENYON REVIEW, 22 (1960), 169-93.

> Hardy's imagination in his shorter poems is "metaphysical" and "in the service of theological passion." These poems may be classified as fables, and they read like "epics in miniature." Ransom discusses several of the "most perfected of the theological or fabulous poems": "Channel Firing," "The Subalterns," "And There Was a Great Calm."

Richardson, James. THOMAS HARDY: THE POETRY OF NECESSITY. Chicago: University of Chicago Press, 1977.

> Richardson's intent is to explore "the interplay of avoidance and investigation, of limitation and multiplicity, of necessity and possibility," which "accounts for the blind of strength and sentiment that characterizes Hardy's lyrics."

St. Claire, George. "Is Hardy, the Poet, a Pessimist?" NEW MEXICO QUARTERLY, 1 (1931), 307-21.

> St. Claire asserts that the poems in each of Hardy's volumes of verse divide into three categories--poems of sorrow, poems of resignation, poems of good cheer. This division is evidence that the poet was unable to "reconcile life's inconsistencies." But the fact that Hardy desired this division does not necessarily label him as a pessimist.

Schwartz, Delmore. "Poetry and Belief in Thomas Hardy." SOUTHERN REVIEW, 6 (1940), 64-77.

> Schwartz contends that a poet's beliefs inhabit poetry in three ways: doctrine is clarified through versification; beliefs of characters are carried and expressed in their thoughts and emotion; beliefs are stated and then modified to suite the demands of rhyme, versification, and metaphor. Schwartz's essay demonstrates how the above operates in Hardy's poetry.

Smith, Robert M. "Philosophy in Thomas Hardy's Poetry." NORTH AMERICAN REVIEW, 220 (1924), 330-40.

> The article asserts that Hardy's philosophy cannot be understood

without an understanding of his poetry. Smith traces Hardy's move from the orthodox theism of his youth to his later embracing of the Immanent Will, and follows the transition as it is expressed in specific poems. Hardy offers two hopes for mankind—the first, "evolutionary meliorism," the second, "the sleep worker" will repair its misdealings with humanity.

Southworth, J.G. THE POETRY OF THOMAS HARDY. Rev. ed. New York: Columbia University Press, 1966.

Southworth deals in part 1 with love, women, God, free will, and fates as they operate in the poems. In part 2 he investigates diction, imagery, prosody, architectonics, and nature. Part 3 is devoted to an estimate of Hardy as "a poet, not as a thinker."

Stedmond, J.M. "Hardy's DYNASTS and Mythical Method." ENGLISH, 12 (1958), 104.

Stedmond asserts that Hardy sought to express historical events through an ironic use of the Aeschylean superstructure. He gave credence to an order imposed by an unconscious and seemingly purposeless Will, whereas Aeschylus believed in an order based on morality and seated in a just and merciful deity. Like Aeschylus, Hardy uses choruses and establishes family relationships between the spirits. Hardy is, however, unable to resolve the paradox of free will and an impotent creator, nor does he utilize a single tragic hero.

Subramanyam, N.S. "Imagery in Hardy's THE DYNASTS." INDIAN JOURNAL OF ENGLISH STUDIES, 2 (1961), 125-29.

Subramanyam presents an analysis of the three major systems of imagery in THE DYNASTS: the "weaving and spinning" imagery which is dominant, the "mechanical world imagery," and the imagery of "deluded small insects and helpless animals."

Swets, Marinus M. "Understanding Hardy's THE RETURN OF THE NATIVE THROUGH HIS POETRY." EXERCISE EXCHANGE, 12 (1965), 4-6.

Hardy's short poems are a key to understanding his ideas. The short poems that contain the ideas expressed in THE RETURN are "The Conversion of the Twain," "Waiting Both," "Hap," "In Time of 'The Breaking Nations,'" "The Man He Killed," "The Darkling Thrush," "At the Draper's," "Ah! are Digging on my Grave?" "In Church," "At Day Close in November," and "Winter in Durnover Field."

Symons, Arthur. A STUDY OF THOMAS HARDY. London: Charles J. Sawyer, 1927.

Symons says that Hardy's poetry deals with the principle of life

(sex, nature) and with the workings of fate in the lives of men
and women.

Teets, Bruce. "Thomas Hardy's Reflective Poetry." ENGLISH LITERATURE IN
TRANSITION, 9 (1966), 183-85.

Teets claims that the lack of recognition of Hardy's poetic achievement has its roots in an overemphasis on the poet as "thinker" and
a "pessimist" and the perceiving of his place as transitional in the
tradition of reflective poetry.

Van Doren, Mark. "The Poems of Thomas Hardy." In FOUR POETS ON
POETRY. Ed. Don Cameron Allen. Baltimore: Johns Hopkins Press, 1959,
pp. 83-107.

Van Doren asserts that Hardy has produced no group or set of
poems that would prove his stature as a poet. All of the poems
are a mixture of perfection and imperfection. Nonetheless, Van
Doren concludes that Hardy is still a great poet.

Wain, John. "The Poetry of Thomas Hardy." CRITICAL QUARTERLY, 8 (1966),
166-73; rpt. as Introd. to SELECTED SHORTER POEMS OF THOMAS HARDY.
London: Macmillan; New York: St. Martin's Press, 1966.

Wain presents a survey of the most outstanding characteristics of
Hardy's poetry.

Zietlow, Paul. MOMENTS OF VISION: THE POETRY OF THOMAS HARDY.
Cambridge, Mass.: Harvard University Press, 1974.

Zietlow's study focuses on COLLECTED POEMS and aims to describe
Hardy's poetic achievement through a detailed descriptive method.
The book opens with a survey of Hardy's first collection of verse,
WESSEX POEMS (1898), and proceeds to a review of the poems
according to type: poems of ironic circumstance, ballads and nar-
ratives, philosophical fantasies, poems of the personal and historical past, love poems, and "moments of vision."

GERARD MANLEY HOPKINS (1844-89)

PRINCIPAL WORKS

Poetry

POEMS OF GERARD MANLEY HOPKINS. 1st ed. Ed. and "Preface to
   Notes" by Robert Bridges. London: Humphrey Milford, Oxford Univer-
   sity Press, 1918.
POEMS OF GERARD MANLEY HOPKINS. 2nd ed. Ed. and introd. Charles
   Williams. London: Oxford University Press, 1930.
POEMS OF GERARD MANLEY HOPKINS. 3rd ed. Ed. and introd. W.H.
   Gardner. London: Oxford University Press, 1948.
POEMS OF GERARD MANLEY HOPKINS. 4th ed. Ed. W.H. Gardner and
   N.H. MacKenzie. London: Oxford University Press, 1967.

Other Works

SERMONS AND DEVOTIONAL WRITINGS (1959), prose.
THE JOURNALS AND PAPERS OF GERARD MANLEY HOPKINS (1959), prose.

BIBLIOGRAPHIES

Cohen, Edward H., ed. THE WORKS AND CRITICISM OF GERARD MANLEY
HOPKINS: A COMPREHENSIVE BIBLIOGRAPHY. Washington, D.C.: Catholic University of America Press, 1969.

Seehammer, Ruth, ed. HOPKINS COLLECTED AT GONZAGA. Chicago:
Loyola University Press, 1970.

Dunne, Tom, ed. GERARD MANLEY HOPKINS: A COMPREHENSIVE BIB-
LIOGRAPHY. Oxford: Clarendon Press, 1976.

BIOGRAPHIES

Keating, Joseph. "Impressions of Father Gerard Hopkins, S.J." MONTH, 114 (1909), 59–68.

> This biographical article discusses Hopkins' influence on Newman and Liddon.

Lahey, G.F. GERARD MANLEY HOPKINS. London: Oxford University Press, 1930.

> Lahey's is the first biography. It is sympathetic and contains some inaccuracies. The principles of his work are discussed and analyzed.

D'Arcy, Martin C. "Gerard Manley Hopkins." In GREAT CATHOLICS. Ed. Claude Williamson. London: Nicholson and Watson, 1938, pp. 438–46.

> D'Arcy presents a biographical essay with emphasis on the poet's spiritual life and character.

Weiss, Theodore. GERARD MANLEY HOPKINS: REALIST ON PARNASSUS. N.p.: Privately printed, 1940.

> Weiss sets out to prove that Hopkins' life attests "not only to the ruthlessness of art in its exposure of the basic inacceptability for him of religion, but also the common incompatibility today between art and religion."

Pick, John. GERARD MANLEY HOPKINS: PRIEST AND POET. London: Oxford University Press, 1942.

> Pick believes that Hopkins' poetical development was enhanced by his life as a Jesuit priest. He supports this thesis by careful explication of forty "religious" poems.

Ruggles, Eleanor. GERARD MANLEY HOPKINS: A LIFE. New York: W.W. Norton, 1944.

> Ruggles' biography includes a study of Hopkins' letters and notebooks, together with the poems. She draws on secondary materials such as descriptions and evaluations of the poet's influence on his contemporaries to flesh out her portrait.

Elliott, Brian. "Gerard Hopkins and Marcus Clark." SOUTHERLY, 8 (1947), 218–27.

> This essay describes the friendship between Hopkins and Marcus Clark at Highgate School.

Srinvasa Iyengar, K.R. GERARD MANLEY HOPKINS. London: Oxford University Press, 1948.

> The author describes Hopkins' character and narrates his life story. He investigates "the problems of religious psychology and the fundamental place of the religious quest in the poet's development." Srinvasa Iyengar presents a detailed treatment of the technique of Hopkins' verse, concentrating on the significance of its metrical innovations, new rhythms and assonances.

Doyle, Louis F. "In the Valley of the Shadow of Hopkins." CATHOLIC WORLD, 169 (1949), 102-08.

> This essay is on Hopkins' failure to adapt to Jesuit religious life.

Kenyon Critics. GERARD MANLEY HOPKINS. London: Dennis Dobson, 1949.

> See "Criticism" below.

Crehan, J.H. "More Light on Gerard Hopkins." MONTH, 10 (1953), 205-14.

> This biographical essay deals with Hopkins' friendship with Alexandre Wood.

Sieveking, Lance. "Gerard Manley Hopkins." In his THE EYE OF THE BEHOLDER. London: Hulton Press, 1957, pp. 275-85.

> This chapter includes important biographical information.

_____. "Remembering Gerard Manley Hopkins." LISTENER, 24 January 1957, pp. 151-52.

> This essay draws on accounts of the poet's contemporaries and members of his family.

Sanbrook, James. A POET HIDDEN: THE LIFE OF RICHARD WATSON DIXON 1883-1900. London: Althone Press, 1962.

> Sanbrook provides information on Dixon's friendship with Hopkins.

O'Donovan, Patrick. "The Tragedy of Gerard Manley Hopkins." OBSERVER MAGAZINE, 18 August 1968, pp. 29-30.

> O'Donovan presents a brief biographical essay.

Bergonzi, Bernard. GERARD MANLEY HOPKINS. New York: Macmillan, 1977.

> Bergonzi presents Hopkins' life in a coherent narrative, drawing from the later editions of the poet's letters, journals, sermons,

and spiritual writings. He discusses Hopkins' poems as they "re-flect the experience of life, with the emphasis on the descriptive more than on the critical."

LETTERS

THE CORRESPONDENCE OF GERARD MANLEY HOPKINS AND RICHARD WATSON DAVIS. Rev. ed. Ed. Claude Colleer Abbot. London: Oxford University Press, 1955.

THE LETTERS OF GERARD MANLEY HOPKINS TO ROBERT BRIDGES. Rev. ed. Ed. Claude Colleer Abbot. London: Oxford University Press, 1955.

FURTHER LETTERS OF GERARD MANLEY HOPKINS. Rev. and enl. ed. Ed. Claude Colleer Abbot. London: Oxford University Press, 1956.

NOTEBOOKS AND PAPERS

SELECTIONS FROM THE NOTE-BOOKS OF GERARD MANLEY HOPKINS. Ed. Theodore Weiss. Norfolk, Conn.: New Directions, 1945.

THE NOTEBOOKS AND PAPERS OF GERARD MANLEY HOPKINS. Rev. and enl. ed. Ed. Humphrey House. London: Oxford University Press, 1959.

THE JOURNALS AND PAPERS OF GERARD MANLEY HOPKINS. Ed. Humphrey House, completed by Graham Storey. London: Oxford University Press, 1959.

CONCORDANCE

A CONCORDANCE TO THE POETRY IN ENGLISH OF GERARD MANLEY HOPKINS. Ed. Alfred Borello, programmed by James Anderson and Angelo Triandafilou. Metuchen, N.J.: Scarecrow Press, 1969.

A CONCORDANCE TO THE POETRY OF GERARD MANLEY HOPKINS. Comp. Robert J. Dilligan and Todd K. Bender. Madison: University of Wisconsin Press, 1970.

PERIODICAL

THE HOPKINS QUARTERLY. Ed. John Hopkins and Richard Giles. Columbia: University of South Carolina Press, 1974-- .

CRITICISM

Abraham, John. "The Hopkins Aesthetic." CONTINUUM, 1 (1963), 32-36.

Abraham defines and discusses the essential aesthetic of Hopkins' "inscape" or "the distinctive design manifest in the harmonious relationship of common nature and individualizing traits of the object contemplated." He goes on to say that "it deserves from a positive, intrinsic content of being, actualizing energy or in-stress, a term pertaining to that which immediately individualizes things, and in the Ignatian commentary, it is the equivalent of Scotian haecaeitas. As the equivalent of the Scotian principle of individuation, it is the ultimate unifying principle of reality and so renders an object of art or nature haec and singular. In virtue of this principle, the integrated object has harmony and wholeness, and from this principle emanates ultimately its splendor of form--the radiance and beauty of inscape."

Bender, Todd. GERARD MANLEY HOPKINS: THE CLASSICAL BACKGROUND AND CRITICAL RECEPTION OF HIS WORK. Baltimore: Johns Hopkins Press, 1966.

Bender presents a study of the ideas behind the intellectual context in which the poet wrote and the context in which his poetry was read.

Boyle, Robert, S.J. METAPHOR IN HOPKINS. Chapel Hill: University of North Carolina Press, 1961.

This study "aims to reveal as the unifying and vitalizing factor in Hopkins' mature imagery his underlying view of divine life flowing into the hearts and acts of the just man."

Bridges, Robert. "Preface to Notes." In POEMS OF GERARD MANLEY HOPKINS. Ed. Robert Bridges. London: H. Milford, 1918, pp. 1-6.

Bridges' aim is to lead readers "to search out the rare masterly beauties that distinguish the work" but at the same time points out his "faults," which include "affectation of metaphor," "perversion of human feeling," "habitual omission of the relative pronoun," "words that are grammatically ambiguous," "insensitivity to the irrelevant suggestions that our numerous homophones cause," and "repellant rhymes."

Chevigny, Bell Gale. "Instress and Devotion in the Poetry of Gerard Manley Hopkins." VICTORIAN STUDIES, 9 (1965), 141-53.

The aim of Chevigny's essay is to "suggest that the poems on their own terms fulfilled an urgent need in Hopkins' spiritual life. The poet's notion of 'instress' may be considered the single key to his aesthetics and his spiritual growth, and a nearly constant controlling factor in his developing poetry."

Coogan, Marjorie. "Inscape and Instress: Further Analogies with Scotus." PUBLICATIONS OF THE MODERN LANGUAGE ASSOCIATION OF AMERICA, 65 (1950), 66-74.

> Coogan attempts to clarify the aesthetic position that the poet found in Duns Scotus.

Cotter, James Finn. INSCAPE: THE CHRISTOLOGY AND POETRY OF GERARD MANLEY HOPKINS. Pittsburgh: University of Pittsburgh Press, 1972. Bibliog.

> Cotter examines "the 'myth' or system of related ideas and images that make up the poet's vision of historical and created reality which religion encompasses, orders, reveals." The book falls into three major sections: one on Christology, one on poetry, one on gnosis.

Devlin, Christopher. "Hopkins and Duns Scotus." NEW VERSE, nos. 1-32 (1935), 12-15.

> The article discusses the manner in which "the minds of Scotus and Hopkins found themselves in unison."

Downes, David A. GERARD MANLEY HOPKINS: A STUDY OF HIS IGNA-TIAN SPIRIT. New York: Bookman Associates, 1959.

> This book, according to its author, is a reading of Gerard Manley Hopkins as a meditative poet whose poetic experience originated primarily from his learning and living THE SPIRITUAL EXERCISES of St. Ignatius Loyola. It is the main intent of this study to ex-amine to what extent Hopkins' art was influenced by Ignatian spirituality.

_____. VICTORIAN POETS: HOPKINS AND PATER. New York: Bookman Associates, 1965.

> Downes intends in this study "to form a composite of two Victorians in and out of their times who, despite the fact that they lived and died well within the last century, saw the road leading to our cen-tury and some of the crossroads we would have to confront."

Empson, William. SEVEN TYPES OF AMBIGUITY. London: Chatto and Win-dus, 1930. Pp. 148-49, 225.

> In sections dealing with Hopkins, Empson focuses on "The Wind-hover," claiming that it demonstrates "a clear sense of the Freud-ian use of opposites, where two things thought of as incompatible but desired intensely by different systems of judgment" coalesce and are forced into open conflict before the readers.

Flanner, Hildegard. "Gerard Manley Hopkins." NEW REPUBLIC, 65 (1931), 331-32.

Flanner discusses Hopkins' prosody, "verbal indulgences," and the
relation of his poetry to "mortal doubt." She concludes that his
work is "essentially enlightened, honest and rebellious, and made
to last."

Gardner, W.H. GERARD MANLEY HOPKINS: A STUDY OF POETIC IDIO-
SYNCRASY IN RELATION TO POETIC TRADITION. 2 vols. New Haven,
Conn.: Yale University Press, 1949.

Gardner's study is primarily critical--he demonstrates that Hopkins
was both traditionalist and revolutionary. He devotes chapters to
Hopkins' relation to his social, cultural, artistic, political, economic, and religious backgrounds, and to the influence of Duns
Scotus and Ignatius Loyola's SPIRITUAL EXERCISES on the poet.
The critical chapters deal with prosody, meter, the problems with
sprung rhythm, and diction and syntax. Gardner presents a chronological survey of the poetry, with detailed analyses of several
poems, including "The Wreck of the Deutschland."

Ghiselin, Brewster. "Reading Sprung Rhythms." POETRY (Chicago), 70 (1947),
86-93.

Ghiselin defends Hopkins against Harold Whitehall's assertion.
See Kenyon Critics, below.

Grigson, Geoffrey. GERARD MANLEY HOPKINS. Writers and Their Work
Series, no. 59. London: Longmans, Green, 1962.

Grigson presents a brief survey of the highlights of Hopkins' life
and work.

_____. "Hopkins and Hopkinsese." NEW VERSE, 1 (1935), 24-26.

Grigson's estimate of the poet is as follows: "Hopkins has been
able to teach those who want to hear several things: the value of
an intended precision in a word (whatever ambiguities come with
it), the value and possibility of a freer musical time and a stricter
verse prosody, the necessity of basing style upon the current speech
of one's own time, raising it above the speech instead of trying to
make it into the language of poetry in the Wordsworthian manner,
the fact that poetry again can be both explosive and intricately
and strictly formal, conveying the greatest difficulties of thought
and finest shades of feeling."

Hartman, Geoffrey. GERARD MANLEY HOPKINS: A COLLECTION OF ES-
SAYS. Englewood Cliffs, N.J.: Prentice-Hall, 1966.

This collection includes "Gerard Manley Hopkins" by F.R. Leavis,
"Gerard Manley Hopkins" by Ivor Winters, "An Idiom of Despera-
tion" by John Wain, "The Oddities of Genius" by Robert Bridges,
"Aesthetic-Theological Thoughts on 'The Windhover'" by Romano

Guardini, "The Analogical Mirrors" by H.M. McLuhan, "The Universal Alchemy" by J. Hillis Miller, "The Dialectical of Sense Perception" by Geoffrey Hartman, "Two Mannerists: James and Hopkins" by Giorgio Melchiori, "Hopkins and Whitman" by F.O. Mathiessen, "Sprung Rhythm and English Tradition" by Walter J. Ong, "Poetry and the Language of Communion" by Gigurd Burkhardt, and "Instress of Inscape" by Austin Warren.

_____. "Hopkins." In his THE UNMEDIATED VISION: AN INTERPRETA-TION OF WORDSWORTH, HOPKINS, RILKE, AND VALERY. New Haven, Conn.: Yale University Press, 1954, pp. 47-67.

Hartman presents a detailed analysis of "The Windhover."

_____, ed. HOPKINS: A COLLECTION OF CRITICAL ESSAYS. Englewood Cliffs, N.J.: Prentice-Hall, 1966.

This collection includes essays by F.R. Leavis, Yvor Winters, John Wain, Robert Bridges, F.O. Matthiessen, Walter Ong, and others. Some of these essays were published previously as articles, and are annotated in the "Criticism" section of this guide.

Holloway, Sister Marcella Marie. THE PROSODIC THEORY OF GERARD MANLEY HOPKINS. Washington, D.C.: Catholic University of America Press, 1947.

The author traces "the development of Hopkins' theories of prosody and presents them in their totality." She devotes chapters to structure, stress, rhythm, meter, and time and measure.

House, Humphrey. "A Note on Hopkins' Religious Life." NEW VERSE, 1 (1935), 3-5.

House discusses various items of religious experience as the direct origins of some of the poet's greatest poems.

Hunter, Jim. GERARD MANLEY HOPKINS. Literature in Perspective Series. London: Evans Brothers, 1966.

Hunter presents a biographical chapter and a chapter relating Hopkins to his times. These chapters are followed by a chronological survey of the poetry, a short description of the early poems, notebooks, and fragments, and three general chapters on poetic techniques. The last chapter examines various literary criticisms of the poetry.

Johnson, J.H. "Reply to Yvor Winters." RENASCENCE, 1-3 (1948-50), 117-24.

Johnson examines Yvor Winters' conceptions of the rational and moral character of the poetic process and his essay on Hopkins (see Winters, below), and concludes that both Hopkins and Winters are intellectually irresponsible.

Johnson, Wendell Stacy. GERARD MANLEY HOPKINS: THE POET AS VICTORIAN. Ithaca, N.Y.: Cornell University Press, 1968.

Johnson's book "relates Hopkins to his Victorian culture, literary as well as artistic."

Keating, John W. THE WRECK OF THE DEUTSCHLAND: AN ESSAY AND COMMENTARY. Kent, Ohio: Kent State University Press, 1963.

Keating presents a detailed analysis of the poem.

Kenyon Critics. GERARD MANLEY HOPKINS. Norfolk, Conn.: New Directions, 1945.

The various essays in this book, with the exception of Leavis' "Metaphysical Isolation," and Austin Warren's biographical piece, "Gerard Manley Hopkins," which first appeared in SCRUTINY, were previously published in the KENYON REVIEW. These include "The Analogical Mirrors" by H.M. McLuhan, "Sprung Rhythm" by Harold Whitehall, "The Sweet and Lovely Language" by Josephine Miles, "Instress of Inscape" by Austin Warren, "Hopkins' Sanctity" by Robert Lowell, and "Victorian Hopkins" by Arthur Mizener.

Leavis, F.R. "Gerard Manley Hopkins." In his NEW BEARINGS IN ENGLISH POETRY. 2nd ed. New York: G.V. Stewart, 1950, pp. 159-93.

This discussion constitutes a defense of Hopkins' style. Leavis considers Hopkins a major poet and "one of the most remarkable technical inventors who ever wrote." He analyzes six poems closely.

Lilly, Gweneth. "The Welsh Influence in the Poetry of Gerard Manley Hopkins." MODERN LANGUAGE REVIEW, 38 (1943), 1925-2205.

Lilly presents a detailed discussion of the stylistic similarities between Hopkins' poetry and Welsh poetry.

MacChesney, Donald. A HOPKINS COMMENTARY: AN EXPLANATORY COMMENTARY ON THE MAIN POEMS 1876-89. London: University of London Press, 1968.

MacChesney presents a detailed analysis of the poems written between 1876 and 1889. It is intended by the author as a guide for the general student who desires a better understanding of the poet.

MacColl, D.S. "Patmore and Hopkins: Sense and Nonsense in English Prosody." LONDON MERCURY, 38 (1938), 217-34.

It is MacColl's contention that Hopkins' sprung lines are actually dipodic lines in the style of Coventry Patmore. Hopkins, because of an ignorance of the function of stress, did not recognize the lines as dipodic.

MacKenzie, Norman. HOPKINS. Edinburgh and London: Oliver and Boyd, 1968.

MacKenzie presents a survey of the poet's life and work.

Madge, Charles. "What Is All This Juice?" NEW VERSE, 1 (1935), 17-21.

Madge compares Hopkins and Whitman. "In Hopkins, the direction remains, to the end, undecided; one may find in him the solipsist rhetoric of dislocated syntax, discordia concors, etc., but none the less it is as an exponent of lacy jags--the violent self-identification with kinaesthetic nature, and the exalted physical states of empathic hyperaesthesia--that he is interesting in 1935."

Mariani, Paul L. A COMMENTARY ON THE COMPLETE POEMS OF GERARD MANLEY HOPKINS. Ithaca, N.Y. and London: Cornell University Press, 1970.

This study comments on "every complete poem and nearly every fragment that we know Hopkins to have written in English."

Milroy, James. THE LANGUAGE OF GERARD MANLEY HOPKINS. London: Andre Deutsch, 1977.

Milroy attempts to explain the poet's language rather than evaluate it. In the first part of the book, Milroy considers Hopkins' declaration that "the poetical language of an age should be the current language heightened." In the second part, he focuses on the methods used by the poet to heighten the language of his poetry.

Milward, Peter, S.J. A COMMENTARY ON G.M. HOPKINS' THE WRECK OF THE DEUTSCHLAND. Tokyo: Hokuseido Press, 1968.

Milward presents a detailed analysis of the poem.

Morris, David. THE POETRY OF GERARD MANLEY HOPKINS AND T.S. ELIOT IN THE LIGHT OF THE DONNE TRADITION. Folcroft, Pa.: Folcroft Library Editions, 1971.

Peters, W.A.M. GERARD MANLEY HOPKINS: A CRITICAL ESSAY TOWARDS THE UNDERSTANDING OF HIS POETRY. London: Oxford University Press, 1948.

The central thesis of the book is that of "inscape-instress." The first two chapters deal with Hopkins' attitudes toward external reality, his philosophy of life, and how they relate to his poetic theories. The last three chapters demonstrate how the poet employed "a personal form of language as the only means by which he could realize the aim of his poetry."

Phare, Elsie E. THE POETRY OF GERARD MANLEY HOPKINS: A SURVEY AND COMMENTARY. Cambridge, Engl.: Cambridge University Press, 1933.

Phare presents an impressionistic exegesis of many of Hopkins' poems. She attempts to discern the school to which he belongs and asserts that his emotional responses are sometimes forced. She links this problem to a suspicion that "becoming a Jesuit must involve some unnatural or undesirable deformation."

Pick, John B. GERARD MANLEY HOPKINS: PRIEST AND POET. Oxford: Oxford University Press, 1942. Rpt. Oxford: Oxford University Press, 1966.

Pick's book relates Hopkins' life and poetry to his religious ideals and standards. Ignatius Loyola's SPIRITUAL EXERCISES were the chief formative agent in the poet's creative life.

_____. ed. THE WINDHOVER. Merrill Literary Casebook Series, no. 14. Columbus, Ohio: Charles E. Merrill, 1969.

This series of essays on the poem includes contributions by Yvor Winters ("The Poetry of Gerard Manley Hopkins"), Carl Woodring ("Once More: 'The Windhover'"), J.R. Ritz ("The Windhover"), Denis Donoghue ("The Bird as Symbol: Hopkins' 'WINDHOVER'"), and Thomas P. Harrison (from "The Birds of Gerard Manley Hopkins").

Forter, Allan. "Difficult Beauty." SPECTATOR, 130 (1923), 66.

Porter defends Hopkins' obscurities. He believes that the difficulties involved in reading the poet's works are well worth it, since the complexity is at the root of Hopkins' "heightened, almost hysterical, acuteness of sense."

Read, Herbert. "Gerard Manley Hopkins." In his FORM AND MODERN POETRY. London: Sheed and Ward, 1933, pp. 45-55.

Read discusses briefly the main features of Hopkins' poetry: his sprung rhythm, vocabulary, imagery, and thought.

_____. "Gerard Manley Hopkins." In his IN DEFENSE OF SHELLEY AND OTHER ESSAYS BY HERBERT READ. London: William Heinemann, 1936, pp. 113-44.

Read's thesis consists of the assertion that Hopkins' creativity was

the result of a state of spiritual tension caused by the conflict between belief and sensibility. He demonstrates this with an analysis of "The Windhover."

Richards, I.A. "Gerard Hopkins." DIAL, 81 (1926), 195-203.

The difficulties of Hopkins' poetry create friction, and this friction
stimulates intellectual interest. The difficulties are, therefore,
functional and integral to the poetry, and should be appreciated
as such.

Ritz, Jean Georges. ROBERT BRIDGES AND GERARD HOPKINS 1863-1889:
A LITERARY FRIENDSHIP. London and New York: Oxford University Press, 1960.

Ritz's study aims at determining the direct and indirect influence
of the priest-poet Hopkins on Robert Bridges and Bridges' influence
on Hopkins.

Russell, J.F.J. A CRITICAL COMMENTARY ON GERARD MANLEY HOP-
KINS' POEMS. Macmillan Critical Commentaries. New York: Macmillan,
1971.

Russell concentrates on Hopkins' poetic development, use of language, belief, and sprung rhythm.

Sapir, Edward. "Gerard Hopkins." POETRY (Chicago), 18 (1921), 330-36.

Sapir reviews POEMS (1918) and states that Hopkins has "easily
one of the half-dozen most individual voices in the whole course
of English nineteenth century poetry." His comments, in the
main, are directed to Hopkins' imagery and prosody.

Schneider, Elisabeth. THE DRAGON IN THE GATE: STUDIES IN THE POET-
RY OF G.M. HOPKINS. Perspectives in Criticism Series, no. 20. Berkeley
and Los Angeles: University of California Press, 1968.

This book concentrates on what are seen as the central facets of
Hopkins' poetic achievement. Most of the attention is given to
the major poems.

Sulloway, Allison. GERARD MANLEY HOPKINS AND THE VICTORIAN TEM-
PER. New York: Columbia University Press, 1972.

Sulloway's study "places Hopkins firmly in the center of the Victorian tradition."

Thomas, Alfred, S.J. HOPKINS THE JESUIT: THE YEARS OF TRAINING.
London: Oxford University Press, 1969.

Thomas' book sets down "exactly and in detail what happened to
Hopkins between the destruction of the early verses and his emer-

gence as a major poet during the final years of his training as a Jesuit."

Thornton, R.K.R. GERARD MANLEY HOPKINS: THE POEMS. Studies in English Literature, no. 53. London: Edward Arnold, 1973.

Thornton offers a background of ideas for the poetry and then proceeds to many detailed analyses of the poems.

Weyland, Norman, S.J., ed. IMMORTAL DIAMOND: STUDIES IN GERARD M. HOPKINS. New York: Sheed and Ward, 1949.

This collection of essays by Jesuit scholars contains introductions to Hopkins' poetic aims and techniques by Fathers Maurice B. McNamee, Arthur MacGillivray, and William T. Noon. Several essays are devoted to close readings of poems. These include Raymond V. Schrader's "What Does 'The Windhover' Mean?", Youree Watson's "The Loss of Eurydice," and Robert Boyle's "The Thought Structure of THE WRECK OF THE DEUTSCHLAND." The collection also includes an "Interpretative Glossary of Difficult Words in the POEMS" by Raymond V. Schrader, and a chronological bibliography compiled by Norman Weyland.

Winters, Yvor. "The Poetry of Gerard Manley Hopkins." HUDSON REVIEW, 2 (1949), 60-93.

Winters says that Hopkins' major fault lies in his inability to organize his poems into integrated units. He states, "Hopkins is a poet of fragments for the most part, and it is only if one can enjoy a chaos of details afloat in vague emotion that one can approve the greater part of his work." Hopkins' organizational problem is rooted in his concern with self-expression ("inscape").

Yeats, William Butler. "Introduction." In his THE OXFORD BOOK OF MODERN VERSE 1892-1935. New York: Oxford University Press, 1936, pp. xxiv-xl.

Yeats discusses Hopkins' work as a "last development of poetical diction."

ALFRED EDWARD HOUSMAN (1859-1936)

PRINCIPAL WORKS

Poetry

A SHROPSHIRE LAD. London: Kegan Paul, 1896.
LAST POEMS. London: Grant Richards, 1922.
MORE POEMS. London: Jonathan Cape, 1936.
COLLECTED POEMS. London: Jonathan Cape, 1939.
COLLECTED POEMS. London: Oxford University Press, 1956.
COMPLETE POEMS. New York: Holt, Rinehart and Winston, 1965.
COLLECTED POEMS. New York: Holt, Rinehart and Winston, 1965.

Other Works

THE NAME AND NATURE OF POETRY (1933), criticism.
SELECTED PROSE (1961), prose.

BIBLIOGRAPHIES

Ehrsam, T.G. A BIBLIOGRAPHY OF ALFRED E. HOUSMAN. Boston: F.W. Faxon, 1941.

Stallman, Robert Wooster. "Annotated Bibliography of A.E. Housman: A Critical Study." PUBLICATIONS OF THE MODERN LANGUAGE ASSOCIATION OF AMERICA, 60 (1945), 463-502.

Carter, John, and John Sparrow. A.E. HOUSMAN: AN ANNOTATED HANDLIST. London: Rupert Hart-Davis, 1952.

BIOGRAPHIES

Housman, Laurence. THE UNEXPECTED YEARS. New York: Bobbs-Merrill, 1936.

>   This work contains many details of the poet's early life.

_____. MY BROTHER: A.E. HOUSMAN: PERSONAL RECOLLECTIONS. London: Jonathan Cape, 1937.

>   See "Criticism" below.

Symons, Katherine E., A.W. Pollard, and Laurence Housman. A.E. HOUS-MAN, BROMSGROVE SCHOOL, 1870-1877. Bromsgrove, Engl.: Bromsgrove School for the Housman Memorial Fund, 1937.

>   This collection of memoirs was written by friends of Housman and
>   published at Bromsgrove School as a tribute to his memory. There
>   is an abundance of biographical materials in the contributions
>   which include "Boyhood" by Katherine Symons, "Some Reminis-
>   cences" by A.W. Pollard, "A London Memoir" by R.W. Chambers,
>   and "Poet" by John Sparrow.

Withers, Percy. A BURIED LIFE: PERSONAL RECOLLECTIONS OF A.E. HOUSMAN. London: Jonathan Cape, 1940.

>   See "Criticism" below.

Robinson, Oliver. ANGRY DUST. Boston: Bruce Humphries, 1950.

>   In the third chapter, Robinson evaluates biographical incidents in
>   an attempt to explain the relationship between Housman's life and
>   the philosophy behind his poetry. This book contains bibliographies
>   of first editions and critical works on Housman.

Watson, George. A.E. HOUSMAN: A DIVIDED LIFE. Boston: Beacon Press, 1958.

>   See "Criticism" below.

Scott-Kilvert, Ian. A.E. HOUSMAN. Writers and Their Work Series, no. 69. London: Longmans, Green, 1965.

>   Scott-Kilvert's book contains a brief, but well-stated biography.

Graves, Richard Percival. A.E. HOUSMAN: THE SCHOLAR POET. London and Henley, Engl.: Routledge and Kegan Paul, 1979.

>   Graves's chief aims are to present "a balanced sympathetic account
>   of a remarkable but troubled life" and to "introduce a new genera-
>   tion to the neglected beauties of A.E. Housman's poetry." This is

the first general biography on the classical scholar and poet. The appendix includes the Housman letters at Bromsgrove and a bibliography.

LETTERS

A.E. HOUSMAN: SOME POEMS, SOME LETTERS AND A PERSONAL MEMOIR BY HIS BROTHER LAURENCE HOUSMAN. London: Jonathan Cape, 1937.

LETTERS FROM A.E. HOUSMAN TO E.H. BLAKENEY. Ed. E.H. Blakeney. Winchester, Engl.: Printed at Mr. Blakeney's Private Press, 1941.

THE LETTERS OF A.E. HOUSMAN. Ed. Henry Maas. Cambridge, Mass.: Harvard University Press, 1971.

CRITICISM

Aiken, Conrad. "A.E. Housman." NEW REPUBLIC, 89 (1936), 51-52.

Aiken contends that Housman's range is "extraordinarily narrow," the "classic" perfection and severity of his style is better termed "pseudo-classic," the texture of his verse, at best, is "thin." The result "is a charming but incomplete and essentially adolescent poetry."

Allison, A.F. "The Poetry of A.E. Housman." REVIEW OF ENGLISH STUDIES, 19 (1943), 276-84.

Allison believes that Housman rigidly restrained his emotions in dealing with his fellow men. These emotions sought expression in his poetry, and it is "this intensity of submerged feeling that gives to his verses something of their special character." A SHROPSHIRE LAD (1896) is considered "an expression of common emotion intensely felt."

Andrews, S.G. "Housman's 'The Carpenter's Son.'" EXPLICATOR, 19 (1960), item 3.

Andrews asserts that the words of the carpenter's son in Housman's poem are the means by which the reader comes to a greater understanding of the significance of the Crucifixion.

Bishop, R. "The Poetry of A.E. Housman." POETRY (Chicago), 56 (1940), 144-53.

Bishop presents a general survey of Housman's subject matter and themes, techniques, and attitudes. Bishop states, "Romantic poetry as Housman received it was in need of correction. He corrected it. The romantic conflict of man against society, of man against immutable forces is still there, but presented by a man who had the classical craftsman's respect both for himself and his craft. The form is concise and accurate but for all their lightness, his poems never lose the sense of earth, for all their grace, they are tough enough to sustain a considerable irony. The limits within them he felt intensely, and both strictness and intensity are in his verse." Bishop asserts that a "perfect understanding of his poems depends on knowledge of his personal plight."

Boomsliter, Paul C., and Warren Creel. "The Secret Springs: Housman's Outline on Metrical Rhythm and Language." LANGUAGE AND STYLE, 10 (1977), 296-323.

In Housman's THE NAME AND NATURE OF POETRY (1933), he declared an interest in "the latent base, comprising natural laws by which all versification is conditioned." This article "explores these natural laws, building on an outline that Housman himself provided as a footnote in the printed book, fleshing out his points with pertinent contemporary developments in linguistics, phonetics, and the study of perception."

Bronowski, Jacob. "A.E. Housman." CRITERION, 24 (1937), 518-22.

Bronowski claims that Housman's poems contain a false stoicism. They are "pathetic, self-belittling, and betray maudlin feelings. His poetry condemns itself."

Brooks, Cleanth. "The Whole of Housman." KENYON REVIEW, 3 (1941), 105-07.

Brooks comments on "the total value of Housman and his work." He investigates the poet's "world view," his position as a Romantic poet, not a classical poet ("no amount of talk about classic influence, classic lucidity, etc., should delude us into thinking him otherwise"), his use of irony and understatement, his sentimentality.

Connolly, Cyril. "A Note on the Poetry of A.E. Housman." NEW STATESMAN AND NATION, 11 (1936), 800.

Connolly asserts that Housman's derivations are from Heinrich Heine, not from the classics. A SHROPSHIRE LAD (1896) is Romantic, pre-Raphaelite in its very first line, not "the purest espressions in English poetry of the spirit of the Greek anthology." There are reminiscences of Belloc, Newbolt, Kipling, and the Georgians in various parts of A SHROPSHIRE LAD.

Dobree, Bonamy. "The Complete Housman." SPECTATOR, 164 (1940), 23.

It is Dobree's opinion that Housman's beliefs cannot be accepted;

however, it is the "voice the belief is uttered in" rather than the belief that is important for a poetry reader.

Franklin, Ralph. "Housman's SHROPSHIRE." MODERN LANGUAGE QUARTERLY, 24 (1963), 164-71.

Franklin examines "the frequency and the accuracy of Housman's Shropshire references in an attempt to determine to what extent his work is actually poetry of that local scent."

Garrod, H.W. "Housman: 1939." ESSAYS AND STUDIES, 25 (1939), 7-21.

Garrod discusses R.L. Stevenson's influence on Housman. He presents biographical criticism of the poetry, relating it to what he sees as the poet's personal tragedy.

Haber, Tom Burns. A.E. HOUSMAN. Twayne English Authors Series, no. 46. New York: Twayne, 1967.

The main objectives of Haber's book are "tracing the outstanding events of Housman's seventy-seven years, the beginnings of his poetry, its literary sources and its development, and assaying his influence upon his time and the present."

_____. "A.E. Housman and 'YE ROUNDE TABLE.'" JOURNAL OF ENGLISH AND GERMANIC PHILOLOGY, 61 (1962), 797-809.

This article describes the copy of the short-lived Oxford and Cambridge magazine YE ROUNDE TABLE, to which Housman in his first year at St. John's contributed, under a pseudonym, thirteen pieces of prose and verse. It is located in the Sterling Library of Yale University.

_____. "Housman and Lucretius." CLASSICAL JOURNAL, 58 (1963), 173-82.

An investigation of the "Lucretian turns of thought and language" in Housman's poetry.

_____. THE MAKING OF "A SHROPSHIRE LAD": A MANUSCRIPT VARIORUM. Seattle and London: University of Washington Press, 1966.

_____. "The Spirit of the Perverse in A.E. Housman." SOUTH ATLANTIC QUARTERLY, 40 (1940), 368-78.

Haber explores the possibility that a spirit of perversity dominates a considerable part of Housman's verse.

Hawkins, Maude M. A.E. HOUSMAN: MAN BEHIND A MASK. Chicago: Regnery, 1958.

Alfred Edward Housman

Hawkins agrees with George Watson (A.E. HOUSMAN: A DIVID-
ED LIFE, 1958) that Housman's personal tragedy had its roots in
the poet's unorthodox affection for Moses Jackson.

Highet, Gilbert. "Professor Paradox." In his THE POWERS OF POETRY.
New York: Oxford University Press, 1960, 114-21.

This essay attempts to explain the nature of Housman's bitterness.

Housman, Laurence. MY BROTHER, A.E. HOUSMAN: PERSONAL RECOL-
LECTIONS. London: Jonathan Cape, 1937.

The book contains about a hundred pages of Housman's letters,
eighteen lost poems, some light verse and parodies. Included
also is a summary of the contents of four notebooks and other
odds and ends of a literary nature that have now been destroyed.

Kowalczyk, Richard L. "Horatian Tradition and Pastoral Mode in Housman's
A SHROPSHIRE LAD." VICTORIAN POETRY, 4 (1966), 223-35.

Kowalczyk holds that the Latin themes are the only influence on
Housman: "Housman's poetry has been subject to attack precisely
because critics fail to see the connection between his classicism
(both in attitude and theme) and his display of poetic techniques
reminiscent of the Latin poets." He attempts in this article to
"survey the environs of Housman's Shropshire as an emanation of
the classical, pastoral world which the poet sees as a dramatic
myth for conveying his poetic vision of a man as a minute, but
tragically honorable, particle in the impersonal universe."

Laven, J.A. "Housman's 'The Deserter.'" NOTES AND QUERIES, 9 (1962),
113.

Lavin states that a possible source for "The Deserter" is "A Bold
Dragoon," which appears in James Reeves's THE EVERLASTING
CIRCLE (1960).

Leavis, F.R. "Imagery and Movement." SCRUTINY, 13 (1945), 133-34.

Leavis compares Edward Thomas' use of imagery to A.E. Housman's.
The difference between the two consists in patterns of movement:
"Housman's depends on our being taken up in a kind of lyrical
intoxication that shall speed us on in exalted thoughtlessness.
Thomas' invites pondering and grows in significance as we ponder
it."

Leggett, B.J. HOUSMAN'S LAND OF LOST CONTENT: A CRITICAL STUDY
OF A SHROPSHIRE LAD.

Leggett's study undertakes a detailed explanation of the thematic
and structural unity of A SHROPSHIRE LAD.

_____ . THE POETIC ART OF A.E. HOUSMAN: THEORY AND PRACTICE.
Lincoln and London: University of Nebraska Press, 1978.

Leggett's study considers several issues--the poet's "fate at the
hands of the new critics, his conception of poetry, the links between his theory and practice, the relation of his view of art to
those of more influential poets, the presence in his poetry of a
theory of art which is now identified with Freud and contemporary
psychoanalytic criticism." Leggett's main emphasis is on Housman's
theory. His secondary emphasis is on the thematic and formal
elements of the poetry.

Leighton, Laurence. "One View of Housman." POETRY, 52 (1938), 94-97.

Leighton holds that Housman's forms are mechanical, his subject
matter general "and at the same time remarkably limited." His
style "is easy but its very ease betrays its essential carelessness,"
and his symbols are "concrete and coherent," but meaningless
without an act of faith on the part of the reader.

Macdonald, J.F. "The Poetry of A.E. Housman." QUEEN'S QUARTERLY,
21 (1923), 137.

Macdonald states that Housman's influence "is due to his thought
existing in the mainstream of ideas." No other contemporary poet
has had such an effect on the work of his fellow-craftsmen.

MacNeice, Louis. "Housman in Retrospect." NEW REPUBLIC, 102 (1940),
583.

MacNeice praises Housman for the "brilliance of phrase," and
"extraordinary identity of mood" displayed in his poems. He
characterizes Housman as a paradox--he produced seemingly simple
poetry but was an extremely complex man. The irony in his poetry reveals this. Housman is the last of the Romantics and "a pre-
cursor of the new classicism heralded by T.E. Hulme."

Marlow, Norman. A.E. HOUSMAN: SCHOLAR AND POET. Minneapolis:
University of Minnesota Press, 1958.

Marlow investigates the poetry of Housman, focusing on literary
influences. Chapters are devoted to diction and meter, criticism
of the poetry and nonsense verse.

Muir, Edwin. "A.E. Housman." LONDON MERCURY, 35 (1936), 62-63.

Muir contends that the two salient features of the best of Housman's
poetry are "an evocative power" and an "epigrammatic power."
The evocative power is absent from the collection MORE POEMS
(1936); however, this absence throws into relief Housman's "essentially epigrammatic cast of thought," and shows how deeply it
determined the shape of all his poetry.

Pearsall, Robert Brainard. "Housman Versus Vaughan Williams: 'Is My Team Plowing?'" VICTORIAN POETRY, 4 (1966), 42-44.

> Pearsall defends Ralph Vaughan Williams' decision to drop the third and fourth stanzas of "Is My Team Plowing?" when he set it to music.

Pitts, Gordon. "Housman's 'Be Still, My Soul.'" VICTORIAN POETRY, 3 (1965), 136-38.

> Pitts investigates Housman's use of irony and ambiguities in "Be Still, My Soul," Lyric xlviii in A SHROPSHIRE LAD (1896).

Priestley, J.B. "The Poetry of A.E. Housman." LONDON MERCURY, 7 (1922), 171-84.

> Priestley devotes his attention to the attitude that prompted A SHROPSHIRE LAD (1896). He states, "The mood which inspired these poems seems to me absolutely essential."

Randall, David A. "A SHROPSHIRE LAD with a Variant Title Page." BOOK COLLECTOR, 9 (1960), 458-59.

> Randall has found that the Callamore Collection in the Lilly Library at Indiana University contains a copy of A SHROPSHIRE LAD (1896) with a title page different from that of the first edition. The difference is described in this note.

Ransom, John C. "Honey and Gall." SOUTHERN REVIEW, 6 (1940), 6-12.

> Ransom compares Housman and Hardy as "ironists" and "regional" poets.

Richards, Grant. HOUSMAN, 1897-1936. New York: Oxford University Press, 1941.

> Richards published Housman's works and was his friend for forty years. This book gives an account of the friendship, includes letters hitherto unpublished, and presents a series of appendixes that includes recollections and notes on Housman's poems by Professor N.B.A. Fletcher, who reveals Housman's debt to Shakespeare, Heine, Arnold, and Stevenson. It contains a valuable index.

Ricks, Christopher, ed. A.E. HOUSMAN: A COLLECTION OF CRITICAL ESSAYS. Englewood Cliffs, N.J.: Prentice-Hall, 1968.

> This book contains essays on Housman's poetry by Ezra Pound, Kingsley Amis, Edmund Wilson, John Wain, W.H. Auden, Randall Jarrell, Cleanth Brooks, F.W. Bateson, John Sparrow, and others.

_____ . "The Nature of Housman's Poetry." ESSAYS IN CRITICISM, 14 (1964), 268-84.

Ricks argues that "in the best of Housman's poems, the childish-ness of what is said is part of the effect, but only part, and is absorbed to produce something fine and true--though often some-thing that is, quite legitimately, in two minds."

Robb, Nesca Adeline. "A.E. Housman." In her FOUR IN EXILE. London and New York: Hutchinson, 1948, pp. 11-54.

This essay "aims at making clear conclusions the author has drawn of the vision and life projected in A SHROPSHIRE LAD (1896)."

Robinson, Oliver. ANGRY DUST. Boston: Bruce Humphries, 1950.

Robinson presents a sketch of Housman's life and investigates the matter and manner of his poetry.

Scott-Kilvert, Ian. A.E. HOUSMAN. Writers and Their Work Series, no. 69. London: Longmans, Green, 1965.

The author "offers a critical and sympathetic analysis of Housman's character and of the relationships between his labors as a scholar and his achievement as a poet. It shows how his style was formed early and how little his poetry altered or developed throughout his life."

Seigel, Jules Paul. "A.E. Housman's Modification of the Flower Motif of the Pastoral Elegy." VICTORIAN POETRY, 2 (1964), 47-50.

Seigel asserts that in A SHROPSHIRE LAD, lyric xlvi ("Bring in this timeless grave to throw"), "there is a definite echo of the specific flower passage from the classical pastoral elegy, a utili-zation of the classics which has thus far gone unnoticed. Hous-man's lyric depends totally upon that particular element of the traditional pastoral elegy, the invocation to bring flowers to the bier of the deceased to comfort him, a motif going back to Theo-critus and used by Vergil, Spenser, Marot, Milton, and others." Seigel demonstrates the manner in which Housman has employed this device in his own creative manner.

Skutsch, Otto. ALFRED EDWARD HOUSMAN, 1859-1936: AN ADDRESS DE-LIVERED AT THE CENTENARY CELEBRATIONS IN UNIVERSITY COLLEGE, LONDON, DURING THE THIRD INTERNATIONAL CONGRESS OF CLASSICAL STUDIES. London: Athlone Press, 1960.

Skutsch devotes this address to the nature and quality of Housman's achievement and personality.

Spender, Stephen. "The Essential Housman." HORIZON, 1 (1940), 295-301.

Spender identifies "a fairly well-defined core which one might call 'the essential Housman,' of perhaps less than fifty poems, in which Housman really says all he has to say."

Spivey, Edward. "Housman's 'The Oracles.'" EXPLICATOR, 21 (1963), item 44.

Spivey contends that the line "Tis true there's better booze than brine,/but he that drowns must drink it" is one of the main harmonizing agents of the poem. It alludes to a legendary occurrence at Dodona, the image of which becomes the unifying symbol of the poem.

Strozier, Robert I. "A.E. Housman: Image, Illogic and Allusion." COLBY LIBRARY QUARTERLY, 7 (1966), 257-63.

Strozier examines a few of Housman's poems that end in "the subtly climactic epigram." The author wishes to demonstrate how the poet keeps the epigram from being didactic and platitudinous.

Watson, George L. A.E. HOUSMAN: A DIVIDED LIFE. Boston: Beacon Press, 1958.

Watson attempts to clarify the meaning of Housman's poetry through biography. He appraises Housman's involvement with his Oxford roommate, Moses Jackson and its influence on the poetry.

Whitridge, Arnold. "Vigny and Housman: A Study in Pessimism." AMERICAN SCHOLAR, 10 (1941), 156-69.

Whitridge speaks of the "irreconcilable" pessimism of Alfred de Vigny and Housman, its value, and its attraction for the reader. The similarities and differences in the attitudes of the two writers are discussed.

Withers, Percy. A BURIED LIFE: PERSONAL RECOLLECTIONS OF A.E. HOUSMAN. London: Jonathan Cape, 1940.

Recollections of Withers' friendship with Housman during the last nineteen years of the poet's life.

Wysong, J.N. "A.E. Housman's Use of Astronomy." ANGLIA, 80 (1962), 295-301.

Wysong demonstrates that Housman used astrological images in his poetry to "give startling and effective descriptions of cosmic sweep and grandeur," to "convey his deepest and most heartfelt emotion," and to "express the heart of A.E. Housman--his painful awareness of his lyrically sardonic comment on the ironies of human life."

Zabel, Morton. "The Whole of Housman." NATION, 150 (1940), 684-85.

Zabel investigates irony, ambiguity, syntax arrangements, and use of folk speech in Housman's poetry.

D[AVID] H[ERBERT] LAWRENCE (1885-1930)

PRINCIPAL WORKS

Poetry

LOVE POEMS AND OTHERS. London: Duckworth, 1913.
AMORES: POEMS. London: Duckworth, 1916.
LOOK! WE HAVE COME THROUGH! London: Chatto and Windus, 1917.
NEW POEMS. London: Martin Secker, 1918.
BAY: A BOOK OF POEMS. London: Martin Secker, 1918.
TORTOISES. New York: Thomas Seltzer, 1923.
BIRDS, BEASTS, AND FLOWERS: POEMS. New York: Thomas Seltzer, 1923.
COLLECTED POEMS. 2 vols. London: Martin Secker, 1928-32.
PANSIES: POEMS. London: Martin Secker, 1929.
NETTLES. London: Faber, 1930.
LAST POEMS. Florence: R. Aldington and G. Orioli, 1932.
THE SHIP OF DEATH AND OTHER POEMS. London: Martin Secker, 1933.
SELECTED POEMS. London: Martin Secker, 1934.
POEMS. 2 vols. London: Heinemann, 1939.
FIRE AND OTHER POEMS. San Francisco: Grabhorn Press, 1940.
SELECTED POEMS. New York: New Directions, 1947.
THE COMPLETE POEMS OF D.H. LAWRENCE. 3 vols. London: Heinemann, 1957.
COLLECTED POEMS. 2 vols. London: Heinmann, 1964.

Other Works

SONS AND LOVERS (1913), fiction.
THE RAINBOW (1915), fiction.
WOMEN IN LOVE (1920), fiction.
STUDIES IN CLASSIC AMERICAN LITERATURE (1923), criticism.
LADY CHATTERLEY'S LOVER (1928), fiction.
COMPLETE SHORT STORIES (3 vols., 1955), criticism.
SELECTED LITERARY CRITICISM (1956), criticism.
THE SHORT NOVELS (2 vols., 1956), fiction.
COMPLETE PLAYS (1966), drama.

D[avid] H[erbert] Lawrence

BIBLIOGRAPHIES

McDonald, Edward, ed. A BIBLIOGRAPHY OF THE WRITINGS OF D.H. LAWRENCE. Philadelphia: Centaur Bookshop, 1925.

_____. THE WRITINGS OF D.H. LAWRENCE 1925-30: A BIBLIOGRAPHICAL SUPPLEMENT. Philadelphia: Centaur Bookshop, 1931.

Aldington, Richard, ed. LAWRENCE: A COMPLETE LIST OF HIS WORKS: TOGETHER WITH A CRITICAL APPRAISAL. London: William Heinemann, 1935.

White, William, ed. D.H. LAWRENCE: A CHECKLIST OF WRITINGS ABOUT HIM, 1931-1950. Detroit: Wayne State University Press, 1950.

Roberts, Francis Warren, ed. A BIBLIOGRAPHY OF D.H. LAWRENCE. Soho Bibliography Series. London: Hart Davis, 1963.

Beards, Richard D., comp. "Ten Years of Criticism, 1959-1968. A Checklist." D.H. LAWRENCE REVIEW, 1 (1968), 245-85.

Beards, Richard D., comp., assisted by Barbara Willens. "D.H. Lawrence: Criticism, 1968-69: A Checklist." D.H. LAWRENCE REVIEW, 3 (1970), 70-86.

Heath, Alice C., ed. "The Checklist of D.H. Lawrence Criticism and Scholarship, 1971." D.H. LAWRENCE REVIEW, 5 (1972), 82-92.

_____. "The Checklist of D.H. Lawrence Criticism and Scholarship, 1972." D.H. LAWRENCE REVIEW, 6 (1973), 100-108.

Ferrier, Carole, ed. "D.H. Lawrence's Pre-1920 Poetry: A Descriptive Bibliography of Manuscripts, Typescripts, and Proofs." D.H. LAWRENCE REVIEW, 6 (1973), 333-59.

_____. "The Checklist of D.H. Lawrence Criticism and Scholarship, 1973." D.H. LAWRENCE REVIEW, 7 (1974), 89-98.

_____. "The Checklist of D.H. Lawrence Criticism and Scholarship, 1974." D.H. LAWRENCE REVIEW, 8 (1975), 99-105.

_____. "The Checklist of D.H. Lawrence Criticism and Scholarship, 1975." D.H. LAWRENCE REVIEW, 9 (1976), 157-66.

Stoll, John E., ed. D.H. LAWRENCE: A BIBLIOGRAPHY 1911-1975. Troy, N.Y.: Whitston Publishing Company, 1977.

BIOGRAPHIES

Lawrence, Ada, and G. Stuart Gelder. YOUNG LORENZO: THE EARLY LIFE OF D.H. LAWRENCE. Florence: G. Orilo, 1931.

> Ada Lawrence presents in the first part of the book a sympathetic account of Lawrence's life from childhood to the death of their mother. The second part of the book consists of letters from Lawrence to the author dating from 1911 to 1930. The third part contains early and hitherto unpublished short stories and articles. She includes many reproductions of pictures painted by Lawrence.

Luhan, Mabel Dodge. LORENZO IN TAOS. New York: Alfred Knopf, 1932.

> Luhan presents an account of Lawrence and his wife, Frieda, during their years in New Mexico. It is a psychological study which includes Lawrence's letters to Luhan.

Nin, Anais. D.H. LAWRENCE: AN UNPROFESSIONAL STUDY. Paris: Ward W. Titus, 1932.

> Nin's book describes Lawrence's world as "above all the world of poets" and proceeds on the premise that "it is the preponderance of the poet in him that is the key to his work." In addition to a chapter on the poetry, she presents others on Lawrence's language and style and symbolism, his controversial years, the works TWILIGHT IN ITALY (1916), WOMEN IN LOVE (1920), FANTASIA OF THE UNCONSCIOUS (1932), KANGAROO (1963), THE PRINCESS (1925), and LADY CHATTERLY'S LOVER (1928).

Murry, J.M. REMINISCENCES OF D.H. LAWRENCE. London: Jonathan Cape, 1933.

> Murry's recollection of his relationship with Lawrence is, in the main, an answer to what he considers "Catherine Carswell's sustained attack" upon him in her THE SAVAGE PILGRIMAGE (1932). The reminiscences are printed word for word as they originally appeared in the ADELPHI and contain relevant portions of Lawrence's letters to Murry, the actual text of all reviews of Lawrence's books written and published by Murry, and the anonymous obituary notice that Murry wrote on the news of Lawrence's death.

Lawrence, Frieda. NOT I BUT THE WIND. New York: Viking, 1934.

> Frieda describes her marital relationship with Lawrence. She includes many letters Lawrence wrote to her and her mother-in-law, the Baroness von Richthofer. The latter reveal clearly Lawrence's

D[avid] H[erbert] Lawrence

human and affectionate side. Contains excellent photographs.

E.T. (Jessie Chambers). D.H. LAWRENCE: A PERSONAL RECORD. London: Jonathan Cape, 1935.

> E.T. is Jessie Chambers, the Miriam of SONS AND LOVERS. Her account of her relationship with Lawrence gives a coherent picture of his boyhood and youth. It is an important source for the study of the early development of mind and character.

Merrild, Knud. A POET AND TWO PAINTERS: A MEMOIR OF D.H. LAWRENCE. London: George Routledge, 1938.

> Merrild presents a clear view of Lawrence's complicated personality in his account of their friendship during the winter of 1922-23 when he, Kai Gotzche and Lawrence lived in an isolated community on the Del Monte Ranch above Taos.

Bynner, Witter. JOURNEY WITH GENIUS: RECOLLECTIONS AND REFLECTIONS CONCERNING D.H. LAWRENCE. New York: John Day, 1951.

> Bynner presents candid portraits of Lawrence and his wife, Frieda.

Moore, Harry T. THE LIFE AND WORKS OF D.H. LAWRENCE. New York: Farrar, Straus and Young, 1951.

> Moore presents a comprehensive biography that includes unpublished items previously ignored. He offers a detailed account of the first half of Lawrence's life. In the narrative of the author's years of fame, Moore concentrates on his works. The appendixes contain a complete bibliographic checklist of Lawrence's writings, a survey of critical material on Lawrence, comments on "The Lawrence Country," and an analysis of Jessie Chamber's papers. Moore's focus is mainly on Lawrence's language which, he claims, is what makes his work lasting.

_____. THE INTELLIGENT HEART: THE STORY OF D.H. LAWRENCE. New York: Farrar, Straus and Young, 1955.

> Moore presents a thorough biography with new material, including many letters, unpublished up to this time. Moore conferred with many of Lawrence's intimates in an attempt to draw a portrait that gives Lawrence's works a legitimate biographical context.

D.H. LAWRENCE: A COMPOSITE BIOGRAPHY. 3 vols. Ed. Edward Nehls. Madison: University of Wisconsin Press, 1957.

> Volume 1 presents, in chronological order, opinions of Lawrence offered by contemporaries of the author during his boyhood and youth. Nehls assembles extracts from Lawrence's work and the

published and unpublished writings of his relations, neighbors, teachers, and fellow writers Middleton Murry, Bertrand Russell, Katherine Mansfield, and others, in an effort to record Lawrence's story. Volume 2 covers the years 1919 to 1925 and traces his travels through Italy, Ceylon, Australia, New Mexico, and Mexico. Descriptions of Lawrence at this time of his life are offered by Compton MacKenzie, Rebecca West, Middleton Murry, Mabel Dodge Luchan, his wife, Frieda, and others. Volume 3 describes the last five years of Lawrence's life (1925-30) which were plagued by bad health, bad publicity over LADY CHATTER-LEY'S LOVER, and difficulties over his art exhibit in London.

Lawrence, Frieda. THE MEMOIRS AND CORRESPONDENCE OF D.H. LAWRENCE. Ed. E.W. Tedlock. London: Heinemann, 1964.

Tedlock's book is an assemblege of essays, letters, and Frieda Lawrence's unfinished memoirs. It reads well as an accompaniment to Lawrence's letters edited by Aldous Huxley and Harry T. Moore.

Corke, Helen. D.H. LAWRENCE: THE CROYDON YEARS. Austin: University of Texas, 1965.

Corke was a fellow teacher and intimate of Lawrence's when he was an elementary teacher at Croydon. It was through her that he met Jessie Chambers. Her book contains two memoirs, "Portrait of D.H. Lawrence, 1909-1910" and "D.H. Lawrence's 'Princess': A Memory of Jessie Chambers." The first memoir is an account of the healing effect of Corke's relationship with Lawrence during a period of grief. The second contains extraordinary letters on Lawrence written by Jessie Chambers after his death.

LETTERS

THE LETTERS OF D.H. LAWRENCE. Ed. Aldous Huxley. London: William Heinemann, 1932.

D.H. LAWRENCE: REMINISCENCES AND CORRESPONDENCE: LETTERS TO EARL H. AND ACHSAH BREWSTER. London: Martin Secker, 1934.

LETTERS OF D.H. LAWRENCE. Selected by Richard Aldington. Harmondsworth, Engl.: Penguin Books, 1950.

EIGHT LETTERS OF D.H. LAWRENCE TO RACHEL ANN AND TAYLOR. Foreword by Majl Weing. Pasadena, Calif.: Grant Dahlstrom, 1956.

THE SELECTED LETTERS OF D.H. LAWRENCE. Ed. with introd. Diana Trilling. New York: Doubleday, 1958.

D[avid] H[erbert] Lawrence

THE COLLECTED LETTERS OF D.H. LAWRENCE. Ed. with introd. Harry T. Moore. 2 vols. London: Heinemann, 1962.

THE MEMOIRS AND CORRESPONDENCE OF D.H. LAWRENCE. Ed. Frieda Lawrence. New York: Knopf, 1964.

LAWRENCE IN LOVE: LETTERS TO LOUIS BURROWS. Ed. with introd. notes James T. Boulton. Nottingham: University of Nottingham Press, 1968.

THE QUEST FOR RANANIM: D.H. LAWRENCE'S LETTERS TO S.E. KOTELIAN-SKY, 1914-1930. Ed. with introd. George J. Zytaruk. Montreal and London: McGill-Queen's University Press, 1970.

Moore, Harry T. "D.H. Lawrence to Henry Savage: Two Further Letters." YALE UNIVERSITY GAZETTE, 46 (1972), 262-67.

PERIODICAL

D.H. LAWRENCE REVIEW. Ed. James C. Cowan. Fayetteville: University of Arkansas Press, 1968-- . 3 per year.

CRITICISM

Alvarez, A. "D.H. Lawrence." In his THE SHAPING SPIRIT: STUDIES IN MODERN ENGLISH AND AMERICAN POETS. London: Chatto and Windus, 1958, pp. 140-61.

> Alvarez asserts that Lawrence is "the only native English poet of any importance to survive the First World War." The excellence of his poetry comes from "a complete truth of feeling." Alvarez presents a discussion of the poetry from this position and includes a lengthy analysis of "End of Another Home Holiday."

Auden, W.H. "D.H. Lawrence." In his THE DYER'S HAND. London: Faber, 1963, pp. 277-95.

> Auden states, "What fascinates me about the poems of Lawrence which I like is that I must admit he could never have written them had he held the kind of views about poetry of which I approve." He expatiates on this statement and includes other observations on Lawrence's poetry.

Bartlett, Phyllis. "Lawrence's COLLECTED POEMS: The Demon Takes Over." PUBLICATIONS OF THE MODERN LANGUAGE ASSOCIATION OF AMERICA, 66 (1951), 583-93.

> Bartlett presents an account of Lawrence's revision, during the

winter of 1927-28, of his early poems. The occasion of this revision was the forthcoming collection of his poems to be published
by Martin Secker in 1928-32.

Blackmur, R.P. "D.H. Lawrence and Expressive Form." In his LANGUAGE
AS GESTURE. London: Allen and Union, 1954, pp. 284-300.

> This essay outlines an attack on Lawrence on the grounds that "the
> strength of his peculiar insight lacks the protection and support of
> a rational imagination, and that it fails to its own disadvantage
> to employ the formal devices of the art in which it is couched."

Bordinat, Philip. "The Poetic Image in D.H. Lawrence's 'The Captain's Doll.'"
WEST VIRGINIA UNIVERSITY PHILOLOGICAL PAPERS, 19 (1972), 45-49.

> Bordinat investigates the poetic quality of Lawrence's story and
> asserts that he achieves his effect by a skillful employment of
> the poetic image.

Brashear, Lucy M. "Lawrence's Companion Poems: 'Snake' and 'Tortoises.'"
D.H. LAWRENCE REVIEW, 5 (1972), 54-62.

> Brashear's essay considers "Snake" and the six tortoise poems as
> companion pieces and calls attention to their similarities and com-
> mon theme. The result is a reinterpretation of "Snake" with the
> serpent symbolized on several levels.

Cipolla, Elizabeth. "The Last Poems of D.H. Lawrence." D.H. LAWRENCE
REVIEW, 2 (1969), 103-19.

> Cipolla discusses the last poems of Lawrence as final meditations
> on life and death and as manifestations of his life-long interest in
> the religion and mythology of the ancient Mediterranean world.
> He concludes: "Through a spiritual return to the past, Lawrence
> had sought and found a message for the future."

Cox, C.B., and A.E. Dyson. "D.H. Lawrence: 'Bavarian Gentians' in Modern Poetry." In their STUDIES IN PRACTICAL CRITICISM. London: E. Arnold, 1971, pp. 66-71.

Davis, Herbert. "The Poetic Genius of D.H. Lawrence." UNIVERSITY OF
TORONTO QUARTERLY, 3 (1934), 439-53.

> Davis contends that Lawrence's poetry "is always direct, spontane-
> ous, always a completely individual and characteristic statement.
> There is no lying, no deflection in the interest of convention, or
> prettiness, no current fashions, nothing but a very rare wholeness,
> a terribly complete honesty, which makes his work unique among
> all the numerous recent experiments in verse. There is no senti-
> ment, no vagueness, no obscurity; often a forceful rhetoric, or an
> easy conversational fluency, unlike the meagre cactus-growths

which seem to be the more characteristic product of the aridities of our present existence."

Deutsch, Babette. "D.H. Lawrence." In her THIS MODERN POETRY. London: Faber, 1936, pp. 201-07.

Deutsch says that Lawrence, in the greater part of his verse, lacks control over his material, indulges in slipshod technique, inexact diction, verbosity, and faulty cadences: "His ineptitude is the outward and visible sign of his inward confusion." The article also discusses the influence of Blake, Whitman, and Rimbaud on Lawrence.

Draper, R.P. "Form and Tone in the Poetry of D.H. Lawrence." ENGLISH STUDIES, 49 (1968), 498-508.

Draper discusses Lawrence's gradual departure, throughout the course of his literary career, from the conventional verse of the day.

Enright, D.J. "A Haste for Wisdom: The Poetry of D.H. Lawrence." In his CONSPIRATORS AND POETS. London: Chatto and Windus, 1965, pp. 95-101.

This essay considers "whether it is not Lawrence's technique or lack of it that is resented so much as his range of subject matter, the naturalness of his writing . . . and its effortlessness."

Fairchild, H.N. "Mystics." In his RELIGIOUS TRENDS IN ENGLISH POETRY. Vol. 5. New York: Columbia University Press, 1962, pp. 276-84.

Fairchild claims that Lawrence's "best poetry is his prose." His best verse did not appear until BIRDS, BEASTS, AND FLOWERS in 1923. The pre-1920 poems, "besides contributing importantly to the purely literary history of the Georgian period, embody thoughts and feelings which, under subsequently changing guises, constitute the central core of his prophecy." Fairchild's comments are an attempt to elucidate this assertion and the nature of Lawrence's creative power.

Ferrier, Carole, and Egon Tiedje. "D.H. Lawrence's Pre-1920 Poetry: The Textual Approach: An Exchange." D.H. LAWRENCE REVIEW, 5 (1972), 148-57.

Ferrier answers Egon Tiedje's article (in the fall 1971 volume of the REVIEW; see Tiedje below) suggesting an approach to the significant problems presented by the various manuscript drafts of Lawrence's earlier poetry. She explains why she considers this approach invalid and presents what she calls "a much more productive approach."

Fisher, William J. "Peace and Passivity: The Poetry of D.H. Lawrence."
SOUTH ATLANTIC QUARTERLY, 60 (1956), 337-48.

> The article investigates the expression in Lawrence's poems of a
> drive to be "merged, to be soothed into some harmonious and
> self-obliterating whole." In the poems "the passive conception
> and the passive image prevail: the poet yearns to be taken,
> touched, folded, enclosed; to be eased into darkness; to be im-
> mersed softly and unconsciously."

Gerard, D.E. "Glossary of Eastwood Dialect Words Used by D.H. Lawrence
in His Poems, Plays, and Fiction." D.H. LAWRENCE REVIEW, 1 (1968),
215-37.

Gifford, Henry. "The Defect of Lawrence's Poetry." CRITICAL QUARTERLY,
3 (1961), 164-67.

> Gifford presents his letter to the editor in answer to Pinto's article
> (CRITICAL QUARTERLY, 3 [1961], 5-8; also see Pinto, below)
> agreeing with Pinto's confidence in the "expressive form" of Lawrence's
> poetry. But, Gifford states, Lawrence's poetry is often ruined by
> repetition of words and phrases, and its rhythms "are frequently
> slack and impoverished because he felt no devotion to language.
> He goes on to say that Lawrence "lent himself to the essential
> problem which consists in recognizing poetry as being 'a matter
> of words' and thus demanding attention to words, and to form,
> but he was misguided in his attempts to express this."

_____. "Lawrence's Poetry." CRITICAL QUARTERLY, 3 (1961), 368-69.

> Gifford's response to Pinto's and Gamini Salgado's letters (CRITICAL
> QUARTERLY, 3 [1961], 267-70; see Pinto, below). He again as-
> serts that Lawrence's interest was not "in the fabric of verse" and
> that his poetry suffers much from lack of such interest.

Gilbert, Sandra. ACTS OF ATTENTION: THE POEMS OF D.H. LAWRENCE.
Ithaca, N.Y.: Cornell University Press, 1972.

> Gilbert traces the development of Lawrence's art in verse from its
> beginnings to its conclusions, focusing on the relation of the poems
> to the Romantic traditions in which they are rooted.

Gregory, Horace. PILGRIM OF THE APOCALYPSE. London: Martin Secker,
1934.

> Gregory attempts "to interpret Lawrence's work as one might deal
> with the remains of any other major Romantic poet." Gregory as-
> serts that "poetry lies at the root of everything he had to say.
> Unconsciously, but unerringly, he follows in the tradition of the
> great Romantic English poets and believed with Shelley that the
> distinction between poetry and prose was a vulgar error."

D[avid] H[erbert] Lawrence

Grigson, Geoffrey. "The Poet in D.H. Lawrence." LONDON MAGAZINE, 5 (1958), 66-69.

> Grigson formulates his thesis on the assertion that "The poet Lawrence is inside the novelist, who is inside the prophet; and his potentiality was to have been a more considerable poet . . . than his fiction--or his prophetic activity--allowed him to be."

Gutierrez, Donald. "Circles and Arcs: The Rhythm of Circularity and Centrifugality in D.H. Lawrence's 'Last Poems.'" D.H. LAWRENCE REVIEW, 4 (1971), 291-300.

> Gutierrez explains: "The guiding idea in this paper is that many of the poems in Lawrence's LAST POEMS (1933) cohere as a larger artistic design through a pattern of figurative centrifugality and circularity. These conceptual constructs denote, respectively, a movement outward from a center and an endless movement around a center. Applied to human experience and sensibility, centrifugality can be taken to connote selflessness, and circularity selfishness."

Henderson, Philip. "BIRDS, BEASTS AND FLOWERS." In his THE POET AND SOCIETY. London: Secker and Warburg, 1939, pp. 172-201.

> Henderson devotes this chapter to an investigation of Lawrence's poetry as "an attempt to deny all social responsibilities and restraints."

Hughes, Glenn. "D.H. Lawrence. The Passionate Psychologist." In his IMAGISM AND THE IMAGISTS. London: H. Milford, Oxford University Press; Stanford, Calif.: Stanford University Press, 1931, pp. 167-96.

> Hughes presents a general discussion of Lawrence's themes, subject matter, and techniques. Hughes asserts that there was no radical change in Lawrence's poetry as a result of his association with the imagists.

Kirkham, Michael. "D.H. Lawrence's LAST POEMS." D.H. LAWRENCE REVIEW, 5 (1972), 97-120.

> In the first part of this essay, Kirkham suggests that LAST POEMS (1933) is best read "as a single work, forming a loosely connected sequence of thought." In the second part he discusses the central themes of the sequence and in the third part illustrates, through a close analysis of several poems, Lawrence's poetic embodiment of his themes.

Marshall, Tom. THE PSYCHIC MARINER: A READING OF THE POEMS OF D.H. LAWRENCE. New York: Viking, 1970.

> Marshall states that "there is a continuous development of the unique and quite individual free-verse idiom from the time of

BIRDS, BEASTS AND FLOWERS to the end of his life" and proceeds to investigate in detail Lawrence's growth as a poet, paying
attention to both his ideas and his personal history as expressed
in the poetry.

Maurois, Andre. "D.H. Lawrence." In his POETS AND PROPHETS. London:
Cassell, 1936, pp. 173-207.

Maurois devotes this chapter to general comments on Lawrence's
life and works. Emphasis is placed on his effort to "transcend
the civilized man and reach again the natural man and communion
of bodies; and the hope of achieving this through the senses and
. . . the intercession of woman."

Megroz, R.L. "D.H. Lawrence." In his FIVE NOVELIST POETS OF TODAY.
London: Joiner and Steele, 1933, pp. 224-35.

Megroz presents a general discussion of the subject matter, themes,
and techniques of Lawrence's poetry and Lawrence's emotional
development, and the influence of the latter on his poetry.

Moorthy, P. Rama. "The Poetry of D.H. Lawrence." COMMONWEALTH
QUARTERLY, 2 (1977), 69-78.

Moorthy discusses Lawrence's poetry as constituting a "creative
cosmos, a Noah's ark where every creature achieves its creative
self-hood and creative fullness of being." He claims the poems
"involve the reader in the story of creation . . . its wonder and
mystery, liberating us from our little selves in the vast marvel of
creation."

Murfin, Ross C. SWINBURNE, HARDY, AND LAWRENCE. Chicago: University of Chicago Press, 1978.

Murfin writes on the poetic influence of Algernon Swinburne on
Thomas Hardy, and on Swinburne and Hardy's influence on D.H.
Lawrence.

Oates, Joyce Carol. "The Hostile Sun: The Poetry of D.H. Lawrence." In
her NEW HEAVEN, NEW EARTH: THE VISIONARY EXPERIENCE IN LITERA-
TURE. New York: Vanguard, 1974, pp. 37-81. First published as a monograph under the same title (Los Angeles: Black Sparrow Press, 1973).

Oates presents a study devoted to Lawrence's aesthetics and theory
of man's transformation through spiritual union with other men.

Orell, Herbert M. "D.H. Lawrence: Poet of Death and Resurrection." CRES-
SET, 34 (1971), 10-13.

Orell presents a discussion of Lawrence as a "poet of death and
resurrection" based on the belief that this theme "is the pivot of
his life and writings."

D[avid] H[erbert] Lawrence

Pinto, Vivian de Sola. "D.H. Lawrence: Letter Writer and Craftsman in Verse." RENAISSANCE AND MODERN STUDIES, 1 (1959), 6-34.

The second part of this article describes and analyzes a small notebook containing drafts of many early poems lent to the University of Nottingham in 1955-56 by Mrs. Emily King, the elder sister of D.H. Lawrence.

_____. "Lawrence's Poetry." CRITICAL QUARTERLY, 4 (1962), 81.

This letter that ends the correspondence of Gifford, Pinto, and Salgado regarding the quality of Lawrence's poetic expression (CRITICAL QUARTERLY, 3, 1961). Here Pinto asserts that the correspondence provides evidence that "Lawrence is an important poet of the kind whose poetry is intensely disliked by some very intelligent people like Mr. Gifford and Professor Blackmur" (see Gifford and Blackmur entries, above). Pinto goes on to state, "Similar intense dislike has been incurred by the poetry of Wordsworth and Byron, both of whom, like Lawrence, wrote a lot of inferior verse . . . I would rather be damned with Wordsworth, Byron, and Lawrence than go to a Franco-American heaven with Ezra Pound and his choir of latterday adulators."

Pinto, Vivian de Sola, and Gamini Salgado. "Mr. Gifford and D.H. Lawrence." CRITICAL QUARTERLY, 3 (1961), 677-70.

These letters from Pinto and Salgado to the editor challenge Henry Gifford's position on Lawrence's poetry (CRITICAL QUARTERLY, 3 [1961], 5-18). Pinto and Salgado agree that Lawrence does, indeed, fail to approximate to conventional metrical rules, but maintain that his poetry is, nevertheless, artistically acceptable and effective.

_____. "Imagists and D.H. Lawrence." In his CRISIS IN ENGLISH POETRY. London: Hutchinson's University Library, 1951, pp. 135-40.

Pinto's comments establish Lawrence as "neither a Georgian nor an Imagist" but a "passionately religious man" who might, had he lived long enough, become a "religious poet of a very high order." His poetry suffered because he "in his own words, was 'torn off from the body of mankind' and lacked social background and a tradition."

_____. "Introduction." COMPLETE POEMS OF D.H. LAWRENCE. Collected ed. with notes, Vivian de Sola Pinto and Warren Roberts. 2 vols. London: Heinemann, 1964.

Lawrence's poems, claims Pinto, have "organic" and "expressive" form and their rhythms "convey the pulse of the moment at hand." See also Pittock, below.

_____. "Poet Without a Mask." CRITICAL QUARTERLY, 3 (1961), 5-18.

This essay is an answer to R.P. Blackmur's charge (LANGUAGE
AS GESTURE, 1954) that Lawrence fails as a poet because his
work is vitiated by "the fallacy of faith in expressive form."
Pinto states that Lawrence did not assume the "mask of the master-
builder--a mask that would have resulted in 'expressive form.'"
To be looked for, instead, in his poetry, is "the insurgent, naked
throb of the instant moment" which manifests "a poetry that is
'neither star nor pearl but instantaneous like plasm.'"

Pittock, Malcolm. "Lawrence the Poet." TIMES LITERARY SUPPLEMENT, 2
September 1965, p. 755.

Pittock presents a critique, in the form of a letter to the editor,
of the Pinto-Roberts edition of Lawrence's poems. The letter
points out the omission of an earlier draft of the poem "The
Bride" that appeared under the title "The Dead Mother" in the
London edition of Ada Lawrence and Stuart Gelder's EARLY LIFE
OF D.H. LAWRENCE, 1932.

Press, John. "D.H. Lawrence." In his A MAP OF MODERN ENGLISH VERSE.
London and Oxford: Oxford University Press, 1969, pp. 93-401.

Press asserts that Lawrence's main contribution to poetry was "his
extraordinary skill in discovering and embodying in verse the
rhythm that would correspond exactly with the subtle yet overwhelmingly powerful rhythm of his sensual perceptions and emotional life." The chapter investigates this assertion.

Read, Herbert. "The Figure of Grammar: Whitman and Lawrence." In his
THE TRUE VOICE OF FEELING. London: Faber, 1953, pp. 96-100.

Read contends that Lawrence identified the free verse he employed
in his poetry with Whitman's idea of free verse; however, Lawrence
failed in the expression desired, where Whitman succeeded.

Rexroth, Kenneth, ed. "Introduction." SELECTED POEMS OF D.H. LAWRENCE.
New York: New Directions, 1947, pp. 1-23.

Rexroth analyzes Lawrence's purely poetic contribution, which is
one that can now be seen as one of the most significant of our
time in any language. He traces Lawrence's artistic development
toward a more and more intense expression of reality, human joy,
and complex human relationships.

Rosenthal, M.L. "D.H. Lawrence." In his THE MODERN POETS. New York:
Oxford University Press, 1960, pp. 160-69.

Rosenthal presents a discussion of Lawrence's poetry as an expression of what men and women "really are." His poems go straight
to the heart of the matter of sexual mystery. Rosenthal states,

D[avid] H[erbert] Lawrence

"The extraordinary influence of D.H. Lawrence is based on his
evangelistic call for the return of modern men and women to what
he called 'phallic consciousness.'"

Ross, R.H. "The Rise and Fall of the Poetic Ideal." In his THE GEORGIAN
REVOLT. London: Faber, 1967, pp. 89-90.

Ross comments on the controversy over form between Lawrence and
Edward Marsh. Marsh objected to Lawrence's use of vers libre
and this objection goaded Lawrence into a cogent defense.

Sagar, Keith. "The Genesis of 'Bavarian Gentians.'" D.H. LAWRENCE RE-
VIEW, 8 (1975), 47-53.

Sagar believes that the Ms. B version of "Bavarian Gentians,"
which is the generally known one, is the wrong version. He asserts that the version in Ms. A "is not only the final version of
the poem but also the best." The essay defends his choice.

Savage, D.S. "D.H. Lawrence: A Study in Dissolution." In his THE PER-
SONAL PRINCIPLE: STUDIES IN MODERN POETRY. London: Routledge,
1944, pp. 131-54.

Savage's judgment on Lawrence's life and work can be summed up
as follows: "Lawrence's view of life, his 'biologism,' which is a
similarly retrogressive dissolution back into primary life, implies
a refusal of spiritual values. It leads concurrently to the dissolution of personality and the dissolution of art. Lawrence was, of
course, a considerable personality and a considerable artist, all
that is valuable in his work is explained by these two facts. But
his life attitude, growing out of the compulsive personal situation
of which he remained always a victim, led him to strike at the
very foundations of personality and of art, and his attitude leads
directly into a state of being where neither art nor personality
exists."

Shakir, Evelyn. "'Secret Sin': Lawrence's Early Verse." D.H. LAWRENCE
REVIEW, 8 (1975), 1557-75.

Shakir presents an examination of Lawrence's early verse, together
with his comments on it for the purpose of explaining the poet's
"profound mistrust" of art.

Smailes, T.A. "D.H. Lawrence: Poet." STANDPUNTE, 23 (1968), 24-36.

Smailes tests the validity of Lawrence's claim to the rank of poet
by comparing some of his poems to those of Hopkins, Yeats, and
Eliot.

Smith, L.E.W. "Snake." In his TWELVE POEMS CONSIDERED. London:
Methuen, 1963, pp. 131-43.

Smith asserts that "Snake" is "a perfect example of the wedding of form and content." This assertion is demonstrated by close analysis.

Southworth, James. "D.H. Lawrence: A Note on His Political Ideology." In his SOWING THE SPRING: STUDIES IN BRITISH POETRY FROM HOPKINS TO MacNEICE. Oxford: Basil Blackwell, 1940, pp. 64-75.

Southworth presents a discussion of Lawrence's political ideology as expressed in LAST POEMS (1933).

Spender, Stephen. WORLD WITHIN WORLDS. London: Hamilton, 1951, pp. 96-97.

The creative mystery for Lawrence, says Spender, is "the paradox of the fusion of existences which cannot become one another, for from the contact of the individual with what is outside him, with nature, and with other people, there is a renewal of himself."

Sullivan, Alvin. "The Phoenix Riddle: Recent D.H. Lawrence Scholarship." PAPERS IN LANGUAGE AND LITERATURE, 7 (1971), 203-21.

A survey of cross-currents in recent Lawrence scholarship.

Thwaite, Anthony. "D.H. Lawrence." In his CONTEMPORARY POETRY. London: Heinemann, 1957, pp. 50-53.

Thwaite claims that Lawrence's best poems are "those which keep their eyes solidly on the object, describing and evoking without too much of a didactic and moral burden. Thwaite comments on the techniques of several poems including "Snake," "Piano," and "Giorno Dei Morti."

Tiedje, Egon. "D.H. Lawrence's Early Poetry: The Composition Dates of the Drafts in MS E 317." D.H. LAWRENCE REVIEW, 4 (1971), 227-52.

Trail, George Y. "Towards a Lawrentian Poetic." D.H. LAWRENCE REVIEW, 5 (1972), 67-81.

Trail presents an evaluation of the critical work produced during 1970 on Lawrence's writings. Includes comments on important earlier criticism.

Vickery, John. "The Golden Bough and Modern Poetry." JOURNAL OF AESTHETICS AND ART CRITICISM, 15 (1957), 271-88.

The bulk of this study is devoted to a consideration of the myths and symbols that D.H. Lawrence, Edith Sitwell, and W.B. Yeats derived from Sir James Frazer's THE GOLDEN BOUGH (1922).

Wilder, Amos. "Primitivism in D.H. Lawrence." In his SPIRITUAL ASPECTS OF THE NEW POETRY. New York: Harper's, 1940, pp. 153-65.

Wilder presents a discussion of "a rather undistinguished merger of pan-theism and Bergsonism" in Lawrence's poetry.

Youngblood, Sarah. "Substance and Shadow: The Self in Lawrence's Poetry." D.H. LAWRENCE REVIEW, 1 (1968), 114-28.

Youngblood perceives the autobiographical element in Lawrence's work to be a central issue. She states that "almost all the ways of reading Lawrence's poetry lead toward or proceed from its auto-biographical core, its expressive form."

FREDERICK LOUIS MacNEICE (1907-63)

PRINCIPAL WORKS

Poetry

BLIND FIREWORKS. London: Victor Gollanz, 1929.
POEMS. London: Faber, 1935.
THE EARTH COMPELS. London: Faber, 1938.
I CROSSED THE MINCH. New York and Toronto: Longmans, Green, 1938.
AUTUMN JOURNAL. London: Faber, 1939.
THE LAST DITCH. Dublin: Cuala Press, 1940.
POEMS 1925-1940. New York: Random House, 1940.
SELECTED POEMS. London: Faber, 1940.
PLANT AND PHANTOM. London: Faber, 1941.
SPRINGBOARD: POEMS 1941-1944. London: Faber, 1944.
HOLES IN THE SKY: POEMS 1944-1947. London: Faber, 1948.
COLLECTED POEMS 1925-1948. London: Faber, 1949.
TEN BURNT OFFERINGS. London: Faber, 1952.
AUTUMN SEQUEL: A RHETORICAL POEM IN XXVI CANTOS. London:
    Faber, 1954.
VISITATIONS. London: Faber, 1957.
EIGHTY-FIVE POEMS. London: Faber, 1959.
SOLSTICES. London: Faber, 1961.
THE BURNING PERCH. London: Faber, 1963.
SELECTED POEMS. London: Faber, 1964.
COLLECTED POEMS. London: Faber, 1966.

Other Works

THE AGAMEMNON OF AESCHYLUS (1936), translation.
LETTERS FROM ICELAND, with W.H. Auden (1937), miscellany.
OUT OF THE PICTURE (1937), drama.
MODERN POETRY: A PERSONAL ESSAY (1938), criticism.
THE POETRY OF WILLIAM BUTLER YEATS (1941), criticism.
CHRISTOPHER COLUMBUS: A RADIO PLAY (1944), drama.
THE DARK TOWER AND OTHER RADIO SCRIPTS (1947), drama.

Frederick Louis MacNeice

Goethe's FAUST (1951), translation.
THE PENNY THAT ROLLED AWAY (1954), tale.
ASTROLOGY (1964), survey.
VARIETIES OF PARABLE (1965), criticism.
ONE FOR THE GRAVE: A MODERN MORALITY PLAY (1968), drama.
PERSONS FROM PORLOCK AND OTHER PLAYS FOR RADIO (1969), drama.

BIBLIOGRAPHY

McKinnon, William, ed. "Louis MacNeice: A Bibliography." BULLETIN OF
BIBLIOGRAPHY AND MAGAZINE NOTES, 27 (April-June 1970), 31, 79.

Armitage, Christopher, and Neil Clark, eds. A BIBLIOGRAPHY OF THE
WORKS OF LOUIS MacNEICE. London: Kaye and Ward, 1973.

See also Press under "Biography" below.

AUTOBIOGRAPHY

THE STRINGS ARE FALSE: AN UNFINISHED AUTOBIOGRAPHY. London:
Faber, 1965.

BIOGRAPHIES

Press, John. LOUIS MacNEICE. Writers and Their Work Series, no. 187.
London: Longmans, Green, 1965.

> Press's book contains some biographical information, a select bib-
> liography and some listing of critical and biographical resources.

See below, Brown, Terrence, and Alec Reid, eds. TIME WAS AWAY: THE
WORLD OF LOUIS MacNEICE.

CRITICISM

Aiken, Conrad. "COLLECTED POEMS." NEW REPUBLIC, 16 June 1941, pp.
830-32.

> On POEMS 1925-1940 (1941). MacNeice's poetry is too topical
> and reportorial, Aiken asserts; there is a kind of magic in its
> vividness and "easy intellectual range," but it contains little of
> the linguistic intricacy that induces the reader to turn to it re-
> peatedly.

Allot, Kenneth. "Civilized Common Sense." NEW VERSE, 1 (1939), 20-21.

MacNeice's MODERN POETRY (1938) brings an understanding of
poetry to the ordinary man, says Allot. MacNeice's book is direct,
intelligent, and simply stated.

"AUTUMN JOURNAL." TIMES LITERARY SUPPLEMENT, 20 May 1939,
p. 294.

The most original and effective lines of AUTUMN JOURNAL come
when MacNeice takes a close look at his own cultivated background and tastes and pits them against the background of a dis-
tressed world. His worst lines occur when he makes a priggish
attempt to say the right things and what is expected of a poet
of his affiliation.

"AUTUMN SEQUEL." TIMES LITERARY SUPPLEMENT, 26 November 1954,
p. 754.

The best part of this poem, written for the radio in terza rima,
is in the recording of conversation, claims the critic. He further
asserts any criticism of it is a criticism of the limitations of radio
as a primary medium for poetry and that the difficulties of the
verse form and its apparent unsuitability for a sustained conversational use enable the poet to keep the audience in a state of
delighted expectation for the next rhyme or next glide to a new
topic. Much of the work is deeply moving, especially in its
personal and moral passages. The fault of the poem lies in Mac-
Neice's occasional lapses into facetiousness and facile smartness.

Bach, B.C. "COLLECTED POEMS." COMMONWEAL, 12 May 1965, p. 240.

The collection is overweighed with poems not adequately representative of the poet's evolution. The editor (W.H. Auden) does
include poetry translations from the French, German, and Latin,
and these reveal MacNeice's poetic sympathies and metrical versatility. The canon is, however, generally too topical and the
hortatory tone is too foreign from a milieu that embraces existen-
tial nihilism and pessimism. MacNeice's prose-like verse is per-
vadingly archaic.

Baker, D.W. "EIGHTY-FIVE POEMS." MINNESOTA REVIEW, 7 (1961),
118-29.

Baker claims that MacNeice is among the most powerful twentieth-
century poets, first, because he is aware of modern social and
psychological thought; secondly, because he speaks in a strong
colloquial voice with never an uncertainty; and, thirdly, because
he draws on the ancient Western literary tradition for his images
and craft. He fulfills the purpose of poetry, which is to delight.
Baker presents an analysis of "The Streets of Laredo."

Frederick Louis MacNeice

"BLIND FIREWORKS." TIMES LITERARY SUPPLEMENT, 28 March 1929, p. 263.

The author claims that MacNeice succeeds in transforming life into pictorial effervescence. He works under a creative compulsion that is always present behind the artifice. His imagery is both original and plastic, but it almost always lacks a creative center.

Borroff, M. "What a Poem Is: For Instance 'Snow.'" ESSAYS IN CRITICISM, 8 (1958), 393-404.

Borroff asserts that MacNeice's poem is a verbal representation of the train of thought of a fictional speaker. Through a complex intuitive process, the reader perceives the full meaning and implications of the successive poetic statements and experiences sympathetic participation in the speaker's experience and emotions. Once this process is accomplished the poem begins to function as a kind of moral exhortation, causing the reader to desire to emulate the attitudes depicted in it and enlarge his perception of the world around him. Borroff concludes that this effect is valuable and is genuine because the poem has validity in its primary mode of existence as a work of art. Replies to Borroff's analysis appeared in ESSAYS IN CRITICISM, 9 (1959), 209-11, 450-51. See also Collins, below.

Botterill, D. "HOLES IN THE SKY." LIFE AND LETTERS, 60 (1949), 111-13.

Botterill claims that MacNeice faces a crisis in the art he has practiced, inasmuch as it has become inadequate to his needs. Some of the spontaneity so necessary to his colloquial use of language is absent, but the usual technical mastery of loose rhythms is there, along with a nagging touch of despair. This despair is evidence of an emotional change in the writer.

Brennan, Maya. "A Poet's Revisions: A Consideration of MacNeice's "Blind Fireworks." WESTERN HUMANITIES REVIEW, 23 (1969), 159-71.

Brennan presents a history of the revisions of BLIND FIREWORKS (1929).

Brown, Terrence. LOUIS MacNEICE: SKEPTICAL VISION. Dublin: Gill and MacMillan; New York: Barnes and Noble, 1975.

MacNeice's poetry and thought, Brown states, have as their central determining factor "a tense awareness of fundamental questions, rooted in philosophical skepticism." In the first part of the book, Brown examines the poet's themes, attitudes, and responses in the light of this basic skepticism. In the second part, Brown deals with the technical aspects of MacNeice's verse as "the embodiment of the basic skeptical vision which is the center of his work, the idea behind his poetic achievement."

_____. "Louis MacNeice 1907-1963. His Poetry." STUDIES, 59 (1970), 253-66.

Brown presents a study treating the effect on MacNeice's life and work of the childhood loss of his mother, his exile from Ireland, his poetical skepticism, romantic longing, religious doubt, philosophical skepticism, and vision of the incongruities of life.

Brown, Terrence, and Alec Reid, eds. TIME WAS AWAY: THE WORLD OF LOUIS MacNEICE. Dublin: Dolman Press, 1974.

Brown and Reid present the following biographical, memorial, and critical essays: "Louis MacNeice: A Memorial Address" by W.H. Auden; "Trees Were Green" by Elizabeth Nicholson; "MacNeice: Father and Son" by Terrence Brown; "Louis MacNeice at Birmingham" by E.R. Dodds; "'A Fancy Turn, You Know'" by Bernard Share; "Celt and Classicist: The Versecraft of Louis MacNeice" by Robin Skelton; "MacNeice as Critic" by Walter Allen; "The Translation of the AGAMEMNON of Aeschylus" by W.B. Stanford; "The Faust Translation" by E.L. Stahl; "MacNeice in the Theatre" by Alec Reid; "Castle on the Air" by R.D. Smith; "Sound and Vision" by Dallas Bower; "Time and the Will Lie Sidestepped: Athens, the Interval" by Kevin Andrews; "For Louis MacNeice" by Anthony Thwaite; "MacNeice in England and Ireland" by Derek Mahon; "Despair and Delight" by John Montagne; and "Louis MacNeice" by Liam Miller. This edition includes "A Bibliography of Books by MacNeice" edited by Christopher Armitage, "Radio Scripts" by R.D. Smith, and short biographies of the contributors.

Burham, D. "Mind of Man." COMMONWEAL, 21 August 1953, p. 495.

On MacNeice's TEN BURNT OFFERINGS (1949), Burham claims that it is a book that is essentially personal, reflective, speculative, and leavened with vivid, vigorous, "pure description." He discusses MacNeice's use of nonformal language with mature assurance and remarkable flexibility. MacNeice's volume, TEN BURNT OFFERINGS (1949), is comprised of ten long poems written during the year the poet spent in Greece. Burham sees each poem as divisible into four contrasting sections: some rhymed according to diverse prosodies, some unrhymed, some in short lines, some slow-moving, some as swift-moving as popular ballads. He discusses MacNeice's "mature" and "flexible" use of nonformal language and the difficulty of the early poems because of density of meaning and elliptic allusions.

Chapman, Frank. "POEMS." SCRUTINY, 4 (1925), 300-302.

On POEMS (1935). MacNeice is not a great poet, but one of the best of the contemporary poets, Chapman states. He sees MacNeice's work as entirely unaffected, and reflective of the complicated social background of his time and the isolation it imposes. Chapman detects, however, a lack of adequate center in the poetry and asserts that MacNeice gives "a slight air of floppiness to even his best work."

Collins, P.A.W., and R. Draper. "Miss Borroff on 'Snow.'" ESSAYS IN CRITICISM, 9 (1959), 209-11.

Collins complains that Borroff gives equal attention to all the details of the poem rather than selecting those that impress her as the most significant indications of its mature achievement.

Colum, Mary. "Poetry Diminished." FORUM, 10 (1939), 271.

MacNeice places poetry on a low level.

Cook, R.L. "Louis MacNeice: An Appreciation." POETRY REVIEW, 38 (1947), 161-70.

Cook says that MacNeice lays bare truth by brilliant surface descriptions of the trivial objects of modern life that are of such great value to the average Britisher. His gift for this is backed by technical ability. After AUTUMN JOURNAL (1939), Cook asserts, MacNeice revealed a capacity for greater spiritual strength and even more technical assurance, but he needs still to prove himself as a true poet by going beneath the surface and "bringing back permanent poetry--he needs to touch the bone."

Crimmins, P.D. "COLLECTED POEMS." POETRY REVIEW, 41 (1950), 148-49.

Crimmins sees MacNeice as a memorable poet, but claims his work projects an attitude of utter defeatism.

Crowder, R. "Mr. MacNeice and Miss Sitwell." POETRY (Chicago), 63 (1944), 218-22.

Crowder discusses the influences of Edith Sitwell on MacNeice, especially regarding the themes of the plight of the aged and of childcult, and the use of nursery rhyme principles and rococo ornament.

Daiches, David. "The Honest Man Alone." POETRY (Chicago), 57 (1940), 152-57.

Daiches perceives the poems in THE LAST DITCH (1940) hovering between "pedestrian jog" and restrained lyricism. The collection is not an important contribution to MacNeice's poetic output.

Dickey, William. "In the Convention." POETRY (Chicago), 104 (1964), 375-78.

On SELECTED POEMS (1940). Many poems in this edition, Dickey asserts, suffer from imprecise and colorless diction.

Dupree, F.W. "Lewis and MacNeice." NATION, 13 October 1945, p. 380.

Dupree says poems in SPRINGBOARD (1944) are disappointing, inasmuch as they are tired and lacing in spirit. There is, however, a power of individuality that comes through. He says the language is without color and verse.

"THE EARTH COMPELS." TIMES LITERARY SUPPLEMENT, 7 May 1938, p. 318.

The author claims that these poems about Iceland are a subdued comment of striking sensibility. MacNeice describes the most rarified and private emotions of his visit there.

"EIGHTY-FIVE POEMS." TIMES LITERARY SUPPLEMENT, 27 February 1959, p. 114.

The critic states that the book is the best basis so far for a discriminating critical study of the poet. None of the poems present MacNeice as the stereotyped, hostile "1930s poet." They exude wit, irony, neatness, and "the sense of there being a good many sides to every question."

Elman, R.E. "Legacy of Louis MacNeice." NEW REPUBLIC, 26 October 1963, pp. 19-21.

Elman presents an overview of MacNeice's work. He investigates the poet's sense of the speech of the moment, and use of accidental meters and primitive style.

Fiscalini, J. "Sympathetic Poet." COMMONWEAL, 4 July 1958, p. 357.

There are excellent poems in VISITATIONS (1957), claims Fiscalini, but it also contains a good deal of bad verse. MacNeice, in the last section of the book, and seemingly without good reason, doubles verbs and epithets and cultivates a filmsy, inflated rhythm. Fiscalini concludes that the poems will not satisfy the intellectual or imaginative reader.

Fitts, Dudley. "Belles Lettres." SATURDAY REVIEW OF LITERATURE, 25 February 1939, p. 20.

Fitts says that MODERN POETRY (1938) was not written for students but for the intelligently interested reader. MacNeice has put a great deal of sensitive criticism and hard thought into it. Although much of the criticism in it is "exceptionable," it is all "a cantankerous, keen, and wholly delightful book."

_____. "MacNeice on Yeats." SATURDAY REVIEW OF LITERATURE, 3 May 1941, p. 6.

Fitts states that the best book on Yeats is still Edmund Wilson's

AXEL'S CASTLE (1931), but MacNeice's THE POETRY OF WILLIAM BUTLER YEATS (1941) is, nevertheless, a charmingly written cele-bration of Yeats, that, while avoiding profundity and the com-plexities of its subject, is worth reading. The greatest disappoint-ment, Fitts claims, is MacNeice's casual approach and superficial, anecdotal style.

French, Samuel. "EARTH COMPELS." POETRY (Chicago), 53 (1939), 280-83.

MacNeice still occasionally identifies with Auden's style instead of his own, states French, solidifies his point of view and gives evidence that he is writing for an increasingly large audience.

Gitzen, John. "Louis MacNeice: The Last Decade." TWENTIETH CENTURY LITERATURE, 14 (1968), 133-41.

Gitzen presents a summary of MacNeice's movement from structural images to parable, from the autobiographical to the impersonal viewpoint, from conversational to rigid meters, and from complex to simplified diction. Gitzen concludes that MacNeice's last years were marked by a strict discipline and agonizing simplicity that resembled that of the aging Yeats.

Gregory, Horace. "The New January." POETRY (Chicago), 74 (1949), 301-04.

Gregory asserts that the verse in HOLES IN THE SKY (1948) lacks wit and brilliance, is sometimes toneless, obscure, and mediocre.

Gunn, Thom. "Modes of Control." YALE REVIEW, 53 (1964), 447-58.

THE BURNING PERCH (1963) is MacNeice's best book. His ten-dencies toward journalistic generalization and jingle writing are present, but used for a good purpose instead of being extraneous as they sometimes are in the earlier works.

Hamilton, Ian. "Louis MacNeice." LONDON MAGAZINE, 3 (1963), 62-66.

Heppenstall, R. "A Demise of Poets." LONDON MAGAZINE, 6 (1967), 57-65.

Heppenstall presents an account of his acquaintance with MacNeice.

"HOLES IN THE SKY." TIMES LITERARY SUPPLEMENT, 5 June 1948, p. 315.

An uncertainty has entered into the poet's style. MacNeice's emo-tions are sincere and valid, but he has become awkwardly self-conscious in tone and an official flavor has permeated the language.

"I CROSSED THE MINCH." TIMES LITERARY SUPPLEMENT, 9 April 1938, p. 247.

The book presents a true picture of the Hebrides if one can delve beneath MacNeice's jokes and self-consciousness of expression.

Irwin, John T. "MacNeice, Auden, and the Art Ballad." CONTEMPORARY LITERATURE, 11 (1970), 58-79.

Irwin's essay concentrates on MacNeice's subtle interpretation of the ballad tradition. The poet has a modernist viewpoint combined with an old naive romanticism. This is especially evident in "The Streets of Laredo," a poem in which he imitates the surface form of the original to help establish and enrich the irony in his view of modern London.

Jack, Peter Monro. "AUTUMN JOURNAL." NEW YORK TIMES BOOK RE-VIEW, 18 February 1940, p. 2.

Jack claims that AUTUMN JOURNAL is written in a sound tradi-tional form and that it has something of Wordsworth's PRELUDE; Tennyson's IN MEMORIAM, and Bridges' TESTAMENT OF BEAUTY. Its style, however, is new--typical, lively, personal, argumentive, and taking nothing for granted. Whatever words that seem effec-tive at the moment are employed. MacNeice manages this mix with intelligent control. Jack concludes that AUTUMN JOURNAL is "probably the finest sustained achievement of the younger poets."

_____. "Louis MacNeice on MODERN POETRY." NEW YORK TIMES BOOK REVIEW, 19 March 1939, p. 2.

MODERN POETRY (1938), asserts Jack, does not have the disci-pline and force of a critical study, though it has the interest and pleasure of a poet's personality. Desultory chapters on imagery, rhythm, and diction appear. Jack calls attention to the many interesting things MacNeice says about the younger English poets, much of which comes from the poet's personal acquaintance with them. It is this familiar touch, he concludes, that is the book's most valuable asset.

Jarrell, Randall. "From That Island." KENYON REVIEW, 1 (1939), 468-71.

Jarrell says that MODERN POETRY (1938) is an apologia for MacNeice's friends' poetry and for his ignorance of American poetry. MacNeice's book is rarely brilliant.

Jeffares, Norman A. "Poetry of Yeats." ENGLISH STUDIES, 27 (1946), 29-31.

The main value of THE POETRY OF WILLIAM BUTLER YEATS (1941), Jeffares claims, lies in its lively comparisons, its attempts to estimate the reality or the importance to Yeats of certain pre-

Frederick Louis MacNeice

dominant ideas. MacNeice writes knowingly of Yeats but attaches too much importance to Pater's influence.

Kennedy, X.J. "Underestimations." POETRY (Chicago), 103 (1964), 330-33.

Kennedy says that THE BURNING PERCH (1963) is occasional and often diffuse, but its best pieces still have "the power of moving out of flat objects into a sharp conclusion, that curious hesitation between two and three dimensions that the convention was invented to exploit."

"THE LAST DITCH." TIMES LITERARY SUPPLEMENT, 8 June 1940, p. 282.

The critic claims that MacNeice's great virtue is that he presumes nothing and almost never strains beyond what he knows to be his reach. He is tentative and conversational, and even his cleverness is spontaneous and unsophisticated. The defect in this virtue is a tendency to lapse into the trivial and the tentative, and this defect is evident more than usual in these poems. The vital idiosyncrasy of his style is the most impressive quality in the collection.

Leavis, Q.D. "MODERN POETRY." SCRUTINY, 8 (1939), 72-73.

Leavis asserts that this account of MacNeice's friends and their work "reads like a book written by a schoolboy for schoolboys."

Lienhardt, R.G. "PLANT AND PHANTOM." SCRUTINY, 10 (1941), 91-93.

MacNeice should confine himself to simple journalism in verse. The volume is self-indulgent and often shallow. An absence of sensitive discrimination of the value of differing experiences is unfortunate. Lienhardt complains that the poet elaborates and distends the tritest of sentiments and ideas, and employs heavily artificial diction.

Mack, Maynard. "Critical Synthesis." YALE REVIEW, 28 (1939), 398-402.

In MODERN POETRY (1938), Mack states, "MacNeice never reveals a vigorous sense of the continuing tradition of English poetry, and accordingly never takes a really perspicacious view of the relations of the newer with the older poets. He gives the impression that modern poetry is modern British poetry and that modern poetry is, to an alarming extent, Auden."

McKinnon, William. APOLLO'S BLENDED DREAM: A STUDY OF THE POETRY OF LOUIS MacNEICE. London: Oxford University Press, 1971.

The emphasis in this book is on the "deep and abiding awareness of the poet's need for belief and . . . his equally strong and conscious awareness of the need to find the forms, especially the

tone of voice, appropriate to the creative expression of this belief." The early chapters attempt to "unfold the dominant strands
in the pattern of MacNeice's thinking." Those that follow il-
lustrate the effect of this upon the form of his poetic expression
and communication." The book is designed to "define some of
the ways in which a reborn critical theory will need to function
if it is to achieve a synthesis of modern with traditional poetic
practice."

Mellers, W.H. "AUTUMN JOURNAL." SCRUTINY, 8 (1939), 125-28.

AUTUMN JOURNAL (1939) consists of "ruminations as poetry dished
up as prose dished up as meter." The book is "astonishingly concerned with the contemporary situation but doesn't convince us that
he is, as a poet, aware of anything at all. . . . Shake up all
the Auden-Isherwood-Day Lewis-MacNeice poetic and dramatic
productions of the last few years, dump them out helter-skelter,
and the sense of them would not be substantially altered. . . .
[How] can anyone pretend that this stuff has anything to do with
mysterious processes, the developed sensibility, out of which is
born poetry?"

_____. "The Poetry of W.B. Yeats." SCRUTINY, 10 (1941), 381-83.

MacNeice's study of Yeats (1941) makes no new contribution and
tells us nothing essential about Yeats's background that Yeats has
not told us himself. The book is a failure because it does not
contain criticism and therefore lacks the core of any fixed critical
attitude.

Moore, D.B. THE POETRY OF LOUIS MacNEICE. Leicester, Engl.: Leicester University Press, 1972.

The book deals with the poet's achievement, intentions, and reputation, and provides close examination of many individual poems.
Moore presents MacNeice as a poet of modern city life writing
about the impact of twentieth-century life on his senses.

Nuttall, A.D. "Voices of. Parable." REVIEW OF ENGLISH STUDIES, 17
(1966), 450.

Nuttall asserts that MacNeice investigates in VARIETIES OF PAR-
ABLE (1965) double-level writing, but fails to transform the valuable insight that one should be skeptical of, namely, C.S. Lewis'
distinction between symbolism as a "mode of thought" and allegory
as a "mode of expression," into a strong demonstration. "There
are too many questions raised, assigned a source, and then dropped."

O'Connor, W.V.D. "Master of His Idiom." SATURDAY REVIEW OF LITERA-
TURE, 29 January 1949, p. 27.

Frederick Louis MacNeice

O'Connor says that MacNeice is master of the idiom in HOLES IN THE SKY (1948). The reader is not made to feel that poetic structure is in danger of disintegration. His asides inform the theme, and the symbols recur in a kind of contrapuntal pattern. By holding to central conceits, O'Connor claims, MacNeice achieves a concentration of meaning.

"PLANT OR PHANTOM." TIMES LITERARY SUPPLEMENT, 19 April 1941, p. 194.

The critic asserts that MacNeice commits himself to vitality, neglecting abstract conceptions. He comes nearer to a balance in this book than in others. His talent for pitching his poetry close to the conversational level without letting it slip down into prose is commendable.

Pocock, R. "THE BURNING PERCH." ENCOUNTER, 33 (1969), 70-71.

Pocock presents a remembrance of MacNeice's last days.

"A Poet of Our Time." TIMES LITERARY SUPPLEMENT, 28 October 1949, p. 696.

The critic claims that COLLECTED POEMS 1925-1948 (1949) shows "a small talent and limited achievement and few signs of further development." MacNeice is not the outstanding poet of the 1930s. He does not produce compelling images or phrasing; he indulges in cliché symbolism, is confused over positive values by which he stands, and this leads to a confusion of tone. His technique becomes too easily separable from content.

"Poetry of Yeats." TIMES LITERARY SUPPLEMENT, 29 March 1941, p. 150.

The critic asserts that MacNeice follows with subtlety the course of Yeats's life, but in the end the reader is still unsatisfied and baffled. He goes on to say that Yeats eludes the reader because he eluded himself and that MacNeice does cover thoroughly the early influences and writes well on the relation between poetry and sociology. MacNeice presents in readable fashion the unreadable philosophy of Yeats. This is an acute and learned book overall, concludes the critic.

Press, John. LOUIS MacNEICE. Writers and Their Work Series, no. 187. London: Longmans, Green, 1965.

This is the first substantial study on MacNeice published after his death in 1963. The book contains chapters on his life; the prose, drama, and translations; the early poetry; the war and years and late forties; the verse from 1949 to the mid-fifties; and the final creative period.

"Putting Time On Ice." TIME, 25 April 1969, pp. 109-12.

The critic claims that the reediting of LETTERS FROM ICELAND (1937) in 1969 manifests "probably the only successful verse partnership since the old English firm of Beaumont and Fletcher closed shop."

Raine, Kathleen. "Poetry of Yeats." HORIZON, 4 (1941), 66-71.

Raine says that MacNeice's study fails to attack the problem of the relation between Yeats's system and beliefs and his poetry.

Rodman, Seldon. "AUTUMN JOURNAL." SATURDAY REVIEW OF LITERATURE, 10 February 1940, p. 18.

In a time of confusion the poet seeks order by laughing intelligently at his own weakness, Rodman states. He condemns his own ethical paralysis, looking to Barcelona, into the Greek classroom, and into his personal dilemmas for the origins of a new and more valid set of beliefs. JOURNAL falls halfway between the lyric and the didactic. It is written in an "elastic quatrain" and indicates a development in modern poetry quite at variance with and challenging to the theory of Cleanth Brooks and other New Critics who perceive the "obscure interior drama" of the "metaphysical school" as supreme.

Rosenberger, Coleman. "Two Conspiracies: MacNeice and Arajon." POETRY (Chicago), 68 (1946), 44-49.

Rosenberger argues that Arajon's unique conspiracy was a public and private one: a record of wartime emotions of French soldiers and civilians, "a beacon across France against the Nazis." MacNeice's conspiracy is the familiar one of the practice of poetry as a private act. He writes on the impact of war on the individual and does so with creative sensibility. The poems demonstrate share guilt--his and the enemy's. MacNeice's "Explorations" is "an almost perfect poem."

Ross, Alan. "EIGHTY-FIVE POEMS." LONDON MAGAZINE, 6 (1959), 71.

Ross asserts that MacNeice's collection, divided into eight groups, illustrates the eight phases of the poet's creative life. In each of his eight roles MacNeice remains relaxed, off-hand, devoid of solemnity. A "delicious irony" runs through all his poetry that is always on the verge of turning nostalgia into self-mockery. With journalistic efficiency, MacNeice "brings the virtues of fluency and technical skill to bear on a number of themes, none of them beyond the reach of ordinary (non-literary) people."

Salomon, I.L. "An Irish Oracle at Delphi." POETRY (Chicago), 83 (1954), 232-33.

Salomon states that poems in AUTUMN SEQUEL (1954) are mature,

Frederick Louis MacNeice

reflective, and episodic conceptions of what poetry may be when
an artist fails to achieve the Aeschylean sense of tragedy he once
expected of his fellow craftsmen. MacNeice is still not capable
of writing great poetry, but he has made sense of his world: the
design of the forceful quartets coincides with what is superb in
modern writing. However, the series of quartets wants unity,
and the book is exasperating because the poet never comes to
terms with the series of symbols he has evoked for the initiate.

Savage, D.S. "Poet's Perspective." POETRY (Chicago), 64 (1944), 148-58.

MacNeice's poetry, Savage says, displays a decline from "inte-
grality" to concentration on periphery. His perspective is too
much limited to that of social existence. He has failed in his
task of continuously informing his vision of the world with his
personal quality. Savage claims that Auden, Spender, and Mac-
Neice have all suffered a disruption of poetic continuity through
an inability or refusal to penetrate beneath the surface of life
and relate themselves in some way to the ultimate of existence.

Schwartz, Delmore. "Adroitly Naive." POETRY (Chicago), 48 (1936), 115-
17.

Schwartz asserts that MacNeice belongs to the "Bungalow School"
of poetry over which Geoffrey Grigson presides. His poems are
"dull and coated with chocolate."

Smith, Edward Elton. LOUIS MacNEICE. Twayne English Authors Series,
no. 99. New York: Twayne, 1970.

The three themes developed in Smith's study are MacNeice "as
representative man of his time," as "poet who fulfilled his early
literary promise," and "as poet who ended as he began." The
concern throughout is with the poetry rather than the life of the
poet. The approach is chronological, dealing with the poet suc-
cessively as a bright young writer, a member of the Oxford group,
a budding liberal, a disillusioned liberal, and a classical humanist.

Smith, William J. "The Black Clock: The Poetic Achievement of Louis Mac-
Neice." HOLLINS CRITIC, 4 (1967), 1-11.

Smith claims that MacNeice's poems are easy to understand on the
surface, but they present deeper, less obvious difficulties. A
brilliant topography, extraordinary verbal dexterity, and poise
are demonstrated by command of complicated verse forms. There
is a distance maintained, even when he is being most personal,
that gives his poetry, "at its best a cold classical power, and at
its worst, the casualness of an uncommitted poetic journalist."
It is not until THE BURNING PERCH (1963) that he confronts his
loneliness and otherness head-on, and the result is poems that are
"direct and terrifying," intense, and honest.

Southworth, James G. "Louis MacNeice." In his SOWING THE SPRING: STUDIES IN BRITISH POETS FROM HOPKINS TO MacNEICE. Oxford: Basil Blackwell, 1940, pp. 165-78.

What distinguishes MacNeice from his contemporaries, Southworth says, is his personal independence, experimental prosodic forms, and profusion of rich imagery and illusion.

Spender, Stephen. "Songs of an Unsung Classicist." SATURDAY REVIEW OF LITERATURE, 7 September 1963, pp. 25-33.

MacNeice is one of the best poets of the twentieth century, Spender claims. He is also one of the most neglected. His clarity, honesty, and "the quiet milieu of his Classical humanism" is at the root of this neglect.

Symons, Julian. "Louis MacNeice: The Artist as Everyman." POETRY (Chicago), 56 (1940), 86-94.

Symons states that MacNeice's poetry is autobiographical and reflects the attitudes of the "ordinary man." The lack of commitment to any external force prevents the poems from reaching the highest artistic achievement.

"TEN BURNT OFFERINGS." TIMES LITERARY SUPPLEMENT, 8 August 1952, p. 510.

The critic claims that the book marks a change in MacNeice's poetic form. The poems are primarily a meditative exercise in poetic apprehension. Place, commentary, and moods of the poet once were preeminent; now all operate under the aegis of the main design of the poem. Some energy has been lost in the transition.

Tolley, T.A. "The Thirties Poets at Oxford." UNIVERSITY OF TORONTO QUARTERLY, 37 (1968), 338-58.

Tolley presents an examination of the work and relationships of Auden, MacNeice, Spender, and Lewis.

"VISITATIONS." TIMES LITERARY SUPPLEMENT, 7 June 1957, p. 350.

The poems reveal a return to shorter, more compact forms, claims the critic. MacNeice retains his facility for making striking phrases and images but also retains a tendency to rely unduly on verbal ingenuity. New depth is suggested.

Wain, John. "Louis MacNeice as Critic." ENCOUNTER, 27 (1966), 49-55.

Wain asserts that MacNeice's criticism is free of "cant and bullying." VARIETIES OF PARABLE (1965) is set in perspective against the poet's other critical works.

Walton, Geoffrey. "MODERN POETRY." SCRUTINY, 7 (1939), 437-40.

Walton says, "MacNeice passes off the mediocre and watered down as the excellent and he does it with all the pompousness, irresponsibility, and tendentiousness which characterizes the older generation of middlebrow propagandists whom SCRUTINY used to refer to as literary racketeers. The book is another attempt . . . to discourage artistic revival and to stabilize a taste for the second rate."

Wilson, T.C. "One of the Best." POETRY (Chicago), 57 (1938), 339-44.

Wilson says that MacNeice's poetry reveals extraordinary qualities: wit, imagination, sympathy, intelligence; however, the poet's inability or unwillingness to take sides results in a lamentable absence of impact.

JOHN EDWARD MASEFIELD (1878-1967)

PRINCIPAL WORKS

Poetry

SALT-WATER BALLADS. London: Grant Richards, 1902.
BALLADS. London: Elkin Matthews, 1903.
BALLADS AND POEMS. London: Elkin Mathews, 1910.
THE EVERLASTING MERCY. London: Sidgwick and Jackson, 1911.
THE STORY OF A ROUNDHOUSE AND OTHER POEMS. New York: Macmillan, 1912.
THE WIDOW IN THE BYE-STREET. London: Sidgwick and Jackson, 1912.
THE DAFFODIL FIELDS. London: William Heinemann, 1913.
DAUBER: A POEM. London: William Heinemann, 1913.
PHILIP THE KING AND OTHER POEMS. London: William Heinemann, 1914.
GOOD FRIDAY AND OTHER POEMS. New York: Macmillan, 1916.
SONNETS AND POEMS. Letchworth, Engl.: Garden City Press, 1916.
LOLLINGDON DOWNS AND OTHER POEMS. London: William Heinemann, 1917.
POEMS OF JOHN MASEFIELD. New York: Macmillan, 1918.
ROSAS. New York: Macmillan, 1918.
A POEM AND TWO PLAYS. London: William Heinemann, 1919.
REYNARD THE FOX, OR THE GHOST HEATH RUN. London: William Heinemann, 1919.
ENSLAVED AND OTHER POEMS. London: William Heinemann, 1920.
RIGHT ROYAL. London: William Heinemann, 1920.
KING COLE. London: William Heinemann, 1921.
THE DREAM. London: William Heinemann, 1922.
SELECTED POEMS. London: William Heinemann, 1922.
THE COLLECTED POEMS OF JOHN MASEFIELD. London: William Heinemann, 1923.
A KING'S DAUGHTER: A TRAGEDY IN VERSE. London: William Heinemann, 1923.
TRISTAN AND ISOLT: A PLAY IN VERSE. London: William Heinemann, 1927.
MIDSUMMER NIGHT AND OTHER TALES TOLD IN VERSE. London: William Heinemann, 1928.

POEMS: COMPLETE IN ONE VOLUME. New York: Macmillan, 1929.
THE WANDERER OF LIVERPOOL. New York: Macmillan, 1930.
A TALE OF TROY. London: William Heinemann, 1932.
A LETTER FROM PONTUS AND OTHER VERSE. London: William Heinemann, 1936.
SOME VERSES TO SOME GERMANS. London: William Heinemann, 1939.
GAUTAMA, THE ENLIGHTENED AND OTHER VERSE. London: William Heinemann, 1941.
WONDERINGS (BETWEEN ONE AND SIX YEARS). London: William Heinemann, 1943.
A BOOK OF BOTH SORTS: SELECTIONS FROM THE VERSE AND PROSE. London: William Heinemann, 1947.
ON THE HILL. London: William Heinemann, 1949.
POEMS: COMPLETE EDITION. New York: Macmillan, 1953.
THE BLUEBELLS AND OTHER VERSE. London: William Heinemann, 1961.
OLD RAIGER AND OTHER VERSE. London: William Heinmann, 1964.
IN GLAD THANKSGIVING. London: William Heinemann, 1966.
THE SEA: POEMS. London: William Heinmann, 1978.

Other Works

A MAINSAIL HAUL (1905), essays.
SEA LIFE IN NELSON'S TIME (1905), essays.
ON THE SPANISH MAIN (1906), essays.
A TARPAULIN MUSTER (1907), fiction.
CAPTAIN MARGARET: A ROMANCE (1908), fiction.
MULTITUDE AND SOLITUDE (1909), fiction.
LOST ENDEAVOR (1910), fiction.
WILLIAM SHAKESPEARE (1911), criticism.
GALLIPOLI (1916), history.
RECENT PROSE (1924), fictions, essays.
THE MIDNIGHT FOLK (1927), fiction.
CHAUCER (1931), essay.
THE TAKING OF THE GRY (1934), fiction.
PLAYS: VOLUMES I AND II (1936).
DEAR NED: THE AUTOBIOGRAPHY OF A CORPSE (1938), fiction.
SOME MEMORIES OF W.B. YEATS (1940), biographical essay.
BADON PARCHMENTS (1947), fiction.
ST. KATHERINE OF LEDBURY (1951), essays.

BIBLIOGRAPHIES

Simmons, Charles H., ed. A BIBLIOGRAPHY OF THE WORKS OF JOHN MASEFIELD. New York: Columbia University Press, 1930.

Nevinson, H.W., ed. JOHN MASEFIELD: AN APPRECIATION, TOGETHER WITH A BIBLIOGRAPHY. London: William Heinemann, 1931.

Drew, Fraser, ed. "Some Contributions to the Bibliography of John Masefield: Parts I and II." PAPERS OF THE BIBLIOGRAPHICAL SOCIETY OF AMERICA, 53 (1959), 188-96, 262-67.

Hadley-Taylor, Geoffrey, ed. JOHN MASEFIELD, POET LAUREATE: A BIBLIOGRAPHY. London: Cranbrooke Tower Press, 1960.

AUTOBIOGRAPHIES

IN THE MILL. London: William Heinemann, 1941.

> Masefield's account of the two years in which he worked in a carpet factory in Yonkers. The emphasis is on his self-education. He describes the first stages of a long road from literary ignorance to the poet laureateship of England.

NEW CHUM. London: William Heinemann, 1944.

> Masefield's account of his apprenticeship aboard the H.M.S. CONWAY when he was sixteen.

SO LONG TO LEARN: CHAPTERS OF AN AUTOBIOGRAPHY. London: William Heinemann, 1952.

> This work is strongest in its memories of the author's childhood. There is, however, attention given to the fulminating points in Masefield's career, such as his discovery of Mallory and Chaucer and his introduction to Yeats through an understanding review by H.W. Nevinson in THE LONDON CHRONICLE at the turn of the century.

GRACE BEFORE PLOUGHING. London: Reader's Union, 1966.

> Masefield's account of his first impressions as a child growing up in the town of Ledbury, England.

BIOGRAPHIES

Chase, Stanley P. "Mr. John Masefield: A Biographical Note." MODERN LANGUAGE NOTES, 40 (1925), 84-87.

> See "Criticism" below.

Nevinson, H.W. JOHN MASEFIELD: AN APPRECIATION, TOGETHER WITH A BIBLIOGRAPHY. London: William Heinemann, 1931.

> Nevinson's appreciation contains an outline of Masefield's life.

Peel, J.H.B. "My Neighbor John Masefield is 80." NEW YORK TIMES BOOK REVIEW, 1 June 1958, p. 63.

See "Criticism" below.

Lamont, Corliss. REMEMBERING JOHN MASEFIELD. Introd. Judith Masefield. Teaneck, N.J.: Fairleigh Dickinson University Press, 1971.

See "Criticism" below.

Sternlicht, Stanford. JOHN MASEFIELD. Boston: Twayne, 1977.

See "Criticism" below.

Smith, Constance Babington. JOHN MASEFIELD: A LIFE. New York: Macmillan, 1978.

Smith presents an account of Masefield in all the various stages of his life. This book is the first and so far only full biography of the poet.

LETTERS

Lamont, Corliss. REMEMBERING JOHN MASEFIELD. Introd. Judith Masefield. Teaneck, N.J.: Fairleigh Dickinson University Press, 1971.

Lamont's book contains letters.

CRITICISM

Armstrong, Martin D. "Recent English Poetry." FORTNIGHTLY REVIEW, n.s. 95 (1914), 498-512.

Masefield's poetry, above all, exemplifies "mature manifestations of the spirit of adventure," Armstrong asserts. The poet's greatest gift is his ability to portray "joyous consciousness of life lived at full pressure."

Beers, Henry A. "Book Reviews." YALE REVIEW, 2 (1913), 560-63.

Beers considers ON MULTITUDE AND SOLITUDE (1909), THE EVERLASTING MERCY (1911), THE STORY OF A ROUND HOUSE AND OTHER POEMS (1912). Masefield, he states, is a "new poet of the true old English breed. Wordsworth's attempts at the real language of men" pale beside Masefield's depiction of his people's speech. Beers compares examples of the two poets' attempts at "real speech" in poetry.

Berry, Francis. JOHN MASEFIELD: THE NARRATIVE POET. Sheffield, Engl.: J.W. Northend, 1967.

> Berry presents a tribute to Masefield's narrative techniques in verse.

Bickley, Francis. "John Masefield: A Tentative Analysis." BOOKMAN (London), 46 (1914), 295-99.

> With the exception of the early poems, almost all of what Masefield has done is "tentative": "The struggle between his instinct to shun ugliness and seek beauty, and his conviction that ugliness must be fought and not fled, has a distracting and disintegrating effect on all his work." Bickley continues, "his art can never have that power which only comes of confidence and certainty of direction" as long as these elements in Masefield's character are warring one another.

"A British Taste Battle." BOOKMAN (New York), 36 (1912), 1-6.

> An account of the feud, chronicled in the SATURDAY REVIEW a few weeks previously, between John Masefield and "TWHC," another "minor poet." The origin of the feud was critic J.E. Barton's praise of Masefield's verse.

Broad, Flora M. "Mr. Masefield's Fox Hunting." POETRY REVIEW, 11 (1920), 251-57.

> Broad says that the theme of REYNARD THE FOX (1919) is healthier and less morbid than the previous long poems of Masefield, but the coarse language, low tone, and lack of beauty in most of his work eliminates the possibility of its being true poetry.

Canby, Henry Seidel. "Noyes and Masefield." YALE REVIEW, 3 (1914), 287-302.

> Canby says that Noyes "perpetuates moral ideals which a generation hungry for success forgets or despises." He is a champion of "nobility." Masefield represents "a new and less conventional poetry, a poetry based on the passions of the common man . . . which for many of us is charged with a higher significance." Those looking for "nobility" will find in his work much to be unsympathetic toward. The only resemblance between the two poets is their "rich sentiment."

Chase, Stanley P. "Mr. John Masefield: A Biographical Note." MODERN LANGUAGE NOTES, 40 (1925), 84-87.

> Chase presents a short biographical essay on Masefield that clears up some erroneous notions about the facts of his life and work.

_____. "The Scene of THE EVERLASTING MERCY." SOUTHWEST REVIEW, (1926), 121-35.

Chase claims that despite the reference to Shropshire in the first line of the poem, the scene described is really that of Ledbury, Hertfordshire, in the Western Midlands, where Masefield grew up.

Davison, Edward. "The Poetry of John Masefield." ENGLISH JOURNAL, 15 (1926), 5-13.

Davison says that publication of THE EVERLASTING MERCY (1911) before the war began a definite reaction against the Parnasian type of verse that had survived the Edwardian times. The two major defects of Masefield's early poetry consist in a coarseness of poetic texture that results from haste and carelessness and his practice of providing a verbal photograph of an actual event instead of translating the event into poetry by modifying the everyday language describing the event into its poetic equivalent. Masefield is at his best in THE DAUBER (1913) and REYNARD THE FOX (1919), Davison states. These poems give us "the rarest of his presents, really long outbursts of beautiful, vivid poetry, uninterrupted by the clamors and banalities of his more raucous Muse." These two poems are not sordid and contain none of the gratuitous realism so often found in Masefield's poetry.

Drew, Fraser. "John Masefield and the MANCHESTER GUARDIAN." PHILO-LOGICAL QUARTERLY, 37 (1958), 126-28.

Drew presents a report on the extent and importance of Masefield's early association with the MANCHESTER GUARDIAN.

_____. "John Masefield in New Haven." YALE LIBRARY GAZETTE, 32 (1958), 151-57.

Drew presents a report of Masefield's association with Yale University and a description of the Masefield books in the Crosby Collection of that university's library.

_____. JOHN MASEFIELD'S ENGLAND: A STUDY OF THE NATIONAL THEMES IN HIS WORK. Teaneck, N.J.: Fairleigh Dickinson Press, 1973.

This study examines Masefield's work as representative of the English heritage: countryside, people, games and pastimes, ships, sailors, and soldiers.

_____. "Masefield's DAUBER: Autobiography or Sailor's Tale Retold?" MODERN LANGUAGE NOTES, 72 (1957), 99-101.

Drew says that the long narrative poem had as its germ a tale told to an "eye witness" and grew from this beginning through the intermediate form of the short story, "In the Roost." DAUBER is not, then, fundamentally autobiographical, even though its descriptive detail and theme are clearly Masefield's own.

——————. "In New York with John Masefield." TRACE, no. 27 (1958), pp. 9-12.

Drew presents a memoir of the author's pilgrimage to Masefield's New York and the recollection of the poet's American experience.

——————. "Poetry and Pugilism: John Masefield's Fights." CANADIAN FORUM, 38 (1958), 155-56.

Masefield's THE EVERLASTING MERCY owes its early popularity to its representation of one of the most exciting boxing scenes in English literature, the 1896 Corbett-Fitzsimmons bout, rather than to its evangelical theme, Drew asserts. Masefield further proved that he was a skilled fight commentator in the novel SARD HARKER (1924).

Drinkwater, John. "Mr. Masefield's DAUBER." BOOKMAN (London), 44 (1913), 124-25.

Masefield has an "instinct for tragedy" which prompts him to write about man's struggle with "external circumstance and his own primal passions," rather than an instinct for comedy which would prompt him to deal with "character in conflict." Tragedy can find complete expression only in verse; comedy only in prose.

Firkins, O.W. "Mr. Masefield's Poetry." NATION, 15 March 1919, p. 389.

Firkins asserts that SALT-WATER BALLADS (1902) indicates "vigor awaiting release." THE EVERLASTING MERCY (1911) has a feeling that is "strong and true" even though coarse. THE WIDOW ON THE BYE STREET (1912) is simply "low." One is repelled by the "feasting on calamity" in DAUBER (1913), but the work is touching. THE DAFFODIL FIELDS (1913) is "wolfish" in its greed but "feline in its playfulness"; and in its sonnets, "Mr. Masefield, for the first time, thinks." Masefield takes "a dreamer's point of view" in all his poems.

Gibson, Ashley. "Mr. John Masefield." BOOKMAN (London), 34 (1909), 8-10.

Gibson presents a general survey of Masefield's early literary contributions.

Gierasch, Walter. "Masefield's 'C.L.M.'" EXPLICATOR, 13 (1955), item 25.

Gierasch discusses the incongruities of the first stanza, which are carried with the ironies. These incongruities have their roots in bitterness and exist beyond the main irony of the poem.

John Edward Masefield

Gould, Gerald. "The Poetry of John Masefield." BOOKMAN (London), 66 (1924), 95-97.

> Masefield is responsible, more than anyone else, for making narrative poetry "a living force in English," Gould says. One should look to Masefield for movement, not plot or characterization.

Gregory, Horace. "Masefield: Shock of Rediscovery." SATURDAY REVIEW OF LITERATURE, 20 May 1950, pp. 14-16.

> Gregory claims that no one has seriously written on Masefield's poetry since the entry on the scene of the British poets who wrote a different kind of verse from his. Masefield came to prominence immediately preceding World War II and from that time on it became increasingly difficult to find a name for his verse. However, after the war a change in the literary atmosphere allowed Kipling and Hardy to be reappraised and de la Mare and Sitwell to achieve stature. Now, with the publication of ON THE HILL (1949), the shock of new discovery attends the verse of Masefield. His gifts include "a serene, clear voice," "clarity of vision," and an "unexpected kind of humour . . . that comes from a hidden source of an otherwise grave and melancholy temperament."

Hamilton, W.H. JOHN MASEFIELD: A CRITICAL STUDY. London: George Allen and Unwin, 1922; rpt. Port Washington, N.Y.: Kennikat Press, 1969.

> Hamilton presents a general survey of Masefield's work. He devotes chapters to the early verse and prose, the novels, critical works, plays, THE EVERLASTING MERCY (1911), and the sonnets. The book is designed to introduce Masefield's writings to new readers.

Harrison, Austin. "The Old English." ENGLISH REVIEW, 35 (1923), 512-15.

> An account of the circumstances attending the printing of THE EVERLASTING MERCY in the ENGLISH REVIEW.

Henderson, Alice Corbin. "Mr. Masefield's Lecture [on English Poetry]." POETRY (Chicago), 7 (1916), 301-03.

> Henderson says that Masefield's remarks in this lecture allow that poetry, with its new simplicity of diction, its use of today's speech patterns, and its direct approach to life as it is, is "simply regaining its lost kingdom." The poet is finally coming to his audience.

Hillyer, Robert. "John Masefield." DIAL, 80 (1926), 1235-40.

> Hillyer claims that Masefield is "at once the best and the worst of modern poets." Kipling and Hardy were the "worst possible" influences on the poet. Chaucer was the best. Masefield's greatest achievement is KING COLE (1921). The most accomplished of the shorter poems are "Ships," "Biography," "Cargoes," "Wild Duck,"

"The Wanderer," "The River," "Cap on Head," "The Hounds of
Hell," and "Animula."

"John Masefield's Debt to Geoffrey Chaucer." CURRENT OPINION, 60
(1916), 194-95.

> The critic claims that during a period spent working in a carpet
> factory in Yonkers, Masefield bought a copy of Chaucer's poems
> for seventy-five cents. He read the book and decided to become
> a poet. Thus Masefield brought back to English verse the "Chau-
> cerian temper . . . the vigorous speech and vital contemporaneous
> speech of life."

Lamont, Corliss. REMEMBERING JOHN MASEFIELD. Introd. Judith Masefield.
Teaneck, N.J.: Fairleigh Dickinson University Press, 1971.

> Lamont presents a loving recollection of the author's friendship
> with Masefield, dating from 1924. The volume includes many let-
> ters from Masefield and his wife, Constance, to various persons.

Lloyd, Francis V., Jr. "Masefield's 'Sea Fever.'" EXPLICATOR, 3 (1945),
item 36.

> Lloyd asserts that the poem does not end on an ironic note. The
> work "gypsy" in line 9 may mean "wanderer" and not necessarily
> connote "sly" or "cunning." Examples are given of several other
> poets' use of "gypsy" that clearly means "wanderer."

Middleton, George. "John Masefield's THE EVERLASTING MERCY." BOOK-
MAN (London), 43 (1912), 525-27.

> Middleton presents a discussion of subject matter and themes in the
> work.

Monroe, Harriet. "John Masefield." POETRY (Chicago), 7 (1917), 320-23.

> Monroe considers the poem, LOLLINGDON DOWNS (1917), "an
> inquiry into the meaning of modern life by a modern mind . . . a
> search for the principle of life, a search through and beyond the
> assertions of science."

"Mr. Masefield as a Playwright." NATION, 22 March 1919, p. 432.

> The volume, COLLECTED POEMS AND PLAYS (1919), is a record
> of a period of experimentation in new dramatic forms, claims the
> critic. It includes a realistic tragedy in "low life" (NAN), a
> historic tragedy in realistic prose (POMPEY), a tragedy of revenge
> in poetic prose (THE FAITHFUL), and an adaptation of the Greek
> formula in rhymed verse in various meters (PHILIP THE KING).
> These experiments have varying success and the failure, when it
> occurs, is due to Masefield's error in his theory of tragedy. The

power of tragedy does not come, as he believes, from "a delighted brooding on excessive, terrible things," but rather from "contemplating the spiritual reaction of a great personality confronted by excessive, terrible things." Masefield overemphasizes plot at the expense of character in NAN, POMPEY, and PHILIP THE KING. THE FAITHFUL is a triumphant success.

Murry, John Middleton. "The Future of Mr. Masefield." ATHENAEUM (London), 25 June 1920, pp. 823-24.

Murry claims that Masefield's most valuable qualities are his "creative energy," his "interestingness," and the "nature of his faith." ENSLAVED: AND OTHER POEMS (1920) marks a higher level of achievement than REYNARD THE FOX (1919), which appeared six months previous to ENSLAVED.

_____. "The Nostalgia of Mr. Masefield." ATHENAEUM (London), 23 January 1920, pp. 104-05.

Murry discusses REYNARD THE FOX (1919) as "durable in virtue of its substance and . . . durable in virtue of its form."

Noult, Clifford A., Jr. "Masefield's 'Cargoes.'" EXPLICATOR, 16 (1958), item 31.

The poem can be read as an exaltation of the least "romantic" of the three ships, the coaster--a thoroughly commercial vessel, a true cargo ship.

Palmer, Herbert. "John Masefield: Poet Laureate." CORNHILL MAGAZINE, 156 (1937), 468-81.

Palmer presents a general survey of Masefield's life and work. He discusses his resemblances to Chaucer and Shakespeare and his influence on J. Redford Anderson, Edward Thompson, and T.S. Eliot.

Peel, J.H.B. "My Neighbor John Masefield is 80." NEW YORK TIMES BOOK REVIEW, 1 June 1958, p. 63.

Peel presents a memoir of his visit to Masefield's home, Burcote . Brook, at Clifton Hampton near Oxford.

Price, Clair. "John Masefield Talks on Literature and War." NEW YORK TIMES BOOK REVIEW, 17 March 1950, p. 12.

Price presents an account of his conversation with Masefield on the effect of World War II on art in England.

"Some Dramatic Considerations of PHILIP THE KING and PLASTER SAINTS."
POETRY REVIEW, 5 (1914), 219-23.

> The dignity of the verse suffers from Masefield's inept use of
> rhymed verse. "The happy-go-lucky method of rhyming, so ad-
> mirably adapted to THE EVERLASTING MERCY is painfully alien
> to the spirit of high seriousness which informs PHILIP THE KING."
> The most successful of the other poems in the book is "August
> 1914." The author also discusses Zangwill's PLASTER SAINTS.

Spark, Muriel. JOHN MASEFIELD. London, 1953; London: Macmillan,
1962.

> In the main, Spark offers a consideration of Masefield as a nar-
> rative writer. The author takes as her first task in considering
> the poetry the dissociation of Masefield from the Georgian group.
> She then considers the early short poems (rather than the sonnets
> or lyrics) as they "reveal the narrative poet in the making." This
> investigation is followed by an examination, closely and at length,
> of THE EVERLASTING MERCY (1911), DAUBER (1913), and REY-
> NARD THE FOX (1919).

Sternlicht, Stanford. JOHN MASEFIELD. Boston: Twayne, 1977.

> The first serious study of Masefield's canon after his death, Stern-
> licht's work is an explanation and evaluation of all of Masefield's
> published writing. The first chapter is "the longest, most compre-
> hensive, most accurate" biography of the poet in print; chapter
> 2 treats the poems "Sea Fever" and "Cargoes"; chapter 3 discusses
> the long narrative poems from THE EVERLASTING MERCY through
> KING COLE; chapter 4 deals with the remainder of the poetry,
> in particular with "August 1914" and "The Wanderer"; chapter 5
> evaluates Masefield as dramatist; chapter 6 discusses the novels;
> chapter 7 deals with Masefield's nonfiction; and chapter 8 dis-
> cusses Masefield's literary career as England's most popular poet
> laureate.

Strong, L.A.G. JOHN MASEFIELD. London: Longmans, Green, 1952.

> This brief study investigates selections from the poetry and prose
> that the author considers most representative of Masefield's genius.

Thomas, Gilbert. JOHN MASEFIELD. New York: Macmillan, 1933.

> The author "aims at conveying a vital general impression" of Mase-
> field's vision, concentrating on his most representative writings.
> This study includes chapters on biography, the lyrics and ballads,
> THE EVERLASTING MERCY (1911), the narrative poems, the prose,
> and the plays.

_____. "Mr. Masefield's Poetry." FORTNIGHTLY REVIEW, 99 (1913), 1154-64.

Thomas considers THE WIDOW IN THE BYE STREET (1912), DAUBER (1913), and THE EVERLASTING MERCY (1911) in their relation to new developments in poetry.

Waugh, Arthur. "The New Poetry." QUARTERLY REVIEW (London), 226 (1916), 382.

The article praises the "highly impressive meter" and "glowing passion for morality" in THE EVERLASTING MERCY (1911) and THE WIDOW IN THE BYE STREET (1912).

White, Newman I. "John Masefield--An Estimate." SOUTH ATLANTIC QUARTERLY, 26 (1927), 189-200.

The principal value of Masefield's prose works, White claims, is that they throw light on his poetry. "He is the best living exemplar of Romanticism as the art of wandering in time and space." A recent reviewer, White says, is justified in calling his novels "almost a public scandal," and adds that the impression given by his plays "wears off too early" and "their characters are impermanently realized." White concludes that Masefield's reputation stands on his poetry, the greatest claim of which is a concrete and abstract worship of beauty in which the emotional tone predominates over the intellectual. The greatest fault in the poetry is technical carelessness.

EDWIN MUIR (1887-1959)

PRINCIPAL WORKS

Poetry

FIRST POEMS. London: L. and V. Woolf, 1925.
CHORUS OF THE NEWLY DEAD. London: L. and V. Woolf, 1926.
VARIATIONS ON A TIME THEME. London: J.M. Dent, 1934.
JOURNEYS AND PLACES. London: J.M. Dent, 1937.
THE NARROW PLACE. London: Faber, 1943.
THE VOYAGE AND OTHER POEMS. London: Faber, 1946.
THE LABYRINTH. London: Faber, 1949.
COLLECTED POEMS, 1921-1951. London: Faber, 1952.
PROMETHEUS. London: Faber, 1954.
ONE FOOT IN EDEN. London: Faber, 1956.
COLLECTED POEMS, 1921-1958. London: Faber, 1960.
SELECTED POEMS. London: Faber, 1965.

Other Works

WE MODERNS: ENIGMAS AND GUESSES (1918), prose.
LATITUDES (1924), criticism.
TRANSITION, ESSAYS ON CONTEMPORARY LITERATURE (1926), criticism.
THE MARIONETTE (1927), fiction.
THE STRUCTURE OF THE NOVEL (1928), essay.
JOHN KNOX (1929), biography.
Franz Kafka's THE CASTLE, with Willa Muir (1930), translation.
THE THREE BROTHERS (1931), fiction.
Franz Kafka's THE GREAT WALL OF CHINA, with Willa Muir (1933), transla-
    tion.
Franz Kafka's THE TRIAL, with Willa Muir (1937), translation.
Franz Kafka's AMERICA, with Willa Muir (1938), translation.
THE PRESENT AGE FROM 1914 (1939), criticism.
Franz Kafka's IN THE PENAL SETTLEMENT, with Willa Muir (1948), translation.
ESSAYS ON LITERATURE & SOCIETY (1949), essays.

BIBLIOGRAPHIES

Mellown, Elgin, and Peter Hoy, eds. A CHECKLIST OF WRITINGS ABOUT EDWIN MUIR. University: University of Alabama Press, 1964.

Mellown, Elgin, ed. "A Checklist of Critical Writings about Muir." BULLE-TIN OF BIBLIOGRAPHY, 25 (1968), 157-60.

Hoy, Peter, ed. "A Preliminary Checklist of Addenda to Mellown's BIBLI-OGRAPHY." SERIF, 6 (1969), 27-32.

Mellown, Elgin, ed. BIBLIOGRAPHY OF THE WRITINGS OF EDWIN MUIR. University: University of Alabama, 1970.

AUTOBIOGRAPHY

THE STORY AND THE FABLE: AN AUTOBIOGRAPHY. London: Hogarth Press, 1954.

> Muir tells of his life from age fourteen, when he moved from Ork-ney to Glasgow, to age thirty-five. He records his slow process of self-understanding and self-realization.

BIOGRAPHIES

Gill, Bernard. "Sunset Light: A Poet's Last Days." WESTERN HUMANITIES REVIEW, 14 (1960), 283-88.

> This article is a neighbor's loving account of Muir's last days at Priory Cottage.

Butter, P.H. EDWIN MUIR: MAN AND POET. Edinburgh: Oliver and Boyd; New York: Barnes and Noble, 1966.

> See "Criticism" below.

Muir, Willa. BELONGING: A MEMOIR. London: Hogarth, 1968.

> Willa Muir presents her recollections of her life with the poet. Her book covers the time between 1918, the year of their marriage, and 1959, the year of Muir's death.

CRITICISM

Blackmur, R.P. "Edwin Muir: Between the Tiger's Paw." KENYON REVIEW, 21 (1959), 419-36. Rpt. In FOUR POETS ON POETRY. Ed. Don Cameron Allen. Baltimore: Johns Hopkins Press, 1959, pp. 24-43.

Blackmur presents an examination of Muir's poetry as "the mode of his thoughtful piety, the mode of the mind's action where his piety is not only enacted for him but takes independent action on its own account for all of us."

Butter, Peter H. "Edwin Muir: THE JOURNEY BACK." ENGLISH, 16 (1967), 218-22.

Butter describes THE JOURNEY BACK as Muir's "longest mature poem" and presents his understanding of the poem as the poet's attempt "to treat his ideas on time and human life more comprehensively than before."

_____. EDWIN MUIR: MAN AND POET. Edinburgh: Oliver and Boyd; New York: Barnes and Noble, 1966.

Butter devotes this extended study to both the life and work of the poet. It contains chapters on the influence of Nietszche on the early works, and chapters on the early poems, the poems written between 1932 and 1937, the translations, the poetry of 1938-1945, and Muir's career as a reviewer. The final pages contain a bibliography.

Carruth, Hayden. "An Appreciation of Muir." PRAIRIE SCHOONER, 32 (1958), 148-52.

Carruth presents a discussion of Muir's use of symbolic image as central to his poems.

_____. "The Separate Splendours: Homage to Edwin Muir. I. To Fashion the Transitory." POETRY (Chicago), 88 (1956), 389-93.

Carruth's thesis is that Muir, although closely allied by the problem of time in his poetry to the metaphysics, is "Wordsworthian in tone and manner." This Wordsworthian realism manifests itself in the kind of poetic realism that involves a "matter-of-fact use of the poetic conventions for what they are--the easiest, clearest, and most economical means of coming to terms with the substance of one's imagination." He characterizes Muir as "a fabulist who relies for his effects on a high degree of poetic realism."

"COLLECTED POEMS 1921-1958." LISTENER, 63 (1960), 941.

Muir, says the critic, "succeeds by a quality that does not easily attract attention--the patient and utterly sincere following of his own inner direction, which is a deeply traditional one."

Emig, Janet. "The Articulate Breath." ENGLISH JOURNAL, 52 (1963), 540-41.

On "The Animals." Emig presents a close examination of Muir's poem "The Animals" in an effort to determine what, in the piece, "requests, even urges, contemplation and study."

Galler, David. "Edwin Muir." POETRY (Chicago), 94 (1959), 330-33.

Galler presents an examination of Muir's poetry as operating in the realm of "Contradiction" with guilt, innocence, time, eternity, and "the intransigent will that seeks the ultimate truth and the Platonic passion for denying ends" as its subject matter.

Garber, Frederick. "Edwin Muir's Heraldic Mode." TWENTIETH CENTURY LITERATURE, 12 (1966), 96-103.

Garber devotes this article to a discussion of Muir's use of heraldry to "symbolize order, tradition and history, a meaningful, recognizable continuity in time."

Gardner, Helen Louise. EDWIN MUIR. Cardiff: University of Wales Press, 1961.

Gardner identifies Muir as a "self-educated man" and, therefore, "quite outside the professional pattern of most poets of this century," and proceeds toward a short survey of his poetic achievement.

Grice, Fred. "The Poetry of Edwin Muir." ESSAYS IN CRITICISM, 5 (1955), 243-52.

Grice presents an examination of Edwin Muir's poetry as influenced by the "New Apocalyptic" movement that flourished in England in the late 1920s.

Hall, John Clive. EDWIN MUIR. Writers and Their Work Series, no. 71. London: Longmans, Green, 1956.

Hall presents a brief survey of Muir's literary contribution, attributing his success to a "fundamental quality" described as "the uncompromising individuality of his vision."

Hamburger, Michael. "Edwin Muir." ENCOUNTER, 15 (1960), 46-53.

The distinction of Muir's poetry lies in the "totality of its means and ends," says Hamburger. He "persisted in relating everything to everything, and subordinated every activity to one dominant concern." His "moral vision and his imaginative vision were not in conflict, and both were integral parts of his nature."

Hassan, Ihab H. "Of Time and Emblematic Reconciliation." SOUTH ATLANTIC QUARTERLY, 58 (1959), 427-39.

Hassan's essay explores the poet's preoccupation with time, Christian vision, and use of emblems and allegory. Extended comments on rhythm and imagery.

Hixson, Allie Corbin. EDWIN MUIR: A CRITICAL STUDY. New York:
Vantage, 1977.

> Hixson illustrates Muir's development and accounts for the early
> neglect of his poetry in Britain and continued neglect in the Unit-
> ed States. She gives lengthy treatment to the "Lallans" contro-
> versy and to Muir's translation work.

Hoffman, Daniel. BARBAROUS KNOWLEDGE: MYTH IN THE POETRY OF
YEATS, GRAVES AND MUIR. New York: Oxford University Press, 1967.

> Hoffman presents a full survey of Muir's career and concludes that
> his verse, "like that of Graves and Yeats, depends upon a struc-
> ture of myth, but unlike theirs, his myth is at no point fully re-
> vealed to him. He discovers the parts of it patiently poem after
> poem. . . . An archetypal myth, based upon the image of man's
> fall and his search for the recovery of lost innocence, becomes in
> time Muir's own redemption from the seeming chaos of modern
> life. . . . He begins with all the ancient beliefs available to him
> which Yeats and Graves had in later life to excavate by toil and
> study; but Muir abjures these given structures for a myth of his
> own which reflects his Christian humanism as well as his sense
> that modern Scotland is one with ancient Troy, and that he, a
> contemporary man, relives the fable foretold in the Old Testament."

_____. "Edwin Muir: The Story and the Fable." YALE REVIEW, 55 (1966),
403-26.

> Hoffman devotes this article to a clarification of the mythical
> interpretation of life at the center of Muir's writings.

Holloway, John. "The Poetry of Edwin Muir." HUDSON REVIEW, 13 (1960),
550-67.

> Holloway's critical approach consists of treating Muir's poems as
> "deeds of the imagination which have penetrated into the realities,
> and the humanly important realities, of human life." He asserts
> that an investigation of only the formal qualities of the poems--
> diction, imagery, syntax, et cetera--can only yield secondary
> merits as opposed to the primary merits yielded from seeing the
> poems as he does.

Holroyd, Stuart. "The Celtic Genius in Modern Poetry." POETRY REVIEW,
45 (1954), 21-26.

> Holroyd's thesis is that Celtic literature is more significant today
> than ever because of its "imagination, mysticism and a sense of
> the past." Muir is one of the great Celtic writers. He is a
> mystic "possessing the vision of Blake and the capacity for passion-
> ate thinking of Donne."

Huberman, Elizabeth. THE POETRY OF EDWIN MUIR: THE FIELD OF GOOD AND ILL. New York: Oxford University Press, 1971.

In her study, Huberman "explores, through analysis of the most important poems in each of Muir's volumes, the major themes of his poetry, the directions in which these themes have developed, and the technical resources through which they have been patterned and expressed." She places Muir in the particular poetic tradition in which he belongs, describes his relationship with other poets, and determines his stature by evidence in his poems and the response of contemporary critics.

Jennings, Elizabeth. "The Living Dead--VII: Edwin Muir as Poet and Allegorist." LONDON MAGAZINE, 7 (1960), 43-56.

Jennings traces Muir's development as a visionary poet.

Jocelyn, Sister M. "Herbert and Muir: Pilgrims of Their Age." RENASCENCE, 4 (1963), 127-32.

Sister Jocelyn uses eight poems in the Evergreen edition of the COLLECTED POEMS to demonstrate the resemblances and the differences of Herbert's and Muir's poetry, and also to "provide an accurate illustration of the peculiar amalgam of the seventeenth century and contemporary religious sensibility which we see in Muir."

Mills, Ralph J., Jr. "Eden's Gate: The Later Poetry of Edwin Muir." PERSONALIST, 44 (1963), 58-78.

Mills examines what he views as the apocalyptic vision and prophetic substance of Muir's last poems. He sees the poems as maintaining "a double focus--the condition of the world before man flawed its unity and the human estate as it now is standing side by side." Extended comments are offered on the role of dreams in the poems.

Moore, Geoffrey. POETRY TODAY. London: Longmans, Green, 1958.

Moore comments briefly on Muir's "feeling for simplicity and sobriety"--a feeling that accounts for the popularity of his poetry following the Second World War.

O'Connor, Philip. "Specks of a Golden Age." In his THE LOWER VIEW. London: Faber, 1960, pp. 175-81.

This is an account of an interview O'Connor conducted with Muir a few months before Muir died. Of Muir he states, "he regarded literary work as an enterprise. . . . This enterprising attitude to writing vitiates it from its most profitable concourse with life and culture--any dynamic, creatively modifying concourse . . . Muir invested--with certain creative results--in the idea of teachability,

the explainability of a great deal of literature. This is a wise
inroad into too mysteriously an assessed matter. But preliminary
superficiality, over-rationality, is, of course, a price to pay."

Peschmann, Hermann. "Edwin Muir: A Return to Radical Innocence." EN-
GLISH, 12 (1959), 168-71.

Peschmann's essay is devoted to a clarification of "self-integration,
the keynote of the poet's work." This "self-integration" is described as "a reintegration, a return to that state of 'integrity'
that preceded the Fall." In Muir's late work this quest or journey
of the soul is interpreted more and more in Christian terms.

Raine, Kathleen. "Edwin Muir: An Appreciation." TEXAS QUARTERLY, 4
(1961), 233-45.

Raine presents a general survey of Muir's poetic achievement.

Scholten, Martin. "The Humanism of Edwin Muir." COLLEGE ENGLISH, 21
(1960), 322-26.

Scholten defines Muir's basic viewpoint or philosophical attitude
as "humanistic" and discusses its manifestation in the poetry.

Summers, Joseph H. "The Achievement of Edwin Muir." MASSACHUSETTS
REVIEW, 2 (1961), 240-60.

Summers traces the poet's literary and intellectual development
from the appearance, in 1918, or WE MODERNS to that of ONE
FOOT IN EDEN in 1956. He examines Muir's poetic achievement
and his contributions to fiction and literary criticism.

_____. "Edwin Muir." BOOKS ABROAD, 34 (1960), 123.

A brief survey of Muir's literary career.

Watson, J.R. "Edwin Muir and the Problem of Evil." CRITICAL QUARTERLY,
6 (1964), 231-49.

The problem that informs a great deal of Muir's poetry, Watson
claims, is that of the frustrated hero "striving to find some meaning and purpose in life which can exist beside the realities of
pain and disease and suffering." Watson's article examines this
problem as it manifests itself in the poetry, which he characterizes
as being of serious and compressed utterance, of the Scottish and
also of true European tradition."

WILFRED EDWARD SALTER OWEN (1893-1918)

PRINCIPAL WORKS

Poetry

POEMS. London: Chatto and Windus, 1920.
THE POEMS OF WILFRED OWEN. London: Chatto and Windus, 1931.
THIRTEEN POEMS. Northampton, Mass.: Gehenna Press, 1956.
COLLECTED POEMS OF WILFRED OWEN. London: Chatto and Windus, 1963.

BIBLIOGRAPHIES

Milne, H.H.M. "The Poems of Wilfred Owen." BRITISH MUSEUM QUARTER-
LY, 9 (1935), 19-20.

White, William. WILFRED OWEN, 1893-1918: A BIBLIOGRAPHY. Prefacing
note Harold Owen. Kent, Ohio: Kent State University Press, 1967.

BIOGRAPHIES

Owen, Harold. JOURNAL FROM OBSCURITY: MEMOIRS OF THE OWEN
FAMILY: WILFRED OWEN 1893-1918. 3 vols. London: Oxford University
Press, 1963-65.

> Volume 1 is entitled CHILDHOOD; volume 2, YOUTH; and volume
> 3, WAR.

A TRIBUTE TO WILFRED OWEN. Comp. Thomas J. Walsh. Birkenhead, Engl.:
Birkenhead Institute, 1964.

> This magazine of tributes from the poet's friends includes a brief
> biography by the compiler. A.S. Paton contributed an essay on
> Owen's childhood. See "Criticism" below.

White, Gertrude M. WILFRED OWEN. New York: Twayne, 1969.

> White's book contains some biographical material. See "Criticism" below.

Stallworthy, Jon. WILFRED OWEN. Oxford University Press, 1974.

> Stallworthy presents a survey of Owen's life and work. See "Criticism" below.

LETTERS

THE COLLECTED LETTERS OF WILFRED OWEN. Ed. Harold Owen and John Bell. London and New York: Oxford University Press, 1967.

CRITICISM

Bebbington, W.G. "Jessie Pope and Wilfred Owen." ARIEL: A REVIEW OF INTERNATIONAL ENGLISH LITERATURE, 3 (1972), 82-93.

> This article examines Jessie Pope's role as a patriotic poet and concludes there is little connection between Pope and Owen beyond Owen's dedication to Pope, eventually cancelled, to "Dulce et Decorum Est."

Blunden, Edmund. "Mainly Wilfred Owen." In his WAR POETS 1914-1918. Writers and Their Work Series, no. 100. London: Longmans, Green, 1958, pp. 29-38.

> Blunden's study concentrates on Owen's attitudes, themes, and poetic techniques.

Brophy, James. "The War Poetry of Wilfred Owen and Osbert Sitwell: An Instructive Contrast." MODERN LANGUAGE STUDIES, 1 (1971), 22-29.

Cohen, Joseph. "In Memory of W.B. Yeats and Wilfred Owen." JOURNAL OF ENGLISH AND GERMANIC PHILOLOGY, 58 (1959), 637-49.

> Cohen investigates the reasons behind W.B. Yeats's controversial refusal to include Owen's poems in his OXFORD BOOK OF MODERN VERSE (1939).

_____. "Own Agonistes." ENGLISH LANGUAGE IN TRANSITION, 8 (1965), 253-68.

> Cohen attempts to demonstrate that "a form of homosexuality dominated Wilfred's sexual nature," stating such a demonstration is "the final key to understanding Owen's achievement, and that the position he took toward the war was almost entirely motivated by homosexual elements."

_____. "Owen's 'The Show.'" EXPLICATOR, 16 (1957), item 8.

Cohen asserts that Owen's "The Show," demonstrates the poet's technique of interpreting materials for his poems in terms of his own combat experience. The material in this poem is borrowed from Hardy's THE DYNASTS (1903-08).

_____. "Wilfred Owen: Fresher Field than Flanders." ENGLISH LANGUAGE IN TRANSITION, 7 (1964), 1-7.

Cohen comments on the various editions of Owen's poems prior to C. Day Lewis' edition of the COLLECTED POEMS (1963) and concludes that the Day Lewis edition "is considerably improved over the earlier ones."

_____. "Wilfred Owen in America." PRAIRIE SCHOONER, 31 (1957), 339-45.

Cohen investigates the reasons that explain Owen's failure to achieve popular recognition in America.

_____. "The Wilfred Owen Poetry Collection." LIBRARY CHRONICLE OF THE UNIVERSITY OF TEXAS, 5 (1955), 24-35.

This article is on the formal organization, purposes, and content of the Wilfred Owen War Poetry Collection at the University of Texas.

_____. "Wilfred Owen's Greater Love." TULANE STUDIES IN ENGLISH, 6 (1956), 105-07.

Cohen seeks "to establish the point of view that Owen was above all a spiritual poet and that the distinguishing spiritual element in his poetry is a thoroughly developed religious concept which he called the greater love. Its souce is to be found in the impact on his thinking made by the life of Jesus."

Cooke, William. "Wilfred Owen's 'Miners' and the Minnie Pit Disaster." ENGLISH, 26 (1977), 213-17.

Cooke discusses Owen's poem in its historical context.

Cox, C.B., and A.E. Dyson. "Wilfred Owen: 'Futility.'" In their MODERN POETRY: STUDIES IN PRACTICAL CRITICISM. London: E. Arnold, 1963, pp. 52-56.

Cox and Dyson praise Owen's poem "Futility" for its simple and homely vocabulary, economy, and controlled ironic tone.

Daiches, David. "The Poetry of Wilfred Owen." In his NEW LITERARY VALUES: STUDIES IN MODERN LITERATURE. Edinburgh: Oliver and Boyd, 1936, pp. 52-68.

Daiches presents a brief survey of Owen's achievement with particular emphasis on the quality of universality and penetrating insight revealed in his poems.

Fairchild, Hoxie Neale. "Toward Hysteria." In his RELIGIOUS TRENDS IN
ENGLISH POETRY 1880-1920. Vol. 5. New York: Columbia University
Press, 1962.

Owen is the best of the war poets, Fairchild claims, as well as
the most traditional. "He uses poetry not for the direct relief
of a hysterical state of mind, but as a means of controlling and
sublimating his distress through a loftiness of spirit which subdues
rage to sorrow and pity."

Fletcher, John. "Wilfred Owen ReEdited." ETUDES ANGLAISES, 17 (1964),
171-78.

Fletcher claims that C. Day Lewis' edition of Owen's COLLECTED
POEMS (1963) is "the most valuable so far" because of the critical
apparatus it supplies.

Freeman, Rosemary. "Parody as Literary Form: George Herbert and Wilfred
Owen." ESSAYS IN CRITICISM, 8 (1963), 307-22.

Freeman demonstrates Owen's dependence on Georgian poetic style
to increase the irony of his contrast between a woman's love and
a soldier's sacrifice.

_____. "Wilfred Owen's 'Greater Love.'" ESSAYS IN CRITICISM, 16 (1966),
132-33.

This is a letter questioning James Hill's suggestion "that the biblical allusion at the end of 'Greater Love' (see Hill, below) is
better identified with Christ's rebuke to the woman of Jerusalem
in St. Luke 23:28-29, because the passage implicitly reinforces
the tragic irony that death had more real value than life by
ironically devaluating the natural consequences of a woman's
love, i.e., giving birth to a new life." Freeman asserts that
this view is objectionable inasmuch as it "excludes any interpretation of 'you may touch them not' which is conspicuous in the
encounter between Mary and Christ."

Gose, Elliott B., Jr. "Digging In: An Interpretation of Wilfred Owen's
'Strange Meeting.'" COLLEGE ENGLISH, 22 (1961), 417-19.

Gose analyzes the poem and concludes that "it demonstrates Owen's
realization that what was of transcendent importance to the fight-
ing man should not be his physical suffering contrasted with the
comforts of civilians, but first the dehumanization of war, its
ability to turn men into spiritual automatons, and second the para-
doxical alternative it offered him of learning pity through involvement with suffering."

Hazo, Samuel J. "The Passion of Wilfred Owen." RENASCENCE, 11 (1959), 201-08.

> Hazo traces Owen's passage "from acrimony to pity, from the descriptive to the transfigurative, from the autobiographical to the objective." To exemplify Owen's development, Hazo examines parts of several poems, including "Dulce et Decorum Est," "At a Cloory Near the Ancre," and "Anthem for Doomed Youth."

Hibbard, Dominic. "Introduction." WILFRED OWEN: WAR POEMS AND OTHERS. Ed. Dominic Hibbard. London: Chatto and Windus, 1974, pp. 30-50.

> Hibbard devotes his essay to Owen's early work, Sassoon's influence, the religious aspects, sound devices, and subject matter and images in the poems as a whole.

_____. "Wilfred Owen and the Georgians." REVIEW OF ENGLISH STUDIES, 30 (1979), 28-40.

> Hibbard discusses Owen's reading of the Georgian anthologies and other works, and the poets he may have encountered in his lifetime.

_____. "Wilfred Owen's Rhyming." STUDIA NEOPHILOLOGICA, 50 (1978), 207-14.

> Hibbard's article claims that "Wilfred Owen's invention, which was his own and not borrowed from any other poet, was the use of terminal pararhymes as a consistent rhyme scheme." Hibbard describes pararhymes (a term unknown to Owen) as "differing from half-rhyme in that there is identity not only between the consonants after the stressed vowel but also between those before it."

Hill, James J., Jr. "The Text of Wilfred Owen's 'Purple.'" NOTES AND QUERIES, 10 (1963), 464.

> Hill presents a brief discussion of C. Day Lewis' gloss on the word "King" in line 10 of "Purple."

_____. "Wilfred Owen's 'Greater Love.'" ESSAYS IN CRITICISM, 15 (1965), 476-77.

> Hill presents an objection to Rosemary Freeman's interpretation (see above) of the biblical allusion in the final line of Owen's "Greater Love."

Johnston, John H. "Poetry and Pity: Wilfred Owen." In his ENGLISH POETRY OF THE FIRST WORLD WAR: A STUDY IN THE EVALUATION OF LYRIC AND NARRATIVE FORM. Princeton, N.J.: Princeton University Press, 1964, pp. 155-209.

> Owen, like many of the other war poets, "did not fully exploit

the tragic possibilities of his material," states Johnston. This
failure is due to a stance that is too personal and subjective and
too much reliant on the lyric mode.

Lane, Arthur E. AN ADEQUATE RESPONSE: THE WAR POETRY OF WILFRED
OWEN AND SIGFRIED SASSOON. Detroit: Wayne State University Press,
1972.

> Lane examines both poets' work as "a poetry of experience."
> He contrasts their work with that of their contemporaries and
> explores their attitude toward the war as different from the at-
> titude of those not fighting. Lane states that Owen and Sassoon
> wrote poetry that "was an adequate response to the fact of mod-
> ern warfare" and demonstrated the "inoperability of experience
> and ideals" under such circumstances.

Loiseau, J. "A Reading of Wilfred Owen's Poems." ENGLISH STUDIES, 21
(1939), 97-108.

> Before the war, says Loiseau, "poetry was to Owen, as to many
> of his Victorian predecessors and Georgian contemporaries, a care-
> ful selecting of themes, words, and rhythms." During the war
> Owen "submitted to a perversion of his art" and "was turned
> into a recorder of a mad, cruel world, and, facing this task
> with fortitude, suffered agonies. . . . But from these agonies
> emerged a poetry instinct with such power of expression and
> depth of feeling as he might otherwise not have reached." Loi-
> seau traces this transition.

Masson, David I. "Wilfred Owen's Free Phonetic Patterns: Their Style and
Function." JOURNAL OF AESTHETICS AND ART CRITICISM, 54 (1955),
360-69.

> This article investigates Owen's internal alliterative and asso-
> nance patterns.

Milne, H.H.M. "The Poems of Wilfred Owen." BRITISH MUSEUM QUARTER-
LY, 9 (1935), 19-20.

> Milne presents an account of the Owen documents in the British
> Museum that are pertinent to the study of the poet's development.

O'Keefe, Timothy. "Ironic Allusion in the Poetry of Wilfred Owen." ARIEL:
A REVIEW OF INTERNATIONAL ENGLISH LITERATURE, 3 (1972), 72-81.

> O'Keefe investigates Owen's use of literary and biblical allusions
> in order to effect in his readers a horror of war. He asserts that
> the inability of literary tradition to carry the meaning of modern
> warfare is, paradoxically, what triggered a better method of bring-
> ing the issue home to readers.

Pinto, Vivian de Sola. "Trench Poets." In his CRISIS IN ENGLISH POETRY, 1880-1940. London: Hutchinson's University Library, 1951, pp. 121-40.

Pinto examines several of Owen's works--among them "The Seed," "Exposure," "Greater Love," "Futility," and "Strange Meeting"-- and concludes that Owen was the best of the war poets, the greatness of his poetry lying in its moral power.

Posey, Horace G., Jr. "Muted Satire in 'Anthem for Doomed Youth.'" ESSAYS IN CRITICISM, 21 (1971), 377-81.

Posey asserts that "in this sonnet Owen's underlying sense of a more primitive and purer Christianity lies at the back of a satire which sorrowfully excoriates the pretentious ceremonials of contemporary orthodox, revealing it as empty and ultimately inadequate." Posey's article is an elaboration of this thesis.

Sitwell, Osbert. "Wilfred Owen." ATLANTIC MONTHLY, 186 (1950), 37-42.

The essay constitutes a personal reminiscence.

Spender, Stephen. "Poetry and Pity." In his THE DESTRUCTIVE ELEMENT. Boston: Houghton Mifflin, 1936, pp. 217-21.

Spender contends that "pity is not an adequate emotion in poetry. It tends to become negative, exhaustive, sentimental, masochistic. The only way it can avoid sentimentality is to plunge into extreme subjectivity and become projected as self pity."

Stallworthy, Jon. WILFRED OWEN. Chatterton Lecture on an English Poet, British Academy. London: Oxford University Press, 1970.

Stallworthy presents a survey of Owen's life and work, and focuses attention on the poet's admiration for Keats.

_____. WILFRED OWEN. London: Oxford University Press, 1974.

Stallworthy considers this biography of Owen as complementary to Harold Owen's JOURNAL FROM OBSCURITY and Owen and John Bell's edition of the poet's COLLECTED LETTERS. These three books form the foundation for an edition of the COMPLETE POEMS of Wilfred Owen on which Stallworthy is now engaged.

Walsh, Thomas Jeffrey, comp. A TRIBUTE TO WILFRED OWEN. Birkenhead, Engl.: Birkenhead Institute, 1964.

This work commemorates the opening of the Wilfred Owen Memorial Library at the Birkenhead Institute. It includes memoirs, biographical material, and critical essays by Thomas Jeffrey Walsh, A.S. Paton, Sigfried Sassoon, Joseph Cohen, and others.

Welland, D.S.R. "Half Rhyme in Wilfred Owen: Its Derivation and Use."
REVIEW OF ENGLISH STUDIES, 1 (1950), 226-41.

> Welland claims that theories that assert that Owen learned his
> half-rhyme technique from American and English poets (Emily
> Dickinson, Henry Vaughan, G.M. Hopkins) or from Welsh writ-
> ings cannot be substantiated. Welland also demonstrates that
> French symbolist poet Laurent Tailhade's familiarizing Owen with
> the poetry of Jules Romain is responsible for Owen's continual
> use of half-rhyme.

———. WILFRED OWEN: A CRITICAL STUDY. London: Chatto and Windus, 1960.

> This study is designed for readers already familiar with Owen's
> poetry and concentrates on his craftsmanship rather than on his
> life. In addition to detailed analysis of the poetry, Welland
> offers comments on the importance of Owen's use of half rhyme,
> and gives a history of publications, editions, and criticism of the
> poetry.

White, Gertrude M. WILFRED OWEN. New York: Twayne, 1969.

> The purpose of this study is "to show Owen's growth as a poet,
> the forces that brought him to poetic maturity, and his attainment
> of an individual style."

"Wilfred Owen Against the Background of Two Wars." TIMES LITERARY SUP-
PLEMENT, 28 August 1953, p. xxvii.

> This article identifies Owen (along with Sigfried Sassoon) as re-
> sponsible "for poetry coming to be regarded as the most effective
> means of creating attention among those with social or political
> interests instead of soothing and titillating the sensitive minds of
> people with conventional aesthetic tastes." The critic states,
> "Owen, like Mr. Sassoon, wrote out of obligation: to bring
> home to others a state of affairs whose reality he wishes to ham-
> mer into their consciousness. It was this moral protest that one
> finds echoed by nearly all the poets of any consequence in the
> 1930s."

KATHLEEN JESSE RAINE (1908-)

PRINCIPAL WORKS

Poetry

STONE AND FLOWER: POEMS 1935-43. London: Editions Poetry, 1943.
LIVING IN TIME. London: Editions Poetry, 1946.
THE PYTHONESS AND OTHER POEMS. London: Hamish Hamilton, 1949.
SELECTED POEMS. New York: Weekend Press, 1952.
THE YEAR ONE. London: Hamish Hamilton, 1952.
THE COLLECTED POEMS OF KATHLEEN RAINE. London: Hamish Hamilton, 1956.
THE HOLLOW HILL AND OTHER POEMS, 1960-1964. London: Hamish Hamilton, 1965.
NINFA REVISITED. London: Enitharmon Press, 1968.
SIX DREAMS AND OTHER POEMS. London: Enitharmon Press, 1968.

Other Works

Denis de Rougemont's TALK OF THE DEVIL (1945), translation.
Honoré de Balzac's COUSIN BETTE (1948), translation.
Honoré de Balzac's LOST ILLUSIONS (1951), translation.
WILLIAM BLAKE (1951), criticism.
COLERIDGE (1953), criticism.
BLAKE AND ENGLAND (1960), criticism.
DEFENDING ANCIENT SPRINGS (1967), criticism.
Calderon de la Barca's LIFE IS A DREAM, with R.M. Nadal (1968), translation.
WILLIAM BLAKE AND TRADITIONAL MYTHOLOGY (1969), criticism.

BIBLIOGRAPHY

Mills, Ralph J., Jr., ed. "Selected Bibliography." In his KATHLEEN RAINE. A CRITICAL ESSAY. Grand Rapids, Mich.: Eerdmans, 1967, pp. 47-48. See "Criticism" below.

CRITICISM

Adams, Hazard. "The Poetry of Kathleen Raine." TEXAS STUDIES IN EN-
GLISH, 37 (1958), 114-26.

> Adams divides Raine's poetry into two categories that "invoke dif-
> ferent female powers and express female attitudes toward those
> powers." In the first group he places those poems "in which the
> woman, aware of, and apparently comfortable with, her role of
> pythoness, priestess, and goddess, casts spells and makes invoca-
> tion." In the second are poems "in which the woman is a medium
> for rather than a source of magical powers."

Grubb, Frederick. "Forms of Flight: Herbert Read, Edwin Muir, and Kathleen
Raine." In his A VISION OF REALITY: A STUDY OF LIBERALISM IN TWEN-
TIETH CENTURY VERSE. London: Chatto and Windus, 1965, pp. 105-16.

> Grubb comments thus on Raine's work: "The virtue of the poem
> is: this scientist is feminine in a rare sense. Women poets too
> often run to ecstasy or gentility, the Magna Mater or the Bride
> of Christ pose. Miss Raine has the wisdom, basis, and tact, that
> one associates with Emily Dickinson and Frances Cornford. . . .
> Her learning is fertilized by feminism. Her feminity consists in
> magnanimity--her readiness to entertain her experience; to her,
> science is not a weltanschauung, nor is nature a mine of symbols
> awaiting exploitation. Science is a means to sympathetic under-
> standing and nature is to be invited, rather than forced, to enrich
> the personality." Grubb goes on to discuss the technical strengths
> and weaknesses of STONE AND FLOWER (1943), LIVING IN
> TIME (1946), THE PYTHONESS (1949), and THE YEAR ONE (1952).

Justice, Donald. "Sacred and Popular." POETRY (Chicago), 91 (1957), 41-
44.

> Justice comments on the symbolic structure, themes, and interest
> in "runic spells" manifested in Raine's poetry.

Mills, Ralph J. KATHLEEN RAINE: A CRITICAL ESSAY. Grand Rapids,
Mich.: Eerdmans, 1967.

> Mills perceives Raine as a religious and visionary poet in the tra-
> dition of Blake, Milton, Coleridge, Shelley, Yeats, and Edwin
> Muir, and presents an analysis of her work with emphasis on her
> use of symbolism.

_____. "The Visionary Poetry of Kathleen Raine." RENASCENCE, 14 (1962),
139-54, 159.

> Mills describes Raine as "a seer and visionary" through whose gifts
> "the elements of nature regain voice and image and bring to light
> the secrets of a design that incorporates man as well." He investi-

gates the themes and poetic speech of poems from STONES AND
FLOWERS (1943), THE PYTHONESS (1949), and THE YEAR ONE
(1953).

Nemerov, Howard. "Seven Poets and the Language." In his POETRY AND
FICTION: ESSAYS. New Brunswick, N.J.: Rutgers University Press, 1963,
pp. 213-14.

> Nemerov discusses "the world of the poems" in Raine's THE YEAR
> ONE (1952). He describes this world as one "which has time
> but no history, centered around the mystery of incarnation, that
> most famous Example never appearing on the scene."

Owen, Evan. "The Poetry of Kathleen Raine." POETRY (Chicago), 80 (1952),
32-36.

> More than anything else, Owen asserts, Raine's poetry bespeaks
> "the poet's search for the faith and the love that will integrate;
> that will weld all the broken particles of modern life into the
> perfection of a rose, a tree." Owen comments on the symbolism
> and pantheistic elements in her poetry, and on the relation of the
> poetry to the sculpture of Brancusi and the paintings of Matta.
> He concludes that her close identification with her poetry explains
> why she is not a great poet: "It would appear that in the very
> nature of their being, women cannot attain that degree of aloof-
> ness necessary to the production of the superlative in poetry."

"A Timeless World." TIMES LITERARY SUPPLEMENT, 9 March 1956, p. 148.

> The article presents a survey of Raine's poetry with emphasis on its
> development and Platonic approach.

Zinnes, Harriet. "COLLECTED POEMS Reviewed." PRAIRIE SCHOONER, 31
(1957), 289-93.

> Zinnes presents a discussion of Raine's poetry in the light of her
> preface to COLLECTED POEMS (1957).

DAME EDITH LOUISA SITWELL (1887-1964)

PRINCIPAL WORKS

Poetry

THE MOTHER AND OTHER POEMS. Oxford: Printed for the author, 1915.
TWENTIETH-CENTURY HARLEQUINADE AND OTHER POEMS, with Osbert
    Sitwell. Oxford: B.H. Blackwell, 1916.
CLOWNS' HOUSES. Oxford: B.H. Blackwell, 1918.
FAÇADE. London: Favil Press, 1922.
BUCOLIC COMEDIES. London: Duckworth, 1924.
THE SLEEPING BEAUTY. London: Duckworth, 1924.
POOR YOUNG PEOPLE AND OTHER POEMS, with Osbert and Sacheverell
    Sitwell. London: Fleuron, 1925.
TROY PARK. London: Duckworth, 1925.
RUSTIC ELEGIES. London: Duckworth, 1927.
FIVE POEMS. London: Duckworth, 1928.
GOLD COAST CUSTOMS. London: Duckworth, 1929.
THE COLLECTED POEMS OF EDITH SITWELL. London: Duckworth, 1930.
FIVE VARIATIONS ON A THEME. London: Duckworth, 1933.
SELECTED POEMS: WITH AN ESSAY ON HER OWN POETRY. London:
    Duckworth, 1936.
POEMS, NEW AND OLD. London: Faber, 1940.
STREET SONGS. London: Macmillan, 1942.
GREEN SONG AND OTHER POEMS. London: Macmillan, 1944.
THE SONG OF THE COLD. London: Macmillan, 1945.
THE SHADOW OF CAIN. London: John Lehmann, 1947.
THE CANTICLE OF THE ROSE: SELECTED POEMS 1920-1947. London: Mac-
    millan, 1949.
FAÇADE AND OTHER POEMS 1920-1935. London: Duckworth, 1950.
POOR MEN'S MUSIC. London: Fore Publications, 1950.
SELECTED POEMS: A SELECTION BY THE AUTHOR. Harmondsworth, Engl.:
    Penguin Books, 1952.
GARDENERS AND ASTRONOMERS. London: Macmillan, 1953.
THE COLLECTED POEMS. New York: Vanguard Press, 1954.
THE OUTCASTS. London: Macmillan, 1962.

MUSIC AND CEREMONIES. New York: Vanguard Press, 1963.
SELECTED POEMS OF EDITH SITWELL. Chosen, introd. John Lehmann. London: Macmillan, 1965.

Other Works

CHILDREN'S TALES--FROM THE RUSSIAN BALLET (1920), fiction.
POETRY AND CRITICISM (1925), criticism.
ALEXANDER POPE (1930), criticism.
ASPECTS OF MODERN POETRY (1934), criticism.
VICTORIA OF ENGLAND (1936), biography.
I LIVE UNDER A BLACK SUN (1937), fiction.
LOOK! THE SUN (1941), anthology of poetry.
FANFARE FOR ELIZABETH (1946), biography.
QUEENS AND THE HIVE (1962), biography.

BIBLIOGRAPHIES

Fosenberg, Lois D., ed. "Edith Sitwell: A Critical Bibliography 1915-1950." BULLETIN OF BIBLIOGRAPHY AND MAGAZINE NOTES, 21 (1953-1954), 40-43, 57-60.

Fifoot, Richard, ed. A BIBLIOGRAPHY OF EDITH, OSBERT AND SACHEVERELL SITWELL. Soho Bibliographies, 11. 2nd rev. ed. London: Rupert Hart-Davis, 1971.

Ehrstine, John W., and Douglas D. Rich, eds. "Edith Sitwell: A Critical Bibliography 1951-1973." BULLETIN OF BIBLIOGRAPHY AND MAGAZINE NOTES, 31 (1974), 111-16.

AUTOBIOGRAPHIES

"Some Notes on My Own Poetry." LONDON MERCURY, 31 (1935), 448-54.

> Sitwell analyzes some of her own work. The major emphasis is on sound, that is, her manipulation of vowels and consonants to achieve certain effects. She explains her method of developing "sense values" and of conveying the inner significance of certain objects through the arrangement of verbal texture.

TAKEN CARE OF: AN AUTOBIOGRAPHY. London: Hutchinson, Athenaeum, 1965.

> Sitwell presents a scattered, humorous account of her life that includes anecdotes about famous personalities, renditions of her encounters with her enemies, discussions, of her poetry, and authoritative comments on the nature of eccentricity.

BIOGRAPHIES

Lehman, John. EDITH SITWELL. Writers and Their Work Series, no. 25. London: Longmans, Green, 1952.

> Lehman's book contains brief biographical material. See "Criticism" below.

Salter, Elizabeth. THE LAST YEARS OF A REBEL: A MEMOIR OF EDITH SITWELL. London: Bodley Head, 1967.

> Salter, who was secretary-companion to Sitwell during her last eight years, provides a glimpse into the end of her life, which was ruined by failing health, failing powers, and debt.

Lehman, John. A NEST OF TIGERS: THE SITWELLS AND THEIR TIMES. London: Macmillan, 1968.

> Lehman's book contains only enough biographical material as is necessary to provide a background for the subject, which is the public reaction to the Sitwells and their work, and the Sitwell's reaction to the public. See "Criticism" below.

LETTERS

SELECTED LETTERS OF EDITH SITWELL. Ed. John Lehman and Derek Parker. London: Macmillan, 1970.

CRITICISM

Beach, Joseph Warren. "Baroque: The Poetry of Edith Sitwell." NEW MEXICO QUARTERLY REVIEW, 19 (1949), 163-76.

> Beach presents a brief description of the artistic contribution of the three Sitwells and an evaluation of Edith Sitwell's poetic achievement as an example of the baroque style.

Bottomley, Gordon. "A Consideration of Miss Edith Sitwell's 'Green Song.'" LIFE AND LETTERS, 45 (1945), 34-40.

> Bottomley explores Sitwell's use of syllabic and rhythmic techniques, line repetitions, and constant symbols to build poems of "conscious symphonic design" and mystic sensibility.

Bowra, Cecil M. EDITH SITWELL. London: Anglo-French Literary Services; Monaco: Lyrebird Press, 1947.

> Bowra presents a brief survey of Sitwell's poetry up to 1945. Considers visual sensibility, fullness of texture, sound systems, imaginary worlds, and use of irony and satire.

Braybrooke, Neville. "The Poetry of Edith Sitwell." CANADIAN FORUM, 32 (1952), 58-59.

> Braybrooke presents a survey of Sitwell's work from 1916 to 1952. Discusses her involvement with WHEELS, an annual of contemporary verse that was produced in 1916 and ran for six cycles precipitating the defined split in English poetry into two camps: the reactionary and the avant-garde. Consideration is given to CLOWNS' HOUSES (1918), the first book taken seriously by the critics, and also to the poet's affinities with the French symbolists, especially Rimbaud. Her influence on Dylan Thomas is also discussed.

Brooks, Benjamin G. "The Poetry of Edith Sitwell." FORTNIGHTLY REVIEW, 125 (1926), 189-202.

> The article traces the development of Sitwell's poetry from 1915 to 1926.

Brophy, James D. EDITH SITWELL: THE SYMBOLIST ORDER. Carbondale: Southern Illinois University Press, 1968.

> The first half of the book is devoted to an examination of Sitwell's criticism, the second half to a study of the organization of her poetry around such central symbols as shadow, sun, and darkness.

Burnett, Hugh, and Feliks, Topolski, eds. "Six English Self-Portraits." HARPER'S, 230 (1965), 56-58.

> This interview was conducted by John Freeman for a British Broadcasting Company television series edited by Hugh Burnett. Sitwell recalls her ancestry and childhood and comments on the nature of her creativity.

Clark, Kenneth. "On the Development of Sitwell's Later Style." HORIZON, 16 (1947), 7-17.

> Through an analysis of several of Sitwell's poems, the author shows how the poet's later style was evolved in the ten years between GOLD COAST CUSTOMS (1929) and POEMS, NEW AND OLD (1940), and was the result of a gradually flowering faith. Clark concludes by asserting that Sitwell's place in English literature is with the religious poets of the seventeenth century: "She has experienced imaginatively, not merely intellectually, the evil and misery of the world and has overcome that experience by the conviction . . . that all creation is one under the Divine Love."

Cronin, Vincent. "The Poetry of Edith Sitwell." MONTH, n.s. 18 (1957), 337-43.

> The article asserts that an "orderly variety" expresses Sitwell's development as a poet and a person.

Crowder, Richard. "Mr. MacNeice and Miss Sitwell." POETRY (London), 63 (1944), 218-22.

> An examination of Sitwell's influence on Louis MacNeice. Through a series of examples the author illustrates MacNeice's takeover of the Sitwellian themes of the plight of the aged, the nostalgic look at the world through a "child cult," the use of "rococo ornament," a prediction for figurative language, and a certain manner of rhyme.

Driberg, Tom. "Edith Sitwell at Home." ENCOUNTER, 26 (1966), 51-55.

> This is an anecdotal and informative recollection of the author's friendship with Sitwell. Much of the account is devoted to Saturday afternoon tea parties in the poet's Bayswater flat thirty-five years previous.

Eastman, Max. THE LITERARY MIND. New York: Scribner's, 1931, pp. 84, 191-92.

> The author sees Sitwell as one of the group of modern writers who are "fighting for the right of literary men to talk loosely and yet be taken seriously in the scientific age." Article contains discussions of "Aubade" and of Sitwell's concept that poetry is aimed at "heightening consciousness."

Edwards, P.D. "Watteau and the Poets." MODERN LANGUAGE NOTES, 74 (1959), 295-97.

> Edwards claims that Sitwell, who shares many of the imaginative preoccupations of the French symbolists, has drawn heavily on the "masks" of the old Italian commedia dell'arte: "Harlequin and Pierrot, Pantaloon, Il Magnifico, Il Dottore, Il Capitaneo and the rest crowd ubiquitously into her early poetry. As in Watteau's 'fetes galantes' and in the poetry of the French symbolists, they adapt themselves ideally to the mixture of fantasy and realism of which her early poetry is constituted."

Empson, William. SEVEN TYPES OF AMBIGUITY. London: Chatto, 1930.

> Contains a brief discussion of Sitwell's use of synaesthesia. See pages 16-17.

Gransden, K.W. "Collected Poems." LISTENER, 58 (1957), 533.

> This collection is a landmark in contemporary poetry, says Gransden. Sitwell's early poems are "voices in a dream . . . far from life." Her later verse reveals a religious approach via the poetic art to the acute and terrifying problems raised by recent history.

Graves, Robert. CONTEMPORARY TECHNIQUES OF POETRY. Hogarth Essays, no. 8. London: Hogarth, 1925.

> Graves believes that Edith Sitwell's poetry has many untraditional qualities. The article contains an analysis of "Sleeping Beauty." See pages 44–45.

"GREEN SONG AND OTHER POEMS." TIMES LITERARY SUPPLEMENT, 2 September 1944, p. 428.

> The article discusses Sitwell's ability to make common words "rich and strange."

Gregory, Horace. "Canticle of the Rose: Poems 1917–1949." NEW YORK TIMES BOOK REVIEW, 11 December 1949, p. 5.

> Sitwell, Hardy and Yeats created a unity of traditional and experimental forms among the trans-Atlantic poets, states the critic.

_____. "The 'Vita Nuova' of Baroque Art in the Recent Poetry of Edith Sitwell." POETRY (Chicago), 66 (1945), 148–56.

> Gregory asserts that Sitwell, like Richard Crashaw, the only defined Baroque poet, illustrates a mastery of the Baroque imagination in poetry. Article comments on her poems "A Young Girl" and "O Bitter Love, O Death."

Grigson, Geoffrey. "An Examination of the Work of Edith Sitwell." BOOKMAN (London), 53 (1931), 242–45.

> Grigson presents a general survey of Sitwell's work.

Harrington, David V. "The 'Metamorphosis' of Edith Sitwell." CRITICISM, 9 (1967), 80–91.

> Harrington presents a detailed consideration of the early and late versions of Sitwell's long poem, METAMORPHOSIS. Harrington concludes that both versions should be considered separately and judged on its own terms. The comparison "offers a convenient testing ground for tracing the poet's development and shifts of interest" as her career went forward.

Hassan, Ihab. "Edith Sitwell and the Symbolist Tradition." COMPARATIVE LITERATURE, 7 (1955), 240–51.

> Hassan presents a detailed analysis of modes of poetic expression in the symbolist tradition found in Sitwell's verse: phantasmic image, synaesthesia, images of "conceit," "symbolic image" (verbal conceits drawn from many areas of knowledge and language levels), auditory conceits, incantation and the highly intricate sound patterns.

Hofmann, Ann. EDITH SITWELL: A CONTRIBUTION TO THE STUDY OF MODERNIST POETRY. Immensee, Switz.: Calendaria, 1942.

This book concerns itself with studies of Sitwell's techniques (metre, rhyme, texture, rhythm), imaginative impetus, choice of imagery, and attitudes toward life, death, time, and illusion.

Howarth, R.G. "New Perceptions With Special Reference to the Poetry of Edith Sitwell." In SOME RECENT DEVELOPMENTS IN ENGLISH LITERATURE. Ed. A.J.A. Waldock, R.G. Howarth and E.J. Dobson. Sydney: Australasian Medical, 1935, pp. 18–32.

Howarth interprets Sitwell's poetry as "not an entire break with the past but a return to the great English artists of the 'rhetorical' tradition--that is, the predecessors of Wordsworth, with those of his contemporaries and successors who have not been strongly influenced by him--and an attempt to introduce some of the qualities of modern French poetry."

Khatchadourian, Haig. "Some Major Trends in Twentieth Century English Literature." VISVABHORATI QUARTERLY, 27 (1961), 140–49.

Khatchadourian presents a brief sketch of some of the characteristic features of twentieth-century literature as seen in its historical and cultural environs. The author identifies Sitwell as one of the poets who has found spiritual peace through religious mysticism.

Kitchin, Laurence. "Edith Sitwell: 1887-1964." LISTENER, 72 (1964), 980.

GOLD COAST CUSTOMS, published in 1929, is important, Kitchin says, not so much for its technical virtuosity but for its resort to primitivism. In it, one must look for understanding of machine-age problems in the patterns of more primitive societies, to see change in the terms of reference. In the later volume, THE SONG OF THE COLD (1945), the significant element is the use of symbolism; for it is from this point on that Sitwell depends on a simple fusion of fertility symbols, a reversion to the basic sign language modern man shares with primitive man. Her verbal skills broadened to fit the ultimate subject, war, and the thrust was then not toward perfection but toward survival.

Lehman, John. EDITH SITWELL. Writers and Their Work Series, no. 25. London: Longmans, Green, 1952.

This essay provides information on Sitwell's place in literary history, on her childhood and family background. The author presents lengthy discussion of her poetry and a shorter consideration of her prose works.

_____. A NEST OF TIGERS: THE SITWELLS IN THEIR TIMES. London: Macmillan, 1968.

This book attempts to "describe and make a personal interim assessment of the impact of the three Sitwells on their times, that is, on the last fifty years of literary, artistic and musical history in Britain (and to a certain extent also, of course, in America." It studies at length their most important works of fiction, poetry, travel and autobiography, as well as their social and historical background and changing circle of friends.

Lindsay, Jack. MEETINGS WITH POETS: MEMORIES OF DYLAN THOMAS, EDITH SITWELL, LOUIS ARAJON, PAUL ELUARD, TRISTAN TZARA. London: Muller, 1968.

Lindsay presents a comprehensive account of the author's memories of Sitwell.

_____. "The Poetry of Edith Sitwell." LIFE AND LETTERS, 64 (1950), 39-52.

Lindsay discusses Sitwell's focus on "the deadening and dissociative pressure of modern times on people and culture and the need to establish a new relation to the Romantic movement in which there would be a gentle fusion between the individual poet and the masses."

Megroz, R.L. THE THREE SITWELLS: A BIOGRAPHICAL AND CRITICAL STUDY. Port Washington, N.Y.: Kennikat Press, 1927, reissued 1969.

This study provides family history, an account of the Sitwells' childhoods, discussion of the three as "personalities," and considerations of the literary movement they spurred.

Mills, Ralph. EDITH SITWELL: A CRITICAL ESSAY. Contemporary Writers in Christian Perspective Series. Grand Rapids, Mich.: Eerdmans, 1968.

Mills presents an essay that includes biographical information and an examination of Sitwell's work, form, and developmental and systematic point of view.

_____. "Edith Sitwell: Prophetess to an Age." CHRISTIAN CENTURY, 82 (1965), 652-55.

Mills presents a survey of Sitwell's work with emphasis on the gradual but distinct changes in style and theme as her artistic output continued over a period of fifty years.

_____. "The Poetic Roles of Edith Sitwell." CHICAGO REVIEW, 14 (1961), 33-64.

Mills presents a study of the mask that Sitwell abandoned in her poetry in order to dramatize her viewpoint. Her writing displays several modes of expression and technique which correspond to the different phases of her thought and attitudes. Her work falls into three stages, each with its own voice, rhetoric, interests, and outlook. Mills discusses in detail these modes and stages.

Muir, Edwin. "Edith Sitwell." NATION AND ATHENAEUM, 15 April 1925, pp. 426-27.

Muir presents a consideration of the mystical and naive elements of Sitwell's poetry, vision, and language.

———. "Miss Edith Sitwell." NATION AND ATHENAEUM, 18 September 1926, pp. 698-700.

Muir discusses transposition of imagery, imagination, "childlike vision," and the move from "inhuman vision to pity" in Sitwell's poetry.

Ower, John. "Cosmic Aristocracy and Cosmic Democracy in Edith Sitwell." CONTEMPORARY LITERATURE, 12 (1971), 527-53.

An investigation of Sitwell's ability to evolve in her poetry a complete and rounded philosophy of life. Ower labels her a "cosmos-maker" in the tradition of Dante, Spenser, Blake, Joyce, and Yeats.

———. "Edith Sitwell: Metaphysical Medium and Metaphysical Message." TWENTIETH CENTURY LITERATURE 16 (1970), 253-67.

Ower claims that in order to integrate her later poetry into an organic whole and to reflect her perception of "violent pressures of discord" Sitwell employs such metaphysical techniques as paradox and ambiguity (these generate considerable thematic irony), direct address to an imagined audience, antithesis, juxtaposition, hyperbole, punning, and conceit. This critical opinion is well supported by a discussion of several of her poems.

———. "A Golden Labyrinth: Edith Sitwell and the Theme of Time." RENASCENCE, 26 (1974), 207-17.

Ower examines the treatment of time in Sitwell's work. Particular attention is given to the later poetry.

Parker, Derek. "Edith Sitwell." POETRY REVIEW (London), 56 (1965), 18-23.

Parker discusses the effect of Sitwell's personality on the critical climate in which her work was judged.

"POEMS NEW AND OLD." TIMES LITERARY SUPPLEMENT, 16 November 1940, p. 580.

This article defends the poet against the accusation that there is little beauty in her poems. Sitwell cannot help making beauty, and in this collection it lies essentially in the main theme which is the triumph of death and the triumph of time.

"A POET'S NOTEBOOK." TIMES LITERARY SUPPLEMENT, 15 May 1944, p. 231.

Sitwell's book of notes is described as providing a portrait of her poetic mind. If understood properly, modern poetry and its criticism "are open territory where still young men who fight battles and love women and dare to sing may enter, and use the whole language without cipher or jargon." The notebook contains, besides notes of particular poets (Chaucer, Blake, Byron, Baudelaire, Pope, Herrick, Verlaine), a series of lucid notes on poetry itself: on rhythm, texture, style, form and imagery. Sitwell's strongest point is that when she thinks and writes about poetry, she is always thinking about life itself. She doesn't separate poetry from life or invent a false vital category to fit the limitations of any particular poetic school or category. Her diagnosis and evaluation of Cocteau's doctrine are, however, mistaken, according to this article.

Pearson, John. THE SITWELLS: A FAMILY'S BIOGRAPHY. New York: Harcourt, Brace, 1979.

Pearson presents the emotional, financial, and domestic history of the three Sitwells and defines their place in the English intellectual life of the twentieth century.

Pryce-Jones, Alan. "Edith Sitwell." COMMONWEAL, 14 May 1965, pp. 241-43.

Pryce-Jones says that the severe criticism Sitwell received in her later years is due to the reluctance of the critics to criticize her in her youth because they feared the tedious consequences of doing so. As she grew older, he states, she surrounded herself with sycophants. Her highly subjective assessments of the influence of vowel sounds and consonantal patterns on the imagination constitute a useless approach to criticism. He concludes that loneliness accounts for her conversion, at sixty-eight, to Catholicism.

Riding, Laura, and Robert Graves. A SURVEY OF MODERNIST POETRY. London: Heinemann, 1927.

Riding comments on the burlesque and humorous qualities of Sitwell's poetry. See pages 230-35, 247-49.

Robb, Margaret. "The Growth of a Poet." COLORADO QUARTERLY, 13 (1964), 151-64.

Robb presents a study of Sitwell's growth as a poet over fifty years. Robb claims that she had native gifts and the motivation to become an artist, and that this will, geared to sensibility and awareness, was nourished by wide reading and experience with art forms. She engaged in a practice period of finger exercises and experimentation wherein she learned what she wished to create. She imitated the masters for a period but soon grew in her own taste, gradually developing her awareness of human beings and also her compassion for and appreciation of them. Robb concludes that her ability to communicate through language increased accordingly.

Salter, Elizabeth. THE LAST YEARS OF A REBEL: A MEMOIR OF EDITH SITWELL. London: Bodley Head, 1967.

Sitwell's secretary gives a personal account of the last year of the poet's life.

Sandt, Sister Mary Callistus, O.S.F. A CRITIQUE OF DAME EDITH SITWELL'S THREE POEMS OF THE ATOMIC AGE. New York: Pageant Press, 1962.

Sandt presents a study of symbolism as the chief device in expressing the theme of sin and redemption in Sitwell's poems, "Dirge for the New Sunrise," "The Shadow of Cain," and "The Canticle of the Rose."

"SELECTED POEMS." TIMES LITERARY SUPPLEMENT, 4 July 1936, p. 559.

The article points out that Sitwell's "far-fetched and unqualified" comparisons in her introduction to SELECTED POEMS (1936) are more palatable when left vague and that her explanations of the poems' origins render the whole process of association rather trifling.

Shawe-Taylor, Desmond. "Queen Edith." NEW STATESMAN AND NATION, 23 January 1954, pp. 96-97.

The real fascination in Sitwell, Shawe-Taylor claims, is exerted not by her poetic achievement but by her perception of what is. Her life-long triumph is that of character acting and make-up.

Singleton, Geoffrey. EDITH SITWELL'S "THE HYMN TO LIFE." London: Fortune Press, 1960.

Singleton presents a full-length critical study of Sitwell's development as a major twentieth-century literary figure.

"The Sitwells." NEW YORKER, 6 November 1948, pp. 26-27.

This is an account of an interview with Edith and Osbert Sitwell.

Sitwell, Osbert. WHO KILLED COCK ROBIN? London: Daniel, 1921, p. 15.

Osbert Sitwell comments on Edith's nonuse of free verse.

"THE SONG OF THE COLD." TIMES LITERARY SUPPLEMENT, 26 January 1946, p. 45.

> This collection gives evidence that Sitwell can conceive of important and tragic themes and give expression to them. Her technique has matured so that she is now in command of all the intricacies of language with which she had formerly experimented; the result is an infinitely more subtle and flexible poetry than her earlier works. Her use of words is also more economical and controlled and her vision has matured.

Sparrow, John. SENSE AND POETRY. New Haven, Conn.: Yale University Press, 1934.

> Sparrow discusses Sitwell's use of association and her striving to convey meaning. See pages 53-55, 57-59, 63-64, 132-36.

Stanford, Derek. "Dame Edith Sitwell and the Transatlantic Muse." MONTH, n.s. 24 (1960), 13-21.

> Stanford claims that Sitwell's work is to be associated with the organicist esthetic of romanticism, in opposition to a "classical" ideal of poetry as "something possessed of irony, paradox, wit, elegance, and imaginative logic--as a form of art which contains contrarieties within a firm structure."

"STREET SONGS." TIMES LITERARY SUPPLEMENT, 7 February 1942, p. 70.

> Sitwell's handling of the three kinds of love that form the subject of this collection is discussed.

Tindal, William York. FORCES IN MODERN BRITISH LITERATURE. New York: Knopf, 1947.

> Tindal presents a consideration of the French influence on Sitwell's poetry. See pages 273-75.

Villa, Jose Garcia, ed. A CELEBRATION FOR EDITH SITWELL. Norfolk, Conn.: New Directions, 1948.

> Written on the occasion of Edith Sitwell's first visit to the United States, the book contains contributions from, among others, Stephen Spender, Osbert Sitwell, Jack Lindsay, Kenneth Clark, Gertrude Stein, W.B. Yeats, and Frederic Prokosch.

Ward, A.C. TWENTIETH CENTURY LITERATURE. London: Methuen, 1928.

> Ward claims that Sitwell uses objects, as in "Aubade," to convey impressions in her poetry. See pages 157-58.

Weeks, Edward. "The Peripatetic Reviewer." ATLANTIC MONTHLY, 215 (1965), 135-36.

> This article is the author's recollection of his friendship with Sitwell from 1923 until her death.

Williams-Ellis, A. AN ANATOMY OF POETRY. Oxford: Blackwell, 1922.

> Williams-Ellis presents a discussion of Sitwell's style and use of synaesthesia and of her serious poetry. See pages 240-46.

Wykes-Joyce, Max. TRIAD OF GENIUS. London: Peter Owen, 1953.

> Wykes-Joyce presents a survey of the work of Osbert, Sacheverell and Edith Sitwell. The book is divided into three sections, the titles of which are "Ancestry," "Biographical," and "Appreciative." There is a select bibliography.

STEPHEN HAROLD SPENDER (1909-)

PRINCIPAL WORKS

Poetry

NINE EXPERIMENTS BY S.H.S.: BEING POEMS WRITTEN AT THE AGE OF
    EIGHTEEN. Hampstead, Engl.: The author, 1928.
20 POEMS. Oxford: Basil Blackwell and Mott, 1930.
POEMS. London: Faber, 1933.
VIENNA. London: Faber, 1934.
THE STILL CENTRE. London: Faber, 1939.
SELECTED POEMS. London: Faber, 1940.
POEMS OF DEDICATION. London: Faber, 1946.
RETURNING TO VIENNA. Pawlet, Vermont: Banyan Press, 1947.
RUINS AND VISIONS. London: Faber, 1947.
EDGE OF BEING. London: Faber, 1949.
COLLECTED POEMS 1928-1953. London: Faber, 1955.
SELECTED POEMS. New York: Random House, 1964.
THE GENEROUS DAYS. London: Faber, 1971.

Other Works

THE DESTRUCTIVE ELEMENT (1935), criticism.
THE BURNING CACTUS (1936), fiction.
FORWARD FROM LIBERALISM (1937), prose.
TRIAL OF A JUDGE (1938), play.
F. García Lorca's POEMS, with J.L. Gili (1939), translation.
Rainer Maria Rilke's DUINO ELEGIES, with J.B. Leishman (1939), translation.
THE BACKWARD SON (1940), fiction.
EUROPEAN WITNESS (1946), prose.
Paul Eluard's LE DUR DÉSIR DE DURER, with F. Cornford (1950), translation.
LEARNING LAUGHTER (1952), prose.
THE MAKING OF A POEM (1955), criticism.
ENGAGED IN WRITING (1958), fiction.
THE STRUGGLE OF THE MODERN (1963), criticism.

Stephen Harold Spender

GHIKA: PAINTINGS, DRAWINGS, SCULPTURE, with P. Leigh Fermor (1964), prose.
THE YEAR OF THE YOUNG REBELS (1969), prose.

BIBLIOGRAPHY

Kulkarni, Hemant B., ed. STEPHEN SPENDER: AN ANNOTATED BIBLIOG-
RAPHY OF HIS WORKS AND CRITICISM. New York: Garland, 1975.

AUTOBIOGRAPHY

WORLD WITHIN WORLD. London: H. Hamilton, 1951.

> Spender recollects his life and literary career from childhood up to
> and including his middle years. He recounts his attempt to live
> according to a political "ideal self" and a sexual "real self."
> The book is an account of the interrelation of Spender's private
> and public lives.

CRITICISM

Cami, Ben. "Stephen Spender Engaged in Writing." NIEUW VLAAMS TIJD-
SCHRIFT, 10 (1958), 1103-06.

Cowan, S.A. "Spender's 'He Will Watch the Hawk With An Indifferent Eye.'"
EXPLICATOR, 28 (1970), item 67.

Fremantle, Anne. "Stephen Spender." COMMONWEAL, 54 (1951), 119-21.

> Although the article is mainly concerned with Spender's autobiog-
> raphy WORLD WITHIN WORLD (1951), there are several observa-
> tions on the poet's creative processes.

Gerber, Philip L., and Robert J. Gemmett. "A Conversation with Stephen
Spender: The Creative Process." ENGLISH RECORD, 18 (1968), 2-10.

> The article consists of the transcription of a videotaped discussion
> that appeared on educational television in Rochester, New York,
> as a production of the Brockport College Television Center of the
> Division of Instructional Resources. The occasion was Spender's
> serving, during 1967, as Distinguished Visiting Professor of the
> English Departments of the Brockport-Cortland-Geneseo-Oswego
> Consortium of the State University of New York. Participants in
> the discussion include Spender, Armand Burke, John Chesnut, Paul
> Curran, and Robert Gemmett. The topic is Spender's creative pro-
> cess.

Gerstenberger, Donna. "The Saint and the Circle: The Dramatic Potential of an Image." CRITICISM, 2 (1960), 336-41.

An examination of Spender's use of the traditional image of the turning wheel and the still point in TRIAL OF A JUDGE (1938). Comparisons to Eliot's use of the image and Yeats's use of the image are made.

Herzman, Ronald B. "Stephen Spender: The Critic as Poet." NOTES ON CONTEMPORARY LITERATURE, 3 (1973), 6-7.

Jacobs, Willis D. "The Moderate Poetical Success of Stephen Spender." COLLEGE ENGLISH, 17 (1956), 374-78.

Jacobs claims that Spender's failure to achieve the literary status promised in his earliest work can be attributed to "bathos, eruptions of false notes, and dismaying errors in taste." Particularly during his political period he "often betrayed the integrity of poetry in his effort to preach." It is in his elegies of "man's loneliness and death," that his talent as a minor poet asserts itself, Jacobs concludes.

_____. "Spender's 'I Think Continually of Those.'" MODERN LANGUAGE NOTES, 65 (1950), 491-92.

Jacobs devotes this short article to the "intentional, enriching ambiguity" of the final lines of the poem.

Knieger, Bernard. "Spender's 'Awakening.'" EXPLICATOR, 12 (1954), item 30.

Knieger discusses the theme, imagery, and complexity of the poem.

Kulkarni, H.B. STEPHEN SPENDER: POET IN CRISIS. Glasgow: Blackie, 1971.

Kulkarni's study examines the thesis that "Spender provides a clear example of how creative impulse is shaped by the stresses and strains of political, social, and personal crises."

Marcus, Mordecai. "'Walden' as a Possible Source for Stephen Spender's 'The Express.'" THOREAU SOCIETY BULLETIN, no. 75 (1961), p. 1.

Marcus asserts that the details and overtones in one of Thoreau's descriptions of a railway train in WALDEN are similar to those in Spender's "The Express," and it is probable that Thoreau provided Spender with the concept and important details for his poem.

Seif, Morton. "The Impact of T.S. Eliot on Auden and Spender." SOUTH ATLANTIC QUARTERLY, 53 (1954), 61-69.

Seif claims that under Eliot's influence Spender manifested a pre-

occupation with the tradition of European culture, considered political solutions as less important than his own integrity as artist,
searched for the resolution of the world's disharmonies through individual action, and appropriated a "sensitive, inward vocabulary
of feeling and intuition."

"A Self-Revealing Poet." TIMES LITERARY SUPPLEMENT, 31 December 1971,
pp. 1629-30.

This article presents a survey of Spender's contribution to twentieth-
century poetry. Spender's poetry is characterized as "an attempt
at redemptive and quasi-religious self-searching" rather than as
the fruit of social or political concern.

Smith, Hallett. "Spender's 'I Think Continually of Those.'" EXPLICATOR, 4
(1944), item 33.

Smith discusses the Laurentian images found in the poem.

Stanford, Derek. STEPHEN SPENDER, LOUIS MacNEICE, CECIL DAY LEWIS.
Contemporary Writers in Christian Perspective Series. Grand Rapids, Mich.:
Eerdmans, 1969.

In this essay, Stanford examines the "sensibility, perception, and
feeling tone" of Spender's poems. See pages 11-23.

Thompson, Leslie M. "Spender's 'Judas Iscariot.'" ENGLISH LANGUAGE
NOTES, 8 (1970), 126-30.

Thompson suggests that Spender's idea of Judas as liberator betrayed
by Christ has precedents in the poetry of Oscar Wilde, W.B. Yeats,
and D.H. Lawrence.

Walcutt, Charles C. "Spender's 'The Landscape Near an Aerodome.'" EXPLI-
CATOR, 5 (1947), item 37.

Walcutt discusses the theme and images of the poem.

Weatherhead, A.K. "Stephen Spender: Lyric Impulse and Will." CONTEMPO-
RARY LITERATURE, 12 (1970), 451-65.

In this essay, Weatherhead considers two impulses at work in Spender's poetry that remain at odds, often rendering the poems inef-
fectual. These two impulses are "the will . . . which is to work
in the outside world, and the senses . . . that work in their own
leisure to spell out the lyrical poetry."

_____. STEPHEN SPENDER AND THE THIRTIES. Lewisburgh, Pa.: Bucknell
University Press, 1975.

Most of Weatherhead's book is devoted to the "formal perfection" of Spender's poetry. The brief introductory chapter is followed by chapters on politics and poetry, the work of other poets of the thirties, Spender's poetry as it appeared volume by volume with concentration on "the essence of his poetry--the heart of the matter."

DYLAN MARLAIS THOMAS (1914-53)

PRINCIPAL WORKS

Poetry

18 POEMS. London: Sunday Referee and the Parton Bookshop, 1934.
TWENTY-FIVE POEMS. London: J.M. Dent, 1936.
THE MAP OF LOVE. London: J.M. Dent, 1939.
THE WORLD I BREATHE. Norfolk, Conn.: New Directions, 1939.
NEW POEMS. Norfolk, Conn.: New Directions, 1943.
DEATHS AND ENTRANCES. London: J.M. Dent, 1946.
SELECTED WRITINGS OF DYLAN THOMAS. Norfolk, Conn.: New Directions, 1946.
TWENTY-SIX POEMS. London: J.M. Dent, 1950.
COLLECTED POEMS 1934-1952. London: J.M. Dent, 1952.
IN COUNTRY SLEEP AND OTHER POEMS. Norfolk, Conn.: New Directions, 1952.

Other Works

PORTRAIT OF THE ARTIST AS A YOUNG DOG (1940), fiction.
THE DOCTOR AND THE DEVILS (1953), filmscript.
QUITE EARLY ONE MORNING (1954), broadcasts.
UNDER MILD WOOD (1954), drama.
ADVENTURES IN THE SKIN TRADE (1955), fiction.
A CHILD'S CHRISTMAS IN WALES (1955), fiction.
A PROSPECT OF THE SEA (1955), fiction.
COLLECTED PROSE (1969), prose.
EARLY PROSE WRITINGS (1971), prose.

BIBLIOGRAPHIES

Buff, W.H., comp. "Bibliography." In THE POETRY OF DYLAN THOMAS.
Ed. Elder Olson. Chicago: University of Chicago Press, 1954.

Rolph, J. Alexander, ed. DYLAN THOMAS: A BIBLIOGRAPHY. London: Dent, 1956.

Brinnin, John Malcolm, ed. A CASEBOOK ON DYLAN THOMAS. New York: Crowell, 1960.

> See "Criticism" below.

Theison, Sister Lois, ed. "Dylan Thomas: A Bibliography of Secondary Criticism." BULLETIN OF BIBLIOGRAPHY AND MAGAZINE NOTES, 26 (1969), 9-28, 32, 36, 59-60.

Maud, Ralph, and Albert Glover, eds. DYLAN THOMAS IN PRINT: A BIBLIOGRAPHICAL HISTORY. Pittsburgh: University of Pittsburgh Press, 1970.

BIOGRAPHIES

Brinnin, John Malcolm. DYLAN THOMAS IN AMERICA. Boston: Little, Brown, 1955.

> Brinnin presents an account of Thomas' visits to America from February of 1950 to November of 1953.

Fraser, G.S. DYLAN THOMAS. London: Longmans, Green, 1957.

> Fraser's book contains a sketch of Thomas' life. See "Criticism" below.

Thomas, Caitlin. LEFTOVER LIFE TO KILL. Boston: Little, Brown, 1957.

> This is an enraged account of Caitlin's life with and without the poet.

DYLAN THOMAS: THE LEGEND AND THE POET. A COLLECTION OF BIOGRAPHICAL AND CRITICAL ESSAYS. Ed. E.W. Tedlock. London: William Heinemann, 1960.

> The first part of this collection consists of twenty-one essays of a biographical nature. The contributors include Pamela Hansford Johnson, Augustus John, Laurence Durrell, Roy Campbell, Theodore Roethke, David Daiches, George Barker, and Louis MacNeice. See "Criticism" below.

Jones, Richard. "The Dylan Thomas Country." TEXAS QUARTERLY, 4 (1961), 34-42.

> Jones presents background material with photographs of key places in the poet's homeland.

Ackerman, John. DYLAN THOMAS: HIS LIFE AND WORK. New York: Oxford University Press, 1964.

> Biographical information is contained in this study that connects Thomas' art to the traditions of the environment in which the poet and his contemporaries grew up and about which they wrote. See "Criticism" below.

Jones, Thomas Henry. DYLAN THOMAS. New York: Barnes and Noble, 1966.

> See "Criticism" below.

Lewis, Min. LAUGHARNE AND DYLAN THOMAS. London: Dennis Dobson, 1967.

> See "Criticism" below.

Fitzgibbon, Constantine. THE LIFE OF DYLAN THOMAS. Boston: Little, Brown, 1975.

> Fitzgibbon treats Thomas' family background and early years, the beginning of his creative years, the stormy relationship with Caitlin, and ends with an account of the poet's four journeys to America. See "Criticism" below.

Ferris, Paul. DYLAN THOMAS. London: Hodder and Stouton, 1977.

> Ferris presents a detailed biography, full of facts previously unknown.

LETTERS

LETTERS OF DYLAN THOMAS TO VERNON WATKINS. Ed. Vernon Watkins. New York: New Directions, 1957.

White, W. "The Poet as Critic: Unpublished Letters of Thomas." ORIENT/WEST (Tokyo), 7 (1962), 63-73.

SELECTED LETTERS OF DYLAN THOMAS. Ed. Constantine Fitzgibbon. Toronto: McClelland and Stewart, 1966.

COMPANION

See Tindall, under "Criticism" below.

NOTEBOOK

THE NOTEBOOKS OF DYLAN THOMAS. Ed. Ralph Maud. New York: New Directions, 1967.

CRITICISM

Ackerman, John. DYLAN THOMAS: HIS LIFE AND WORK. New York: Oxford University Press, 1964.

> This study stresses the importance of the poet's Welsh background and is based on "textual and biographical sources."

Adams, Robert Martin. "Taste and Bad Taste in Metaphysical Poetry: Richard Crashaw and Dylan Thomas." HUDSON REVIEW, 8 (1955), 61-77.

> This is an article that focuses principally on Thomas' "Religious Sonnets," whose central theme is Crucifixion and Resurrection. This is the earliest specific study showing affinities between Thomas and the seventeenth-century metaphysical poets.

Aivaz, David. "The Poetry of Dylan Thomas." HUDSON REVIEW, 3 (1950), 382-404.

> This article stresses the nature and variety of Thomas' highly compressed imagery and his basic theme of "process" seen in his concern with "the generative energy in natural things."

Astley, Russell. "Stations of the Breath: End Rhyme in the Verse of Dylan Thomas." PUBLICATIONS OF THE MODERN LANGUAGE ASSOCIATION OF AMERICA, 84 (1969), 1595-1605.

> This is a detailed study of this feature of Thomas' poetic technique. Astley sees a "general trend away from rebellion toward a rediscovered conservatism" in COLLECTED POEMS (1952).

Bayley, John. "Dylan Thomas." In his THE ROMANTIC SURVIVAL: A STUDY IN POETIC EVOLUTION. London: Constable, 1957, pp. 186-227.

> Bayley presents general observations on the language of Thomas' poetry based on the commonplace distinction between "the word as thing and the word as an indicator." This dual aspect of language is seen as highly important for Thomas' poetry. There is uncertainty about the poet's status because we don't know if language can do what he tried to do with it--that is, if "the consciousness of the receiver can adapt itself to such a variety of linguistic uses and such a multiplicity of verbal stimuli."

Beardsley, Monroe C., and Sam Hynes. "Misunderstanding Poetry: Notes on Some Readings of Dylan Thomas." COLLEGE ENGLISH, 21 (1960), 315-22.

Using "Altarwise by Owl-light," the authors consider four kinds of difficulties critics have with poetic obscurities. This is an essay about explication rather than an essay of explication.

Bloom, Edward A. "Dylan Thomas' 'Naked Vision.'" WESTERN HUMANITIES REVIEW, 14 (1960), 389-400.

This is a wide-ranging analysis of how Thomas worked in his unique way to accomplish what all poets attempt: "revelation," using the poetic process to strip away "all that is extraneous or delusive."

Bloom, Edward A., and Lillian D. Bloom. "Dylan Thomas: His Intimations of Mortality." BOSTON UNIVERSITY STUDIES IN ENGLISH, 4 (1960), 138-51.

Thomas is presented as closely identified with other artists dealing with the confusion and doubt of the twentieth century. However, he is also a "Romanticist," concluding as he did that "regeneration and identification of self" are all important.

Bollier, E.P. "Love, Death and the Poet Dylan Thomas." COLORADO QUARTERLY, 2 (1954), 386-407.

This article discusses Thomas' themes, techniques, and the chief influences on his work.

Bremer, R. "An Analysis and Interpretation of 'Over Sir John's Hill.'" NEOPHILOLOGUS, 53 (1969), 307-20.

The author distinguishes four main interpretations on four different levels, and contends that together they interpenetrate to yield the full meaning of the poem.

Brinnin, John Malcolm, ed. A CASEBOOK ON DYLAN THOMAS. New York: Crowell, 1960.

The essays in this volume are mainly concerned with Thomas' poems and are meant to be read as accompaniment to a careful reading of the poems. The book opens with ten of Thomas' most famous poems. These are followed by thirty-three entries, which include those by John Wain, William Empson, Edith Sitwell, Elizabeth Hardwick, Karl Shapiro, Caitlin Thomas, Pamela Hansford Johnson, Augustus John, Louis MacNeice, and Howard Moss.

_____. "Thomas' 'In the White Giant's Thigh.'" EXPLICATOR, 19 (1960), item 39.

Brinnin clarifies some obscurities in the poem by reference to Welsh legend.

Christensen, Naomi. "Dylan Thomas and the Doublecross of Death." BALL STATE TEACHER'S COLLEGE FORUM, 4 (1963), 49-53.

This article deals mainly with the sonnet sequence, "Altarwise by Owl-light," and focuses on Thomas' principal concern with the certain claims of death, against which both human love and the love of Christ are powerless.

Clair, John A. "Thomas' 'A Refusal to Mourn the Death, by Fire, of a Child in London.'" EXPLICATOR, 17 (1958), item 25.

Clair asserts that the structure of the poem, implicit in its four stanzas, integrates symbolism and imagery by establishing a basic chronological progression from the creation to the present. The poem culminates in the poet's stricture: do not mourn needlessly the lives of those who have returned to the source of all life.

Condon, Richard A. "Thomas' 'Ballad of the Long-Legged Bait.'" EXPLICA-TOR, 16 (1958), item 37.

Condon sees the poem as concerned with the loss of Eden, and as a meditation leading the fisherman to salvation by forcing him to discover the tragic incongruities between youthful delusions about the spiritual advantages of sexual love and the actual meaning, purpose, and physical consequences of such love: children and the perpetuation in the flesh of our flawed humanity. The fisherman's voyage is a thinly veiled description of the sexual act in which release is found from the spiritual travail of guilt and sin.

Cox, C.B., ed. DYLAN THOMAS: A COLLECTION OF CRITICAL ESSAYS. Englewood Cliffs, N.J.: Prentice Hall, 1966.

This anthology includes John Wain's review of COLLECTED POEMS, an introductory essay paying tribute to Thomas' celebration of life by David Daiches, John Ackerman's analysis of Welsh influence on Thomas, Elder Olson's study of the early poems, Winifred Nowotny's interpretation of "There was a Saviour," Ralph Maud's analysis of "Over Sir John's Hill," and William Empson's NEW STATESMAN review of COLLECTED POEMS (1952) and UNDER MILK WOOD (1954). Other essays are included--by Raymond Williams, David Holbrook, Annis Pratt, Robert Adams, John Bayley, and Karl Shapiro.

_____. "Dylan Thomas's 'Fern Hill.'" CRITICAL QUARTERLY, 1 (1959), 134-35.

Cox asserts that seeking to "communicate an experience that is almost beyond expression," Thomas celebrates the "divine innocence of a child." He creates both the child's fresh wondrous vision and his adult interpretation of past experience.

Crewe, J.V. "The Poetry of Dylan Thomas." THEORIA, 38 (1972), 65-83.

Crewe discusses the question, "Does Thomas have anything approaching 'classic' vitality?"

Daiches, David. "The Poetry of Dylan Thomas." ENGLISH JOURNAL 43 (1954), 349-56.

Daiches presents an assessment of Thomas' poetry that finds much to praise and some things to blame in his choice and use of themes and techniques.

Davies, Aneirin Talgan. DYLAN: DRUID OF THE BROKEN BODY. New York: Barnes and Noble, 1966.

This book stresses the importance of the religious elements in Thomas' poetic themes. Pushing hard to find "the dim halo of sanctity" in Thomas' poems, Davis investigates the "Christian allusions and archetypal Christian experience" that aid in the demonstration of how the agnostic poet with a protestant background made such a marked use (especially in his later poems) of "Christian sacramental imagery."

Davies, Walford. DYLAN THOMAS. Cardiff: University of Wales Press, 1972.

A brief chronological study of Thomas' life and works.

_____, ed. DYLAN THOMAS: NEW CRITICAL ESSAYS. London: Dent, 1972.

Entries of special importance in this collection are listed separately above and below under "Criticism."

Fitzgibbon, Constantine. THE LIFE OF DYLAN THOMAS. Boston: Little, Brown, 1975.

This biography deals with the public events, with "the recordable man," rather than with Thomas' private life. It is especially strong on the poet's family background and early years. There are few attempts to judge his poetry, although there are many illuminating observations about the poet's own views of his work and its origins.

Fraser, G.S. DYLAN THOMAS. Writers and Their Work Series, no. 90. London: Longmans, Green, 1957.

Fraser presents a sketch that includes discussions of Thomas' life, personality and works: the collections, 18 POEMS (1935), TWENTY FIVE POEMS (1936), THE MAP OF LOVE (1939), DEATHS AND ENTRANCES (1946), and the later poems.

Dylan Marlais Thomas

Frimage, George J., and Oscar Williams, eds. A GARLAND FOR DYLAN THOMAS. New York: Clarke and Way, 1963.

> Eighty-four poems by seventy-eight poets gathered from the 150 or more written between 1953 and 1963 in Thomas' honor are presented as evidence of the love and admiration of Thomas' poet-friends.

Gregory, Horace. "The Romantic Heritage in the Writings of Dylan Thomas." POETRY (Chicago), 69 (1947), 326-36.

> Gregory presents an appreciation that seeks to define the context of Thomas' poems, with some attention to "the limitations and ranges" of Thomas' vocabulary.

Greiff, Louis K. "Image and Theme in Dylan Thomas: 'A Winter's Tale.'" THOTH, 6 (1965), 35-41.

> Greiff claims that Thomas stresses the essential unity of sexual love and spiritual love. Using metaphors of "the physical world, of hunger, of sexual passion, and of religious worship," the poem is "pictorial, erotic, and religious."

Grubb, Frederick. "Worms Eye: Dylan Thomas." In his A VISION OF REALITY: A STUDY OF LIBERALISM IN TWENTIETH CENTURY VERSE. London: Chatto and Windus, 1965, pp. 179-87.

> This study describes Thomas' "mindless obscurity which offers no incentive for our efforts to understand it" but acknowledges that the poet has great power when he gives his "physical imagination full play."

Harvill, Olga DeHart. "Thomas' 'O Make Me a Mask.'" EXPLICATOR, 26 (1967), item 12.

> Harvill interprets the poem as concerned primarily with the supplicant's agony in trying to avoid the God whom he is seeking.

Hassan, Ihab H. "Thomas' 'The Tombstone Told When She Died.'" EXPLICATOR, 15 (1956), item 11.

> The poem under investigation, states Hassan, clarifies the poet's "reconciliation with the objective fact of mortality" and his "passionate apprehension of the fact of existence."

Harvard, Robert G. "The Symbolic Ambivalence of 'Green' in García Lorca and Dylan Thomas." MODERN LANGUAGE REVIEW, 67 (1972), 810-19.

> Harvard asserts that as for Lorca, "green" is for Thomas in "Fern Hill" a personalized but consistent color-symbol of conflict and tragic deception, "evolving roughly from positive to negative connotations."

Hawkes, Terence. "Dylan Thomas's Welsh." COLLEGE ENGLISH, 21 (1960), 345-47.

> Although not Welsh-speaking, Hawkes says. Thomas had a command of contemporary Welsh idioms--especially the bawdy.

Holbrook, David. DYLAN THOMAS: THE CODE OF THE NIGHT. London: Athlone Press, 1972.

> Holbrook sees Thomas as a "schizoid individual" and views his poetry as an "anguished attempt to ask and answer for himself King Lear's question: 'Who is it that can tell me who I am?'" The book discusses at length the poet's self-destructive behavior and sees it as painfully representative of the "ethos of schizoid dissociation" central to one strain of contemporary culture.

_____. LLAREGGUB REVISITED: DYLAN THOMAS AND THE STATE OF MODERN POETRY. London: Bowes, 1962. Rpt. DYLAN THOMAS AND POETIC DISSOCIATION. Carbondale: Southern Illinois University Press, 1964.

> Holbrook devotes this study to a detailed examination of what he finds disturbing in Dylan Thomas: "a metaphoric irresponsibility, a lack of maturity, and a tendency toward self-destruction."

Holperen, Max. "Dylan Thomas: A Soliloquy." FLORIDA STATE UNIVERSITY STUDIES: MONOGRAPHS IN ENGLISH AND AMERICAN LITERATURE, 11 (1953), 117-41.

> Holperen asserts that Thomas is "limited in theme and mood, and is repetitious in imagery" in his early work. After 1939, Holperen continues, "Thomas's old themes were reworked in a more mature vein, and new themes and sources of imagery were added, but the additions often became mannerisms in themselves."

_____. "Thomas' 'How Soon the Servant Sun.'" EXPLICATOR, 23 (1965), item 65.

> The poem, claims Holperen, contrasts a "sunnily optimistic" view of time and mutability with a "somberly stoic" and rather grim one.

Holroyd, Stuart. "Dylan Thomas and the Religion of the Instinctive Life." In his EMERGENCE FROM CHAOS. Boston: Houghton Mifflin, 1957, pp. 77-94.

> Holroyd makes comparisons between D.H. Lawrence and Thomas. The latter's finest poems are those that express "a feeling of man's co-existence with nature."

Horan, Robert. "In Defense of Dylan Thomas." KENYON REVIEW, 7 (1945), 304-10.

> This early article takes issue with those who criticize Thomas for

being interested not in the subject "but in the verbalized details of the subject." For Thomas, the "subject is the detail." The poet's unique qualities are stressed, as are his important affinities with traditional and contemporary fellow poets.

Howard, D.R. "Thomas' 'In My Craft.'" EXPLICATOR, 12 (1954), item 22.

"Sullen" is the key word, helping to explain the whole poem, states Howard. It refers principally to "the careful and painstaking process of construction."

Hynes, Sam. "Thomas's 'From Love's First Fever to Her Plague.'" EXPLICATOR, 9 (1950), item 18.

Hynes claims that Thomas' poems are much involved with cycles. Here he is concerned with "human development from simplicity to complexity through increased awareness."

Jackaman, Rob. "Man and Mandala: Symbol as Structure in a Poem by Dylan Thomas." ARIEL, 7 (1976), 22–33.

Jackaman discusses the "brilliant" symbolic structure of Thomas' poem "I See the Boys of Summer."

Jones, Thomas Henry. DYLAN THOMAS. New York: Barnes and Noble, 1966.

Principally a biography of Thomas, it also pays extensive attention to representative poems from each of the four periods into which his life is divided. The author is particularly convincing in his attempts to create a balanced view of the poet's difficult years.

Joselyn, Sister M. "'Green and Dying': The Drama of Fern Hill." RENASCENCE, 16 (1964), 219–21.

Thomas' poem, Sr. Joselyn claims, is a dramatization of what Karl Shapiro calls the "joyous mind" and the "fugitive mind" with the latter in the end simply "overpowering" the former.

Kazin, Alfred. "The Posthumous Life of Dylan Thomas." ATLANTIC MONTHLY, 200 (1957), 164–68.

Kazin presents an analysis of Dylan Thomas as legend and symbol. Presents a general understanding of the power of his poetry and life by its consideration of their effects on his friends and audiences.

Kidder, Rushworth. DYLAN THOMAS: THE COUNTRY OF THE SPIRIT. Princeton, N.J.: Princeton University Press, 1973.

Thomas is viewed by Kidder as preeminently a religious poet employing three types of religious imagery: "the referential, the allusive, and the thematic." These classifications lie behind the analyses of the poet's five published volumes of poetry. An appendix considers the "Tendency Toward Ambiguity in Thomas's Revisions."

Kleinman, Hyman H. THE RELIGIOUS SONNETS OF DYLAN THOMAS: A STUDY IN IMAGERY AND MEANING. Berkeley: University of California Press, 1963.

Kleinman presents an attempt to define a unified world of symbols in the sequence. The primary pattern is seen as autobiographical with the birth, life, Crucifixion, and Resurrection of Christ presented as metaphors for the poet's own experience, "principally his spiritual wrestling with the paradox of the Incarnation and the Passion."

Knieger, Bernard. "Dylan Thomas: The Christianity of the 'Altar-wise by Owl-Light Sequence.'" COLLEGE ENGLISH, 23 (1962), 623-28.

Knieger asserts that a positive Christian note is struck in the very first sonnet so that the sequence emerges as a Christian poem. The sequence is "a failure as a whole, perhaps, but a Christian one nevertheless."

_____. "Thomas' 'Light Breaks Where No Sun Shines.'" EXPLICATOR, 15 (1957), item 32.

The poem, says Knieger, can be read two ways: as dealing with the acquisition of knowledge and its effect or as presenting a description of sexual intercourse.

_____. "Thomas' 'On the Marriage of a Virgin.'" EXPLICATOR, 19 (1961), item 61.

Rather than simply contrasting the state of virginity with that of marriage, Knieger says that the poem may be describing the conception and virgin birth of Christ.

_____. "Thomas' "Sonnett II.'" EXPLICATOR, 18 (1959), item 14.

Knieger says that the theme of the sonnet is that time and death deny man's immortality, "but man's sexual nature, the means of his fall, is the means also of his regeneration."

_____. "Thomas' 'Sonnett III.'" EXPLICATOR, 18 (1959), item 25.

Knieger claims that the key to this poem is the identification of "The Lamb" with Christ. It dramatizes his birth, Crucifixion, and Resurrection.

Korg, Jacob. DYLAN THOMAS. English Authors Series, no. 20. New York: Twayne, 1965.

Korg's study consists of a biographical sketch, a general stylistic analysis, and detailed studies of all of Thomas' works. His poetry gets most of the attention, and Korg's investigations are anchored in his conviction that Thomas' poetry "attempts to make the most, rhetorically, of common spiritual convictions."

_____. "Imagery and Universe in Dylan Thomas's '18 Poems.'" ACCENT, 17 (1957), 3-15.

Korg presents an analysis stressing Thomas' search for "ultimate reality" within himself.

Leach, Elsie. "Dylan Thomas's 'Ballad of the Long Legged Bait.'" MODERN LANGUAGE NOTES, 76 (1961), 724-28.

This study interprets the poems as a narrative of Christ's salvation of mankind. The symbolism is conventionally Christian throughout, thus the sexual act is not the subject of the poem, but one of its metaphors.

Leech, Geoffrey. "'This bread I break'--Language and Interpretation." REVIEW OF ENGLISH LITERATURE, 6 (1965), 66-75.

Leech presents a discussion of Thomas' approach to literary criticism and interpretation.

Lewis, Min. LAUGHARNE AND DYLAN THOMAS. London: Dennis Dobson, 1967.

An affectionate and anecdotal guidebook to the township where Thomas lived and worked, this book throws light on the poet's character and personality.

Loesch, Katherine T. "The Shape of Sound: Configurational Rime in the Poetry of Dylan Thomas." SPEECH MONOGRAPHS, 35 (1968), 407-24.

Loesch presents a detailed study in configurational rime which she describes as involving "a basic cluster of vocalic and consonate phonemes" closely situated to one another and including "at least one core syllable with a vocalic nucleus, together with a basic suprasegmental superfix--but with the slot or slots to be filled in irregularly or unusually positioned rather than positioned according to the standard patterns." This stylistic device is found throughout Thomas' poems and is "centrally important to their inherent design."

Logan, John. "Dylan Thomas and the Ark of Art." RENASCENCE, 12 (1960), 59-66.

Logan employs a biographical approach. He asserts that Thomas used his poems to "keep himself alive" as he anguished over the universal and ubiquitous tensions between construction and destruction.

McKay, D.F. "Aspects of Energy in the Poetry of Dylan Thomas and Sylvia Plath." CRITICAL QUARTERLY, 16 (1974), 53–67.

> This article defends both poets against the charge that their work is deficient in meaning. Most critics seem to relegate the "energy" of both writers' poems to the role of "a stylistic enhancement to the poetry's literal signification." Instead, this energy is essential to the poetry as a source of "an exhilarating sense of kinesis."

Martin, J.H. "Dylan Thomas." TIMES LITERARY SUPPLEMENT, 19 March 1964, p. 235.

> Martin comments on his knowledge of the young poet's (c.1936) stress resulting from a division between what he liked and what he thought he had to do (e.g., writing obscurely, getting drunk). The poet was fascinated with "pure word patterns," their sounds and effects.

Maud, Ralph N. "Dylan Thomas' 'Collected Poems': Chronology of Composition." PUBLICATIONS OF THE MODERN LANGUAGE ASSOCIATION OF AMERICA, 76 (1961), 292–97.

> Maud asserts that the chronological presentation of COLLECTED POEMS (1952) is not definitive. The order in which Thomas wrote his poems differs significantly from that in which they were published, so that statements about poetic development based on their published order have only limited validity. Maud follows the chronology of Dylan Thomas' notebooks (1930–34) and the authority authority of his letters to Vernon Watkins for later pieces. Only published poems are discussed.

_____. "Dylan Thomas's Poetry." ESSAYS IN CRITICISM, 4 (1954), 411–20.

> This essay presents an argument about how Thomas' poetry "works." Its "basic unit" is "the short rhetorically coherent phrase." Its "strangeness" can be overcome if we "insist to ourselves that a poem means literally what it says."

_____. ENTRANCES TO DYLAN THOMAS'S POETRY. Pittsburgh: University of Pittsburgh Press, 1963.

> The book focuses on the difficulties of Thomas' poems while stressing their artistic integrity. The analysis of representative poems is meant to clarify and verify the large claims made for Thomas as a major poet.

_____. "Holbrook vs. Thomas." ESSAYS IN CRITICISM, 13 (1963), 86–88.

> This is a defense of Thomas' poetry as part of a censure of David Holbrook's highly negative critical studies of the poet (see Holbrook, above).

Melchiori, Giorgio. "Dylan Thomas: The Poetry of Vision." In his THE TIGHTROPE WALKERS: STUDIES OF MANNERISM IN MODERN ENGLISH LITERATURE. New York: Macmillan, 1956, pp. 213-42.

The author characterizes mannerism as "dominated by the taste for asymmetry and instability" and puts Thomas in the context of its twentieth-century manifestation, "funambulism." Comparisons are made between Thomas' ways with words, images, general poetic techniques, and "vision" and those of Donne, Blake, Hopkins, and Joyce.

Meyer, Robert H. "Dylan Thomas: The Experience, the Picture, and the Message." ENGLISH JOURNAL, 60 (1971), 199-204.

Thomas' poems are representative of "an art form evolving from real human experience to word pictures" meant to share "a vision or 'flashing' insight into the meaning of existence," asserts Meyer.

Miller, J. Hillis. "Dylan Thomas." In his POETS OF REALITY. Cambridge: Harvard University Press, 1965, pp. 190-216.

Thomas' poetry, says Miller, exemplifies "another vareity of the twentieth century poetry of reality." For Thomas, language is its own world, expressing at once "consciousness, body, cosmos" as "a single continuous realm."

Mills, Ralph J., Jr. "Dylan Thomas: The Endless Monologue." ACCENT 20 (1960), 114-36.

This study of Thomas' poetry focuses on his use of language and imagery and his preoccupation with time processes of life and death.

Moore, Geoffrey. "Dylan Thomas." KENYON REVIEW, 17 (1955), 258-77.

The article seeks to "place" Thomas "in his local physical and spiritual environment and against the unfolding pattern of modern verse as a whole." His Welsh background is stressed, and he is seen as a poet of life and affirmation.

Morton, Richard. "Notes on the Imagery of Dylan Thomas." ENGLISH STUDIES, 43 (1962), 155-64.

Morton states that the essential feature of all Thomas' poetry is its "warring" imagery. In his earlier poems he tended to use "archetypal images" of traditional association and obvious emotional force. His later works contained "artificial images" that were new and whose full significations were worked out specifically within a single poem.

Moynihan, William T. THE CRAFT AND ART OF DYLAN THOMAS. Ithaca, N.Y.: Cornell University Press, 1966.

> Moynihan presents an attempt to demonstrate that although "logical-ly" the poet's work is "mired in confusion," "symbolically" it manifests a "mythic unity." Moynihan also points out that Thomas' poetry is divided into periods of rebellion, debate, and consent.

_____. "Dylan Thomas' 'Hewn Voice.'" TEXAS STUDIES IN LANGUAGE AND LITERATURE, 1 (1959), 313-26.

> This is an explanation and defense of Thomas' preoccupation with "auditory effects" in his later poetry. Three types are predominant: "intonation," "phonetic suggestiveness," and "affinitive patterning." Exploiting these techniques enables Thomas to achieve "pure poetry."

_____. "Thomas' 'In the White Giant's Thigh.'" EXPLICATOR, 17 (1959), item 59.

> Moynihan discusses the poem as concerning the "dead as still liv-ing and creating in their union the evercreating earth."

_____. "Thomas ' 'Light Breaks Where No Sun Shines.'" EXPLICATOR, 16 (1958), item 28.

> The most obvious and unified meaning of the poem comes from an interpretation stressing sexual intercourse and conception, claims Moynihan.

Murdy, Louise Boughan. SOUND AND SENSE IN DYLAN THOMAS'S POETRY. Studies in English Literature, no. 20. The Hague: Mouton, 1966.

> Murdy investigates certain aspects of the sound patterns in twenty-eight of Thomas' poems. She relates sound to sense.

Neill, Michael. "Dylan Thomas's 'Taylor Age.'" NOTES AND QUERIES, 17 (1970), 59-63.

> Neill connects Thomas' tailor image with the "scissorman" associ-ated in Freudian thought with castration fantasies.

Ochshorn, Myron. "The Love Song of Dylan Thomas." NEW MEXICO QUAR-TERLY, 24 (1954), 46-65.

> Ochshorn points out that the search for love is the dominant theme of Thomas' poetry. He takes his illustrations from "I See the Boys of Summer," "The Force That Through the Green Fuse Drives the Flower," and "Fern Hill."

Olson, Elder. THE POETRY OF DYLAN THOMAS. Chicago: University of Chicago Press, 1954.

> Olson discusses the nature of Thomas' symbols and other stylistic

techniques. He considers the sonnet sequence, presents appendixes
that offer prose paraphrases of five poems and also a glossary of
certain key words.

Page, Christopher. "Dylan and the Scissorman." ANGLO-WELSH REVIEW, 24
(1974), 76-81.

Page presents an investigation of the "vindictive figure" of the
"scissorman" as it appears in Thomas' stories and poems. Where
the figure appears, "sexual sadism, mutilation, brutality, and
heavily charged, turbulent symbolism characterize the work."
Thomas' use of the figure "attests to the influence of the mental
world of the poet's childhood upon the writings of his adolescence
and maturity."

Perrine, Lawrence. "Thomas' 'Especially When the October Wind.'" EXPLI-
CATOR, 21 (1962), item 1.

The poem, Perrine claims, is "about the making of a poem," as
well as about the passage of time and the approach of death,
which stings the poet into composition.

Reddington, Alphonsus. DYLAN THOMAS: A JOURNEY FROM DARKNESS
TO LIGHT. New York: Paulist Press, 1968.

The author sees Thomas as "essentially a poet of the internal moral
workings of the soul" concerned with three major conflicts: "death-
life, sin-innocence, doubt-faith." The book attempts to find reso-
lutions to the manifold and complex paradoxes and antitheses in
the poetry.

Rickey, Mary Ellen. "Thomas' 'The Conversation of Prayer.'" EXPLICATOR,
16 (1957), item 15.

Rickey says the poem is about reversings, turnings, and exchangings.
The two people in the poems represent opposite extremes of life,
childhood and maturity, which are paradoxically alike, suggesting
the oneness of childhood and manhood.

Scarfe, Francis. "Dylan Thomas: A Pioneer." In AUDEN AND AFTER. London: George Routledge, 1942, pp. 101-17.

This is an attempt to place Thomas among his contemporaries.
Scarfe stresses Thomas' word inventions as his basic device, in-
evitable in expressing "half-perceived, incoherent sensations and
ideas." The importance of biblical symbolism and sexual symbolism
is discussed. The poet is criticized for an excessive "overlaying
of images."

_____. "The Poetry of Dylan Thomas." HORIZON, 2 (1940), 226-39.

This is a short general introduction to Thomas focusing on his affinities with Joyce as an inventor of words, his use of "mythology"
from the Bible, the importance of sexual symbolism, and the influence of Freud.

Sergeant, Howard. "The Religious Development of Dylan Thomas." REVIEW
OF ENGLISH LITERATURE, 3 (1962), 59-67.

Sergeant asserts that Thomas was a naturally religious poet, pre-
occupied as he was with spiritual values and the ultimate concerns
of existence. He also uses traditional biblical-Christian symbols,
concepts and observations, although in his own unique way. The
poet's ambiguities may arise from his methods of composition and
from a desire for paradox rather than from his uncertainties and
doubts.

Sinclair, Andrew. DYLAN THOMAS: NO MAN MORE MAGICAL. New
York: Holt, Rinehart and Winston, 1975.

Sinclair's book consists of a critical study supplemented by photographs.

Smith, A.J. "Ambiguity as Poetic Shift." CRITICAL QUARTERLY, 4 (1962),
68-74.

Smith studies "Our Eunuch Dreams" as representative of the early
Thomas because it exemplifies the poet's controlled imagination
working with the calculated exploitation of ambiguities.

Spender, Stephen. "Greatness of Aim." TIMES LITERARY SUPPLEMENT, 6
August 1954, p. 6.

Spender presents an over-all assessment of Thomas as a "great poet"
and basically a religious one.

Stanford, Derek. DYLAN THOMAS: A LITERARY STUDY. New York: Cita-
del, 1954.

The main purpose of this book is to offer a commentary on Thomas'
poems. The author, in his introduction, expresses the wish that
the book be considered a companion volume to the poet's COL-
LECTED POEMS (1952) and that the two be read in conjunction.

_____. "Dylan Thomas's Animal Faith." SOUTHWEST REVIEW, 42 (1957),
205-12.

Stanford presents a general commentary seeing Thomas as a poet
who "expresses the self by means of metaphysical exploration."

Stearns, Marshall. "Dylan Thomas's 'After the Funeral' (In Memory of Ann Jones)." EXPLICATOR, 3 (1945), item 52.

> The poem is an elegy describing burial and presenting a young boy's loving homage to a generous and pious unknown woman.

Stephens, Peter John. "Dylan Thomas: Giant Among Moderns." NEW QUARTERLY OF POETRY, 1 (1947), 7-11.

> Stephens presents an assessment of Thomas based on SELECTED WRITINGS (1946), viewing the revolutionary and experimental aspects of his work as representative of modern poetry.

Symons, Julian. "Obscurity and Dylan Thomas." KENYON REVIEW, 2 (1940), 61-71.

> Hostile to Thomas, Symons makes a distinction between obscurity of matter and obscurity of manner and sees Thomas as characterized by the latter in using "extended metaphors, private adjectives and sexual symbols to conceal a simple meaning." The poet's "obscurity of language is not always relevant to his poem's subjects; it is very often imposed from outside." He realized, Symons insists, that his subject matter was not profound and tried to hide this by obscurity of manner.

Tedlock, E.W., ed. DYLAN THOMAS: THE LEGEND AND THE POET: A COLLECTION OF BIOGRAPHICAL AND CRITICAL ESSAYS. London: William Heinemann, 1960.

> Tedlock's collection is divided into two parts. The first consists of twenty one essays of a biographical nature; the second of seventeen essays of a critical nature. Among the contributors to the critical half of the book are Frances Scarfe, D.S. Savage, Edith Sitwell, Geoffrey Gregson, Theodore Roethke, Geoffrey Moore, and Karl Shapiro, David Daiches, and G.S. Fraser.

Thomas, R. George. "Dylan Thomas: A Poet of Wales?" ENGLISH: MAGAZINE OF THE ENGLISH ASSOCIATION, 14 (1963), 140-45.

> Thomas' descriptions of himself as a Welsh poet are misleading, Thomas states, presenting, as they do, a false picture of a "provincial" poet. There are comments about the special aural qualities of Thomas' poetry--qualities which make it essential that it be heard.

Tindall, William York. "The Poetry of Dylan Thomas." AMERICAN SCHOLAR, 17 (1948), 431-39.

> Tindall has high and illuminating praise for Thomas as "the best and most magical English-speaking poet to have appeared since Yeats began to write." The influence of Freud's dream theory on the poet are emphasized.

———. A READER'S GUIDE TO DYLAN THOMAS. New York: Farrar Straus, and Cudahy, 1962.

> This is a poem-by-poem explication of Thomas' five books of poetry, with an introductory chapter briefly discussing biographical and cultural background.

Tritscher, Donald. "The Metamorphic Stop in Time of 'A Winter's Tale.'" PUBLICATIONS OF THE MODERN LANGUAGE ASSOCIATION OF AMERICA, 78 (1963), 422-30.

> This is an investigation of the poem, involving a detailed study of its language and image. Two "metaphoric themes--separation and reconciliation, and death and rebirth" are carefully examined in order to show how the poem involves a metamorphosis from "desolation and despair" to a "redemptive vision of glory."

Werry, Richard. "The Poetry of Dylan Thomas." COLLEGE ENGLISH, 11 (1950), 250-56.

> Werry discusses Thomas' unique ways with language and imagery while seeing the poet as seeking to express his own personality and concern with death.

West, Paul. "Dylan Thomas: The Position in Calamity." SOUTHERN REVIEW, 3 (1967), 922-43.

> In the first part of the article, the author treats the poet as a writer who has integrated the two roles of visionary and clown. In the second part he treats "the rhetoric of his life style." In the third part, he defends Thomas against the attack of David Holbrook in DYLAN THOMAS: THE CODE OF THE NIGHT (see Holbrook, above).

Williams, Harry. "Dylan Thomas's Poetry of Redemption: Its Blakean Beginnings." BUCKNELL REVIEW, 20 (1972), 107-20.

> This article discusses the influence of Blake on Thomas (especially the young Thomas), stressing their similar views about "redemption through annihilation" and their differing techniques.

Wittreich, Joseph Anthony, Jr. "Dylan Thomas's Conception of Poetry: A Debt to Blake." ENGLISH LANGUAGE NOTES, 6 (1969), 197-200.

> Wittreich sees Thomas as borrowing Blake's conception of contraries and transforming it into a theory of poetry.

Woodcock, George. "Dylan Thomas and the Welsh Environment." ARIZONA QUARTERLY, 10 (1954), 293-305.

Woodcock sees many of the characteristic themes of his poetry as derived from Welsh culture and tradition in general rather than from Thomas in particular.

Yeoman, W.E. "Dylan Thomas: The Literal Vision." BUCKNELL REVIEW, 14 (1966), 103-15.

Yeoman presents a "literal reading" of Thomas rather than the usual "symbolic translation" of his poetry. The poet's "mythopoetic view" is indicated by his method, working from "personal event or state toward a cosmic human vision."

Zigerell, James. "Thomas' 'When All My Five and Country Senses See.'" EXPLICATOR, 19 (1960), item 11.

Thomas asserts the primacy of feelings, arguing that the poet's heart, his intuitive part, is supplied by his senses just as is the philosopher's intellect. If his feelings are followed they will lead the poet to see himself as part of the universal scheme.

PHILIP EDWARD THOMAS (1878-1917)

PRINCIPAL WORKS

Poetry

SIX POEMS. Flansham, Sussex: Pear Tree Press, 1916.
POEMS. London: Selwyn and Blount, 1917.
LAST POEMS. London: Selwyn and Blount, 1918.
COLLECTED POEMS. London: Selwyn and Blount, 1920.
SELECTED POEMS. Newton: Gregynog Press, 1927.
TWO POEMS. London: Ingpen and Grant, 1927.
THE TRUMPET AND OTHER POEMS. London: Faber, 1940.
SELECTED POEMS. London: Hutchinson Educational, 1962.
SELECTED POEMS. London: Faber, 1964.
THE GREEN ROADS: POEMS FOR YOUNG READERS. London: Bodley Head, 1965.
EDWARD THOMAS: POEMS AND LAST POEMS. London: Macdonald and Evans Annotated Student Texts, 1973.
EDWARD THOMAS ON THE COUNTRYSIDE. A SELECTION OF HIS PROSE AND VERSE. London: Faber, 1977.
THE COLLECTED POEMS OF EDWARD THOMAS 1878-1917. Oxford, Engl.: Clarendon Press, 1978.

Other Works

THE HEART OF ENGLAND (1906), prose.
CELTIC STORIES (1911), prose.
THE COUNTRY (1913), prose.
THE HAPPY-GO-LUCKY MORGANS (1913), fiction.
THE ICKNIELD WAY (1913), prose.
CHOSEN ESSAYS (1926), prose.
ESSAYS OF TODAY AND YESTERDAY (1926), prose.
THE LAST SHEAF (1928), prose.
THE PROSE OF EDWARD THOMAS (1948), prose.

Philip Edward Thomas

BIBLIOGRAPHIES

Eckert, Robert P., comp. EDWARD THOMAS: A BIOGRAPHY AND A BIB-
LIOGRAPHY. New York: E.P. Dutton, 1937.

Cooke, William, ed. EDWARD THOMAS: A CRITICAL BIOGRAPHY 1878-
1917. London: Faber, 1970.

AUTOBIOGRAPHY

THE CHILDHOOD OF EDWARD THOMAS: A FRAGMENT OF AUTOBIOG-
RAPHY. London: Faber, 1938.

> This fragment covers the first sixteen years of Thomas' life.

THE DIARY OF EDWARD THOMAS. Chettenham, Engl.: Whittington Press,
1977.

BIOGRAPHIES

Thomas, Helen. AS IT WAS. London: William Heinemann, 1926.

> This book is the first part of a fictionalized account of Helen
> Thomas' life with the poet. It covers her relationship with Thomas
> from its beginning to their marriage.

_____. WORLD WITHOUT END. London: Faber, 1931.

> This is the second part of Helen Thomas' fictionalized account of
> her life with the poet.

Eckert, Robert P. EDWARD THOMAS: A BIOGRAPHY AND A BIBLIOGRAPHY.
New York: E.P. Dutton, 1937.

> A full biography of Thomas that contains an exhaustive bibliography,
> photographs, and letters. See "Criticism" below.

Moore, John C. THE LIFE AND LETTERS OF EDWARD THOMAS. London
and Toronto: William Heinemann, 1939.

> Moore presents a careful study of Thomas' life followed by a selec-
> tion of edited letters. The letters to Robert Frost were not avail-
> able at the time of this publication.

Farjeon, Eleanor. EDWARD THOMAS: THE LAST FOUR YEARS. Oxford:
Oxford University Press, 1958.

> Farjeon's book covers the years of her friendship with Edward Thom-

as, from the end of 1912 to the spring of 1917. Their correspondence is printed in full. See "Criticism" below.

Cooke, William. EDWARD THOMAS: A CRITICAL BIOGRAPHY. London: Faber, 1970.

See "Criticism" below.

Thomas, R. George. EDWARD THOMAS. Cardiff: University of Wales Press, 1972.

Thomas discusses Thomas' life, his beginnings as a poet, his relationship with Robert Frost, his ambivalent attitude toward Wales, and his poetic techniques.

Marsh, Jan. EDWARD THOMAS: A POET FOR HIS COUNTRY. London: Paul Elek, 1978.

A literary-biographical study, Marsh's book describes "the poet's evolution as a writer in the context of his life as a whole" and "places him in relation to the literary developments of his time-- The rise of Georgian poetry, the shift from the beautiful to the brutal which made the war poetry of Owen and Rosenberg possible, and the coming of Modernism." Marsh relates Thomas' life and work to the "Back to the Land" movement, popular in England between 1880 and 1920, and discusses the literary influence of Arthur Ransome, Eleanor Farjeon, Rupert Brooke, and Robert Frost. The biography is interwoven with detailed consideration of many poems.

Thomas, Helen. TIME AND AGAIN: MEMOIRS AND LETTERS. Ed. Myfanwy Thomas. Manchester: Carcanet Press, 1978.

Helen Thomas' daughter presents Helen's account of her childhood and adolescent years, of various episodes of her life with Edward, letters she wrote to friends, including Janet Hooten Aldis, and Eleanor Farjeon. The last part of the book is Myfanwy's rendition of Helen's life after Edward was killed in 1917.

LETTERS

Moore, John C., ed. THE LIFE AND LETTERS OF EDWARD THOMAS. London and Toronto: William Heinemann, 1939.

Farjeon, Eleanor, ed. "Letters to Eleanor Farjeon." In THE MEMOIRS OF ELEANOR FARJEON. London: Oxford University Press, 1956.

LETTERS FROM EDWARD THOMAS TO GORDON BOTTOMLEY. Ed., introd. R. George Thomas. London: Oxford University Press, 1968.

CRITICISM

Andrew, John. "Edward Thomas." In STUDIES IN THE ARTS: PROCEEDINGS OF THE ST. PETER'S COLLEGE LITERARY SOCIETY. Ed. Francis Warner. London: Basil Blackwell, 1968, pp. 10-20.

> Andrew relates the attitudes and concerns of Thomas' poetry to those in his prose works.

Ashton, Theresa. "Edward Thomas: From Prose to Poetry." POETRY REVIEW, 28 (1937), 449-55.

> This is a discussion of the stylistic relationship between Thomas' prose and poetry.

Blodgett, E.D. "Mouthful of Earth: A Word for Edward Thomas." MODERN POETRY STUDIES, 3 (1972), 145-60.

> Blodgett discusses the difference between Thomas' sensibility to the war and the sensibilities of the other war poets, especially Henry Newbolt and Wilfred Owen. He contends that the impinging of "war, infinitesimal change and mortality" shaped Thomas into the kind of war poet that he was.

Burrow, John. "Keats and Edward Thomas." ESSAYS IN CRITICISM, 7 (1957), 404-15.

> Burrow's essay suggests that the excellence of Thomas' poems written between 1913 and 1916 is as much the result of the poet's Intelligent reading of Keats--during this time he was working on a biographical and critical study of Keats--as of the acknowledged friendship and direction of Robert Frost.

Bushnell, Athalie. "Edward Thomas." POETRY REVIEW, 38 (1947), 241-52.

> Bushnell presents a study of Thomas' life and poetic achievement.

Cooke, William. EDWARD THOMAS: A CRITICAL BIOGRAPHY 1878-1917. London: Faber, 1970.

> The first part of Cooke's book is biographical and the second part traces the poet's development from what is characterized as the stylized and affected early work to an uncompromising honesty manifested in his last achievements. Cooke also examines the process by which Thomas, through "the intimate relation of his critical judgments to his habits as a poet," achieved the directness so crucial to his poetry.

_____. "Roads to France: The War Poetry of Edward Thomas." STAND, 9 (1968), 11-17.

> Cooke reviews several critics' estimates of Thomas as a war poet

and concludes that they are based "on a fundamental error of approach" since they "take it for granted that Thomas lived to become a trench poet." Cooke asserts that the poet "in no way
looked back from the trenches" but "looked outward from England
to the trenches--to that reality of war which these critics feel
he was somehow incapable of facing."

Coombes, Harry. EDWARD THOMAS: A CRITICAL STUDY. London: Chatto
and Windus, 1956; New York: Barnes and Noble, 1973.

Coombes's study includes a short biography of the poet, an investigation of his prose, a history of his critical reception, and a long
final chapter on his poetry.

_____. "The Poetry of Edward Thomas." ESSAYS IN CRITICISM, 3 (1953),
191-200.

Coombes discusses "the consistent delicacy of the nature observation" in Thomas' poetry.

Danby, John F. "Edward Thomas." CRITICAL QUARTERLY, 1 (1959), 307-17.

Danby defends his assertion that "in spite of surface similarities
between Thomas and his contemporaries" he is really "isolated in
his time. . . . His deafness to current literary voices was in fact
the sign and source of his particular strength--a strength which
enabled him to survive the almost wholesale rejection of the Georgian which has been a feature of the last two generations."

de la Mare, Walter, ed. "Foreword." COLLECTED POEMS OF EDWARD
THOMAS. London: Selwyn and Blount, 1920, pp. 5-13.

De La Mare attempts to portray Thomas "as he was to one who
knew him in his personal life."

Eckert, Robert Paul. EDWARD THOMAS: A BIOGRAPHY AND A BIBLIOG-
RAPHY. New York: E.P. Dutton, 1937.

This is a full biography of Thomas that contains a bibliography of
criticism on his work up to 1937. See "Biographies" above.

Emslie, MacDonald. "Spectatorial Attitudes." REVIEW OF ENGLISH LITERA-
TURE, 5 (1964), 66-69.

Emslie explores the social theme of Thomas' short poem, "The
Watchers."

Farjeon, Eleanor. EDWARD THOMAS: THE LAST FOUR YEARS. Oxford:
Oxford University Press, 1958.

This is the author's reminiscences of her friendship with Thomas
during the last four years of his life.

Garnett, Edward. "Edward Thomas." DIAL, 64 (1918), 135-37.

This is a brief article on the virtues of Thomas' poetry and prose sketches.

Harding, D.W. "A Note on Nostalgia." SCRUTINY, 1 (1932), 8-19.

Harding comments on the pervasive feeling of nostalgia in Thomas' poetry.

Harding, Joan. "Dylan Thomas and Edward Thomas." CONTEMPORARY RE-VIEW, 192 (1957), 150-54.

Harding compares the style of Helen Thomas' AS IT WAS (1927) with Caitlin Thomas' LEFTOVER LIFE TO KILL (1957).

Herring, Robert. "Edward Thomas." LONDON MERCURY, 15 (1927), 279-87.

Herring's essay is devoted to an investigation of the subject matter, themes, and style of Thomas' poetry.

Jacobs, R.A. "Regrets and Wishes." ENGLISH JOURNAL, 54 (1965), 569-70.

Jacobs compares Thomas' poem "The Sign Post" with Frost's "The Road Not Taken" (1916) and e.e. cummings's "anyone lived in a pretty how town" (POEMS 1923-54) and concludes that "whereas the three poems are close thematically and all three use nature as a link with man's journey through life," Thomas' poem reveals "a subtler, more complex, and delicately ironic attitude towards life and death."

Lawrence, Ralph. "Edward Thomas in Perspective." ENGLISH, 12 (1959), 177-83.

Lawrence characterizes Thomas' poetry as filled with a deep love for England, steeped in mysticism, and illuminated by the poet's happiness. He presents a brief survey of the publishing history of the poems.

Lea, F.A. "On Patriotism and Edward Thomas." ADELPHI, 14 (1938), 323-25.

Lea presents an analysis of the poem "The Other." Lea describes it as an exception in Thomas' work, which is generally "pure, passionate experience," involving little intellection.

Leavis, F.R. "Imagery and Movement." SCRUTINY, 13 (1945), 133-34.

Leavis compares Thomas' use of imagery to A.E. Housman's. The difference between the two consists in patterns of movement: "Housman's depends on our being taken up in a kind of lyrical intoxication that shall speed us on in exalted thoughtlessness.

Thomas's invites pondering and grows in significance as we ponder it."

Lehmann, John. "Edward Thomas." In his THE OPEN NIGHT. New York: Harcourt, Brace, 1952, pp. 77-86.

Lehmann characterizes Thomas as a nature poet who made the southern counties of England his "own special raw material."

Lewis, C. Day. "The Poetry of Edward Thomas." In ESSAYS BY DIVERS HANDS. Transactions of the Royal Society of Literature of the United Kingdom, no. 3. Ed. Angela Thirkell. London: Oxford University Press, 1956, pp. 75-92.

Lewis discusses Thomas' poetry as manifesting "both the awkwardness and irresistibleness of absolute sincerity."

Mathias, Roland. "Edward Thomas." ANGLO-WELSH REVIEW, 10 (1960), 23-37.

Mathias explores Thomas' influence on and affinity with the poets of the fifties.

Quinn, Maire A. "Ballad and Folk Song in the Writing of Edward Thomas." ANGLO-WELSH REVIEW, 27 (1979), 50-62.

Quinn's essay presents evidence of Thomas' deep interest in ballad and folk song as found in both his own writings and in the comments of his biographers.

Rajan, Bernard. "Georgian Poetry: A Retrospect." CRITIC, 1 (1947), 11-12.

Rajan asserts that Thomas' poem, "Tears," is one of the best pastoral poems of modern time.

Reeves, James. THE CRITICAL SENSE. London: William Heinemann, 1956, pp. 79-82.

Reeves discusses Thomas' poem, "The Owl," as an expression of true feeling rather than sentimentality.

Scannell, Vernon. "Content With Discontent." LONDON MAGAZINE, 1 (1962), 44-51.

Scannell investigates the extent to which Thomas' poetry is dependent upon and imitative of Robert Frost's poetry.

_____. EDWARD THOMAS. Writers and Their Work Series, no. 163. London: Longmans, Green, 1962.

Scannell presents Thomas as a poet whose work "appeals strongly

to modern sensitivity." He discusses Thomas' critical reputation,
the influence on his poetry by Robert Frost, and the stylistic and
thematic strengths and weaknesses of the poetry.

Thomas, R. George. EDWARD THOMAS. Writers of Wales Series. Cardiff:
University of Wales Press, 1972.

_____. "Edward Thomas: A Memorial Tribute." ENGLISH, 21 (1972), 18-
21.

The article presents a brief memoir and tribute to Thomas and his
wife.

Weygandt, C. "Realists of the Countryside." In his THE TIME OF YEATS.
New York: Russell and Russell, 1969, pp. 336-62.

Weygandt finds the strength of Thomas' poems to lie in their directness, sincerity, and attention to all things English.

Whicher, G.F. "The Writings of Edward Thomas." YALE REVIEW, 9 (1920),
556-57.

Whicher presents a brief survey of Thomas' life and literary achievement.

VERNON PHILLIPS WATKINS (1906-67)

PRINCIPAL WORKS

Poetry

THE BALLAD OF THE MARI LWYD AND OTHER POEMS. London: Faber, 1941.
THE LAMP AND THE VEIL. London: Faber, 1945.
THE LADY WITH THE UNICORN. London: Faber, 1948.
SELECTED POEMS. Norfolk, Conn.: New Directions, 1948.
THE DEATH BELL: POEMS AND BALLADS. Norfolk, Conn.: New Directions, 1954.
CYPRESS AND ACACIA. Norfolk, Conn.: New Directions, 1959.
AFFINITIES. Norfolk, Conn.: New Directions, 1962.
SELECTED POEMS, 1930-1960. Norfolk, Conn.: New Directions, 1967.
FIDELITIES. London: Faber, 1968.
UNCOLLECTED POEMS. London: Enitharmon Press, 1969.

Other Works

Heinrich Heine's THE NORTH SEA (1955), translation.

BIBLIOGRAPHY

McCormack, Jane, ed. "Vernon Watkins: A Bibliography." WEST COAST REVIEW 4, (1969-70), 42-48.

BIOGRAPHIES

Vernon Watkins: 1906-1967. Ed. Leslie Norris. London: Faber, 1970.

Several of the essays in this collection yield biographical information. Among the contributions are "Vernon Watkins 1906-1967"
by Gwen Watkins; "Whose Flight is Toil" by Glyn Jones; "Vernon

Watkins: An Encounter and Re-Encounter" by Philip Larkin; "The Poetry of Vernon Watkins" by Kathleen Raine; "Vernon Watkins: A Memoir" by Michael Hamburger; and "Meetings with Vernon Watkins" by Roland Mathias. See "Criticism" below.

Mathias, Roland. VERNON WATKINS. Writers of Wales Series. Cardiff: University of Wales Press, 1974.

Mathias includes a brief biographical sketch.

CRITICISM

ANGLO-WELSH REVIEW, 17 (1968), 6-23.

This issue includes poems by Watkins, a letter by Watkins, and tributes to him by Eryl Davies, Elizabeth Jones, Neville Masterman, and Ceri Richards.

Barker, George. "THE DEATH BELL." LONDON MAGAZINE, 1 (1954), 86-90.

Barker discusses the "formal and clear code of language and image" manifested in Watkins' poetry. He states that "these poems are poems the same way as mathematics are mathematics—no incidental impedimenta present, no chips from rolled logs, no strings of the placenta, no shrieks from sounding axes, only the poem itself, like a window through which the operations of all things can be observed."

_____. "LADY WITH THE UNICORN." LIFE AND LETTERS, 60 (1949), 161-62.

Barker's opinion of Watkins is expressed as follows: "He may be a fine poet, a poet who dignifies and aggrandizes the times in which he writes, but he isn't ritzy enough by half to elicit the applause of the first night audience or smart enough by three-quarters to tickle the ganglia of the pampered jades of Asia."

Bennett, Joseph. "The Moving Finger Writes." HUDSON REVIEW, 16 (1963-64), 629-30.

Bennett offers a brief comment on the materials out of which Watkins has made his "major poetry": "the classic ecstasy of the myth, simple opposites, light and dark."

Blackburn, Thomas. "George Barker—Vernon Watkins—W.S. Graham—David Gascoyne." In his THE PRICE OF AN EYE. London: Longmans, Green, 1961, pp. 129-31.

Blackburn identifies Watkins as "a Christian poet, like the later

Eliot, concerned with the surrender of the personal will to the in-
tention of God." He criticizes Watkins for blunting his communication by "ironing out his humanity."

Conran, Anthony. "Boys of Summer in Their Ruin." ANGLO-WELSH REVIEW,
10 (1960), 11-12.

Conran includes Watkins in a general discussion of Anglo-Welsh
poetry, its emergence and distinguishing qualities.

Davis, Robert Gorham. "Eucharist and Roasting Pheasant." POETRY (Chicago),
73 (1948), 170-73.

Davis discusses the sea as the central image in SELECTED POEMS
(1948).

Dickey, James. "First and Last Things." POETRY (Chicago), 103 (1964), 319.

This is a brief note on the musical qualities of Watkins' AFFINI-
TIES (1962).

Flint, R.W. "Poets of the Fifties." PARTISAN REVIEW 21 (1954), 680-82.

Flint characterizes Watkins as "a pietist, a prophet of natural
energies and the analogous life of the spirit." He offers comments
on the poem "Niobe."

Furbank, P.N. "New Poetry." LISTENER, 68 (1962), 1102.

Furbank attributes the failure of AFFINITIES (1962) to a lack of
individuality in the characters who inhabit the poems.

Gross, Harvey. "William Empson, Vernon Watkins, and Henry Reed." In his
SOUND AND FORM IN MODERN POETRY. Ann Arbor: University of Michigan Press, 1964, pp. 34, 271-75.

Gross examines the meter in "Ophelia," "Thames Forest," Cantata
for the Waking of Lazarus," and "The Death Bell."

Gunn, Thom. "Certain Traditions." POETRY (Chicago), 97 (1941), 264-66.

Gunn criticizes Watkins' use of imagery "more for its quality than
its meaning."

Heath-Stubbs, John. "Pity and the Fixed Stars: An Approach to Vernon Watkins." POETRY QUARTERLY, 12 (1950), 18-23.

Heath-Stubbs comments on the poetic qualities of each of Watkins'
volumes, pointing out the poet's affinities with Yeats, Hopkins,
Williams, and Hölderlin.

Vernon Phillips Watkins

Herring, Robert. "Poetry in War." LIFE AND LETTERS, 33 (1942), 12-18.

> Herring comments briefly on THE BALLAD OF THE MARI LWYD
> (1941). He says that the unity of Watkins' poetry springs from
> his having had time to find his own myth.

Jones, Gwyn. ANGLO-WELSH LITERATURE: THE FIRST FORTY YEARS.
Cardiff: University of Wales Press, 1957.

> Jones includes Watkins in his discussion of twentieth-century Anglo-
> Welsh authors. He characterizes the poet as "one of the two best,"
> the other being Dylan Thomas.

McCormack, Jane. "Sorry, Old Christian." ANGLO-WELSH REVIEW, 18
(1970), 78-82.

> McCormick discusses the literary relationship that existed between
> Dylan Thomas and Watkins as expressed in Thomas' LETTERS TO
> VERNON WATKINS (1956).

Martz, Louis L. "New Poetry." YALE REVIEW, 44 (1955), 307-09.

> Martz discusses Watkins as "one of the finest religious poets of
> our century" and attributes the success of his poetry to a sense of
> "unity of being" manifested in Christian terms.

Mathias, Roland. "Grief and the Circus Horse: A Study of Mythic and Chris-
tian Themes in the Early Poetry of Vernon Watkins." In TRISKEL ONE. Ed.
Sam Adams and Gwilym Rees Hughes. Llandybie, Carmarthenshire, Wales:
Christopher Davies, 1971, pp. 96-138.

> Mathias' purpose in this article is to "demonstrate that throughout
> Vernon Watkins' early published poetry . . . there is a visible
> dichotomy between mythic inheritance and Christian belief, a
> dichotomy which in key poems stands revealed as antithesis."

_____. "A Note on Some Recent Poems by Vernon Watkins." DOCK LEAVES,
1 (1950), 38-49.

> Mathias' purpose in this essay is to "attempt to assess the qualities
> of Watkins' work which have earned respectful recognition." He
> bases his statements on a dozen poems that appeared in the LISTEN-
> ER between 1948 and 1950.

_____. VERNON WATKINS. Writers of Wales Series. Cardiff: University
of Wales Press, 1974.

> In this study, Mathias "elucidates the poet's preoccupations, fam-
> iliarizes the reader with the symbols he uses . . . attempts some
> evaluation of his technical abilities as a poet and offers the opin-
> ion that Watkins was, as he would have wished to be, one of the
> very few twentieth-century representatives of the great metaphysi-
> cal tradition in English poetry."

Meredith, William. "THE DEATH BELL." HUDSON REVIEW, 7 (1955), 595-96.

> Meredith divides the poems in this volume into the successful half "which seem either to begin or to end in a <u>poetical</u> rather than a real image."

Moore, Geoffrey. POETRY TODAY. London: Longmans, Green, 1958.

> Moore presents brief comments on Watkins' employment of the ballad.

Norris, Leslie. "The Poetry of Vernon Watkins." POETRY WALES, 2 (1966), 3-10.

> Norris presents a survey of the subject matter, themes, and techniques in Watkins' poetry. He discusses THE BALLAD OF THE MARI LWYD (1941), THE LAMP AND THE VEIL (1945), THE LADY WITH THE UNICORN (1948), and THE DEATH BELL (1954).

_____. "Seeing Eternity: Vernon Watkins and the Poet's Task." In TRISKEL TWO. Ed. Sam Adams and Gwilym Rees Hughes. Llandybie, Carmarthenshire, Wales: Christopher Davies, 1973, pp. 88-110.

_____, ed. VERNON WATKINS 1906-1967. London: Faber, 1970.

> This volume contains essays on Watkins' life and work by Gwen Watkins, Philip Larkin, Kathleen Raine, and Michael Hamburger. See "Biographies" above.

Polk, Dora. "Gateway to the Vision of Vernon Watkins." ANGLO-WELSH REVIEW, 20 (1971), 131-40.

> Polk demonstrates Watkins' affinities with medieval meditational and allegorical modes.

_____. VERNON WATKINS AND THE SPRING OF VISION. Atlantic Highland, N.J.: Humanities Press, 1978.

> In this study, Polk focuses on the poem BALLAD OF THE MARI LWYD (1941) and explains "the mystic implication of his poems and tries to establish a link between them and Celtic mysticism."

Pryor, Ruth. "Wisdom Is Hid In Crumbs." ANGLO-WELSH REVIEW, 23 (1974), 94-101.

> Pryor investigates the Dante references in Watkins' poetry. She concludes, "In the poetry of Vernon Watkins, Dante's influence is felt not as coherent philosophy, but in single moments of illumination."

Raine, Kathleen. "Intuition's Lightning." POETRY REVIEW, 59 (June 1968), 47-54.

Raine surveys Watkins' contribution.

_____. "Vernon Watkins: Poet of Tradition." ANGLO-WELSH REVIEW, 14 (Summer 1964), 21-38.

Raine presents a general essay on Watkins and discusses the "trans-human" quality of his work.

Ross, Alan. "Vernon Watkins." In his POETRY 1945-1950. London: Long-mans, Green, 1951, pp. 46-47.

Ross points out the affinities of Watkins with Dylan Thomas, George Barker, and Edith Sitwell, and characterizes his poetry as that of "sound and reverberation, of recapitulation and yearning."

Russell, Peter. "Vernon Watkins and His Ballad." POETRY REVIEW, 40 (1949), 54-57.

In this brief discussion, Russell asserts that the most successful poems in the collections are the ballads, even though "the poems which are not of the song-like genus are . . . on the whole more solid and thoughtful." He comments on the influence of Dylan Thomas and W.B. Yeats.

Simpson, Louis. "A Garland for the Muse." HUDSON REVIEW, 13 (1960), 288-89.

Simpson's short discussion finds its principal focus in an investiga-tion of Watkins' "Ode at the Spring Equinox" which he describes "as large, profound, and grandly moving a poem as any I have read in years."

Singer, Burns. "Sins and Symbols." ENCOUNTER, 3 (1954), 79-82.

Singer discusses Watkins' poetry as part of the symbolist tradition. He criticizes the poet for making objects into symbols in a way that "all practical replies to his statements are lost in a welter of generalities."

Snodgrass, W.D. "Voice as Vision." WESTERN REVIEW, 19 (1955), 235-39.

Snodgrass contends that it is Watkins' public style, not his personal style, that most successfully releases his creative energies.

Spark, Muriel. "THE LADY WITH THE UNICORN." OUTPOSTS, 13 (1949), 32-33.

In this brief review, Spark compliments Watkins for his individuali-ty of idiom and draws attention to Hopkins' influence on his work.

Waidson, H.M. "Vernon Watkins and German Literature." ANGLO-WELSH REVIEW, 21 (1972), 124-36.

Waidson explores Watkins' concern for German imaginative writing and the expression of this interest in his literary achievement.

INDEXES

AUTHOR INDEX

This index includes authors, editors, compilers, and contributors to other works cited in the text. References are to page number and alphabetization is letter by letter.

A

B

Author Index

Author Index

F

Fairchild, Hoxie N.   120, 162, 210
Falck, Colin   55
Farjeon, Eleanor   260, 261, 263
Feliks, Topolski   222
Ferguson, De Lancey   85
Fermor, P. Leigh   234
Ferrier, Carole   156, 162
Ferris, Paul   241
Fifoot, Richard   220
Finneran, Richard J.   73
Firkins, O.W.   193
Fiscalini, J.   177
Fisher, A.S.T.   55
Fisher, William J.   163
Fitts, Dudley   177
Fitzgibbon, Constantine   241, 245
Flanner, Hildegard   134
Fleischmann, Wolfgang Bernard   23
Fletcher, J.G.   100
Fletcher, John   210
Flint, R.W.   269
Ford, Hugh D.   38
Ford, Newell   92
Forrest-Thomson, Veronica   92
Forter, Allan   139
Fosenberg, Lois D.   220
Fowler, H.W.   21
Foxall, Edgar   55
Frankenburg, Lloyd   39
Franklin, Ralph   147
Fraser, G.S.   39, 55, 67, 92,
   101, 240, 245
Frazer, Sir James   169
Freeman, Rosemary   210
Fremantle, Anne   234
French, Samuel   178
Frimage, George J.   246
Fuller, John   55
Fuller, Roy   101
Furbank, P.N.   269
Fussell, Paul   39

G

Galler, David   202
Gallup, Jennifer   26
Ganz, Arthur   25
Garber, Frederick   202

Gardner, Averil   92
Gardner, Helen Louise   202
Gardner, Philip   92
Gardner, W.H.   129, 135
Garnett, Edward   264
Garrod, H.W.   147
Gaskell, Ronald   101
Gelder, G. Stuart   157
Gemmett, Robert J.   234
Gerard, D.E.   163
Gerber, Helmut E.   110
Gerber, Philip L.   234
Gerstenberger, Donna   235
Ghiselin, Brewster   135
Gibson, Ashley   193
Gibson, James   120
Gierasch, Walter   193
Gifford, Henry   163
Gilbert, Sandra   163
Giles, Richard   132
Gili, J.L.   233
Gill, Bernard   200
Gill, Roma   92
Gillie, Christopher   19
Gittings, Robert   112, 113
Gitzen, John   178
Glicksberg, Charles I.   93
Glover, Albert   240
Gose, Elliott B., Jr.   210
Gould, Gerald   194
Gransden, K.W.   223
Grant, Damian   55
Graves, Richard Percival   144
Graves, Robert   224, 228
Green, Andrew J.   74
Greenberg, Herbert   56
Gregory, Horace   85, 101, 163,
   178, 194, 224, 246
Greiff, Louis K.   246
Grice, Fred   202
Grigson, Geoffrey   23, 56, 102,
   135, 164, 224
Gross, Harvey   269
Grubb, Frederick   216, 246
Grundy, Joan   120
Guerard, Albert J.   74, 121
Gunn, Thom   67, 178, 269
Gutierrez, Donald   164

Author Index

Author Index

Z

Zabel, Morton   153
Zeitlow, Paul   128

TITLE INDEX

This index includes all titles cited in the text; in some cases the titles have been shortened. References are to page number and alphabetization is letter by letter.

Title Index

Title Index

Title Index

SUBJECT INDEX

This index is alphabetized letter by letter. Underlined page numbers refer to main entries within the subject.

Subject Index

Housman 145

Blank verse, of Betjeman 66

Blunden, Edmund 36, 39, 40, 44, 46

Book reviews 26, 28

Bottomley, Gordon, correspondence with Thomas (P. E.) 261

Bradley, Henry, correspondence with Bridges 73

Brancusi, Constantin, influence on Raine 217

Brewster, Achsah, correspondence with Lawrence 159

Brewster, Earl H., correspondence with Lawrence 159

Bridges, Robert Seymour 42, 46, 71-76, 132, 140, 179

Brooke, Rupert 39, 44
literary influence of 261

Browning, Robert 82, 117

Buchanan, Robert, influence on Hardy 120

Burlesque, elements of in Sitwell's poetry 228

Burrows, Louis, correspondence with Lawrence 160

Byron, George Gordon, Sitwell on 228

C

Caitlin, Thomas, relationship with Dylan Thomas 240, 241

Campbell, Joseph 39

Caudwell, Christopher 42

Censorship 20

Chambers, Jessie, relationship with Lawrence 158, 159

Characters and characterization 19, 20
in Auden's poetry 59
in Empson's theory of criticism 94
in Hardy's works 114, 126
in Masefield's poetry 194, 196
in Watkins' poetry 269

Chaucer, Geoffrey
influence on Masefield 189, 194-95, 196
Sitwell on 228

Children's poetry, by de la Mare 83, 85, 86

Chorus, use of in Hardy's poetry 120, 127

Christianity. See Religion in poetry

Church of England, in Betjeman's poetry 68

City life
in Betjeman's poetry 70
in MacNeice's poetry 181

Clark, Marcus, friendship with Hopkins 130

Classicism
in Bridges' poetry 74
in Housman's poetry 146, 148, 149, 151
in MacNeice's poetry 184, 185

Cocteau, Jean, Sitwell on 228

Coleridge, Samuel Taylor
de la Mare compared to 84
Raine compared to 216

Colum, Padraic 39

Comfort, Alexander 45, 77-79

Comic poetry
of Auden 60
of Betjeman 67, 69
See also Wit and humor

Commedia dell'arte (Italian), influence on Sitwell 223

Copyright 20

Corke, Helen, relationship with Lawrence 159

Cornford, Frances, Raine compared to 216

Cornford, John 42

Coward, Noel, Auden compared to 61

Crane, Hart 35

Crashaw, Richard 224

Criticism. See Literary criticism; names of individual poets

Crucifixion. See Religion in poetry

cummings, e. e. 39
Thomas (P.E.) compared to 264

D

Daniel, Arnault, influence on Pound 119

Daniel, C.H.O., correspondence with Bridges 75

Dante Alighieri
Hardy compared to 118
influence on Watkins 271
Sitwell compared to 227

Darwin, Charles, influence on Hardy 115

Subject Index